Advance Praise for
WHO GETS IN

"Norman Ravvin's *Who Gets In* is a compelling detective story that deciphers Canada's less than welcoming entrance regime in the 1930s. Tracing the labyrinthine journey of his Jewish grandfather's immigration from Poland to Canada and his subsequent efforts to bring his wife and children to join him, this narrative offers a glimpse into the bureaucratic confidence game that so many newcomers tested. Ravvin's wonderfully researched and imagined context intrigues, and his engrossing chronicle speaks for the many forgotten stories that survive between official lines. Ultimately a tale of how tenacity prevails over the reluctance of officialdom, it is also a profoundly kinetic story of perseverance." —ARITHA VAN HERK, author of *No Fixed Address,* finalist for the 1986 Governor General's Literary Awards

"In recounting his grandfather's quest to bring over his wife and children from 1930s Poland, Norman Ravvin uncovers an untold aspect of Canadian immigration history. Rich in archival reconstruction, this engaging, highly readable book is a welcome addition to Canadian Jewish history, narrating the rarely acknowledged story of Jewish Saskatchewan in the early twentieth century." —AARON KREUTER, author of *Shifting Baseline Syndrome,* finalist for the 2022 Governor General's Literary Awards

"A carefully researched, elegantly told tale of the struggle of a Jewish newcomer in rural Saskatchewan to bring his family to Canada in the face of distant Ottawa's restrictive immigration regulations, and the stone-hearted officials who maintained them." —RICHARD MENKIS, Associate Professor of Modern Jewish History, University of British Columbia

"In tracing the course of his grandfather's departure from Poland and arrival in Vancouver, followed by a five-year struggle to secure entry to Canada for his wife and two children, Norman Ravvin uncovers the history of Jewish farming settlements in southern Saskatchewan, Canada's racist past and restrictive immigration policies, and the near impossibility for Jews to gain admission to this country in the 1930s. *Who Gets In* celebrates a grandfather's determination to reunite with his family and a grandson's desire to pay him tribute. Readers will lose themselves in this story of detail and anecdote made compelling by Ravvin's narrative flair." —RUTH PANOFSKY, editor of *The New Spice Box: Contemporary Jewish Writing*

"Norman Ravvin's book is a masterwork of contrasts. It is a thrilling tale of archival research and analysis, a page-turner about bureaucratic processes, and a personal family history that examines national and universal themes, including colonialism, Jewish erasure, and the shifting concept of what it means to be Canadian. This atypical story challenges what we thought we knew about Jewish immigration to Canada at a crucial moment in time." —HARRY SANDERS, Calgary historian

WHO
GETS

AN IMMIGRATION STORY

IN

NORMAN RAVVIN

University of Regina Press

Printed and bound in Canada at Imprimerie Gauvin. The text of this book is printed on 100% post-consumer recycled paper with earth-friendly vegetable-based inks.

COVER AND TEXT DESIGN: Duncan Noel Campbell
COPY EDITOR: Dallas Harrison
PROOFREADER: Nancy Mackenzie
INDEXER: Sergey Lobachev, Brookfield Indexing Services
COVER PHOTO: Library and Archives Canada c-009798

Library and Archives Canada Cataloguing in Publication

TITLE: Who gets in : an immigration story / Norman Ravvin.

NAMES: Ravvin, Norman, 1963– author.

DESCRIPTION: Includes bibliographical references and index.

IDENTIFIERS: Canadiana (print) 20220496021 | Canadiana (ebook) 20220496056 | ISBN 9780889779228 (softcover) | ISBN 9780889779259 (hardcover) | ISBN 9780889779242 (EPUB) | ISBN 9780889779235 (PDF)

SUBJECTS: LCSH: Eisenstein, Yehuda Yosef. | LCSH: Jews,—Canada—Biography. | LCSH: Jews—Poland—Biography. | LCSH: Immigrants—Canada,—Biography. | LCSH: Antisemitism—Canada. | LCSH: Xenophobia—Canada. | LCGFT: Biographies.

CLASSIFICATION: LCC FC106.J5 R38 2023 | DDC 971.004/9240092—dc23

10 9 8 7 6 5 4 3 2 1

University of Regina Press

University of Regina, Regina, Saskatchewan, Canada, s4s 0A2
TEL: (306) 585-4758 FAX: (306) 585-4699
WEB: www.uofrpress.ca

We acknowledge the support of the Canada Council for the Arts for our publishing program. We acknowledge the financial support of the Government of Canada. / Nous reconnaissons l'appui financier du gouvernement du Canada. This publication was made possible with support from Creative Saskatchewan's Book Publishing Production Grant Program.

CONTENTS

PART ONE

ANOTHER SHIP,
ANOTHER TIME

Sometimes a story begins where you don't expect it to. This is a book about travel to Canada from Poland in the 1930s, about Jewish life in southern Saskatchewan, about migration, the abandonment of home, and the power of government authorities to crush individuals. It includes detours into the offices of a prime minister, parliamentarians, immigration bureaucrats, and community organizers and activists. But to be fair to its deeper rhythms and revelations—to a story focused on one man, which also opens a view of Canada that's new—it must step back from 1930s Poland and Saskatchewan in favour of a short account of Canada's west coast, circa 1914.

On a May morning in that year, the Japanese-based steamer *Komagata Maru* arrived in the Vancouver harbour. A big deal this was and not just at the city's port. The prospect of the ship's arrival had received much advance notice in Ottawa, with Prime Minister Robert Borden being kept informed of its arrival. Attention was being paid throughout the British Empire, including in colonial India, where most of the ship's passengers were from. It was the *Komagata Maru* Incident, as the events that followed over the summer came to be called, that ushered in a new immigration regime in Britain's Dominion of Canada. The immediate targets of this new regime were

"Asiatics," the term widely used at the time for Indian subjects of the British Crown. Canada had an onerous head tax to keep out the Chinese, and it had signed a "gentleman's agreement" with the Japanese government to limit the arrival of Japanese on Canada's Pacific coast. But Indian travellers remained outliers, with their home country part of the empire. Many of those seeking access to Canada had fought alongside British troops in colonial wars, so a shared imperial identity presented a complicating factor. Why shouldn't Punjabis who had fought in Indian contingents of the British army be allowed to travel from colony to Dominion as they wished? Steamship companies had recognized a market and inaugurated a Calcutta-Vancouver run that Canadian immigration representatives saw as a threatening source of unskilled labour, dubbed "coolies."

As early as 1908, in response to these developments, the Canadian government applied what it called the "continuous journey" regulation, aimed at blocking Indian travellers who set out for a Canadian port, not directly from home but via Japan or Hawaii. The regulation asserted that "Asiatic" travellers had to come to Canada only by embarking from their home country; from Indian ports, this was an impossibility. Canadian officials aimed, at the same time, to halt the Calcutta-Vancouver route.[1] Two further government actions—crucial backroom orders-in-council enacted by the prime minister's cabinet (or Privy Council)—took these efforts further. One prohibited the arrival at BC ports of unskilled labourers, and the other insisted that Indian emigrants must have $200 "in the pocket." This regulation operated like the Chinese "head tax," setting an exorbitantly high entry fee as a de facto block against Indian immigrants. It effectively set an unofficial quota of zero for Indians aiming to land in the Dominion.

The *Komagata Maru* sat in the Vancouver harbour from late May to the third week of July 1914. A shore committee of Vancouver and Victoria Sikhs and Muslims provided the passengers with necessities, which the Canadian authorities claimed were not their responsibility, while a board of BC judges considered the legality of the captain's demand to land. Almost as soon as the *Komagata Maru* anchored, reporters and photographers boarded the ship along with immigration inspectors. This ensured that there would be a vast array of documentary photographs of the ship from its arrival to its departure. Its presence became a kind of spectacle, with crowds of Vancouverites routinely going down to the pier to see the news event that put their small city on view in the international press.

The best-known photographer of this spectacle was the German-born Jew Leonard Frank, who came to British Columbia in the late nineteenth century looking for a gold stake on Vancouver Island. His photographic career first took shape from his home in the island lumber port of Alberni, where he mixed landscape and portrait work with newspaper freelancing. One of his photographs—maybe the most iconic—of the *Komagata Maru*'s passengers appeared on the front page of the Vancouver *Daily Province* on May 26, three days after the ship anchored. It ran beneath the title "First Pictures of Hindus Aboard the 'Komagata Maru'" (the bulk of the ship's passengers were Punjabi Sikhs; scholars number the Hindus on board at twelve). Frank's photo highlights Gurdit Singh, the man who chartered the ship, and his seven-year-old son, who crossed the Pacific in his father's first-class cabin. The men with them pose formally, almost as if Frank took the time to stage a portrait. At the end of it all, in July, Frank took an almost unearthly photograph of the *Komagata Maru* as it sailed off toward the east, its tall stack smoking, the placid harbour waters cut in a wide V by the ship's prow.

Frank's photography is one point, though not the only one, where the ship's travails in the summer of 1914 overlap with Jewish immigration to Canada in the early twentieth century. Book illustrators routinely use Frank's photographs without attribution and without wondering what it might have meant for a Jew, who'd come to this country from northwest Germany at a time of open borders, to be a representative of a national culture that Canadian authorities included near the top of their hierarchy of "suitable" "white" immigrants. Frank's Germanness would have trumped his Jewishness, and one would like to see his landing documents to learn whether the Canadian government simply knew Frank as a German national. There is nothing from historians regarding how the photographer himself felt or thought about the spectacle that he photographed with such impressive effect, clarity, even beauty—the crowds of men on board taking on a kind of painterly order, with the ship creating a frame for their gathering, their faces and comportment a complicated code of discomfort, pride, and patience in the face of the immigration representatives who flung themselves over the ship's balustrades to inspect the passengers. Surely the clarity of Frank's photographs could not have been accomplished without some kind of awareness of what it meant to be accepted, or not accepted, at a Canadian port. Ironically, his German Jewish photographic eye would create a substantial record of a later Canadian disaster, the internment of the west coast population of Canadian-born and émigré Japanese. In 1942, Frank was hired by the BC Security Commission, which oversaw the removal of all Japanese Canadians from the BC coast, to make a dispassionate photographic record of this undertaking. Is it possible, in 1942, the year of the most heinous mass killing of Jews in Europe by his own German folk, that his eye did not consider what he saw at Hastings Park to be a travesty and a human catastrophe? That year, at Hastings Park on the east side of the city, like the summer departure of the *Komagata Maru*, was a winning season for the proponents of "White Canada." Frank's camera captured the enterprise with care.

The *Komagata Maru* has direct links with the story that I aim to tell. The ship was built at the famous Glasgow Clyde River shipyards for a Hamburg-based shipping line, and initially it was christened the *Stubbenhuk*. The Hansa line advertised the *Stubbenhuk* in Canadian newspapers as a freight carrier making return trips to Europe, but it was designed as an archetypal immigrants' ship with accommodation for only a few in first class and 620 in third class.[2] On late-nineteenth-century sailings, many of these were Jewish passengers leaving Europe from Hamburg and Antwerp for ports at Quebec City and Montreal. Sailing in 1891, it arrived at the port of Montreal with a passenger list of Europeans, among them Russian Jews. The Jews were held for a time at the port's immigration buildings since they were deemed "not of a class suited for any labour" and not to have any "friends" or "means of support" by Montreal immigration authorities.[3] Ultimately, they were allowed to disembark.

When Frank saw the ship twenty-five years later, with its fresh Japanese moniker and its Punjabi passengers, this history most likely eluded him. Still, there he stood on the pier alongside the harbour immigration sheds, camera ready to capture high points in the battle for "White Canada": at its beginning, the arrival of the *Komagata Maru*; at its close, the image of the ship being escorted out of the harbour by one of the Royal Canadian Navy's two warships, picturesquely called the *Rainbow*. Frank, on the boardwalk, and the ship under steam, are framing points for another kind of immigration story, set at a later date, but in response to the same efforts to hold the bar against an influx of people deemed unsuitable to the Dominion. My story begins roughly fifteen years after the *Komagata Maru* Incident, on the central Polish plain in a village called Radzanów.

❀ ❀ ❀

Almost everyone involved in the story that I have to tell is dead, so photographs, if we know what's going on in their backgrounds, have a great deal to offer. They are priceless artifacts, akin to Frank's mysterious port images of 1914. I have three to choose from at the outset, each with something different to offer, each one dating from the 1920s.

The first photo is a strange and mysterious thing—like an illustration for a mesmerist's unlocking of a ghost story. It hides as much as it reveals. The photo presents a young man in his early twenties. He stands before a large wooden building. It is made of planks a foot and a half wide, great knotty pieces of flat wood like those used on the house fronts of chiefs at Haida Gwaii. But these are Polish boards, likely pine, hewn somewhere on the central Polish plains and brought to their building site in the village of Radzanów, some 115 kilometres northwest of Warsaw. The young man stands with his hand on the back of a chair, while the other hand holds what looks like a paper-covered book. On the seat of the chair lies a bouquet. Roses? More likely wildflowers. It looks as if he is on his way to a celebration. He wears his best duds: a dark jacket with three buttons set close together at the midriff, under the jacket a vest and a high-collared white shirt and black tie. A vest pocket handkerchief—nowadays the stores call them pocket squares—pokes raggedly from his breast pocket, as if it is there for its actual use: blowing one's nose.

The young man's expression is serious, the corners of his mouth turned down in the early-twentieth-century manner of portrait sitters and standers. This is a portrait—a young man on his way to a celebration—even though it is taken outdoors, without the care of a studio photographer. The chair, the bouquet, the mysterious object in his hand, all play like props that might be on offer in a proper studio.

In the 1920s, Radzanów, a village of 1,000 Poles, roughly a third of them Jewish, spread out from its central market over farmland with country houses. The village square was surrounded by furriers' shop fronts, glaziers and butchers, bakers and rabbinical scholars. But to sit in a photo studio one had to travel by horse cart some thirty kilometres northeast to Mława, a proper little city with a brick train station,

old and new market squares, and its share of urban pleasures, which included Zygmunt Lipszyc's Fotografia studio in the old market square.

The second photograph was taken not at Lipszyc's studio but at a similar place in the country's capital, Warsaw, where our young man, in 1923, was serving as a Polish army officer's adjutant. This was a good military duty in a time of brutal front postings. It put him in uniform, like the one he wears in his studio photo.

This photo, like the previous one, doubled as a postcard—they are printed on card stock and bear on their reverse sides the telltale right-hand address lines, with a vertical line in the cards' centre indicating address on the right, message to a recipient on the left. In this case, the young Polish military adjutant used the address lines for his message, so the card might have been slipped into an envelope upon being mailed. The note in Yiddish reveals that the photo was sent to one of the writer's brothers, though it doesn't say which of the three. The message is signed in flowing fountain pen ink, which thins and fattens with each stroke: "Yehudah Yosef Eizenshtein." I spell the family name this way to convey its proper pronunciation in the Polish Yiddish milieu of the 1920s. In English, more simply, it is spelled Eisenstein.

The third photo is a reprise or riff on the second.

I have it as a good copy of the original print on more contemporary photographic paper. In the second photo, the young army man is seated, solitary, brow set in thought, an appropriate pose to send home to family in the village. In the third photo, he is joined by two compatriots in matching uniforms—dark jodhpur pants tucked into high laced boots, what must be gold or silver embroidery in zigzag on the collar, caps with the Polish eagle at the peak. The three have gone together to a Warsaw photo studio to have their portrait taken. The studio has provided a wicker chair, a wooden bench, backdrops that imitate Fragonard, all of which lend the subjects a romantic, even epic, feel. And so they should. Poland in the mid-1920s was an epic project. A new nation ravaged by war, which had beaten back a predatory Soviet incursion, it was asserting itself on the world stage. In their army uniforms, these young men were proof of the country's independence. Its unique flair. Its future in a modern world.

❀ ❀ ❀

These are a few of the stories that these pictures tell. Let me tell another divergent one.

Who is our young man? I might begin by calling him Z because of the Kafkaesque quality of his struggle and then, because in his efforts he was always the littlest of men, seemingly unaware of his vulnerability and lack of influence, at the end of a lineup of powerful players who, on a whim, could simply ignore or reject his requests. But also because Z he was to me, as in Zaida, though I knew him only in my first years and have no memory of him not formed by other people's conversations or photographs. There is one snapshot of him from my childhood that I particularly liked. He is seated, holding me. I am two years old, laughing, open-mouthed, in the way that two year olds do. We are in a room that many years later I would know well, on Willow Street in Vancouver's Fairview Slopes, where Jews bought houses in the wartime. In the room, with its paned, east-facing windows, there were books, including a tall leather-bound set of the Talmud printed in nineteenth-century Lemberg. A console record player, which held hardcover folders of 78s. Some of them were popular records, but others were of cantorial music, Koussevitzky and Rosenblatt. My grandfather put them on and sang along, facing the window. This sounds like ethnic melodrama, but that was Z, whose story now seems as timely as any I could tell.

For most of my life, he was a cipher. My mother said almost nothing about her father. Memorializing him was of no interest to her, though she talked often of family in other contexts, whether in ancestral Poland or in Canada. When, as a young woman, she visited her father's sister in Los Angeles, her sage advice for amusing herself as a young visitor in the big city was to "go stand at the corner of Hollywood and Vine." Her father's older brother, the one who'd made his way from Poland to the United States in the early 1920s, was a tailor but fancied himself a poet and kept a ready example of his creativity on a scrap of paper in his breast pocket.

The party line on Z was that he'd left Poland alone with clear intentions to bring his young wife and children after him. My first efforts at uncovering this story drew a blank. He'd played a role in well-documented early settlement projects on the Saskatchewan prairie, where he'd taken up the responsibilities of a community religious functionary. He'd lived in the shadows of impressive men and women recalled in memoirs of the 1930s. But it was as if I'd made him up, concocted his years in southern Saskatchewan and his efforts there to right his life, which had been fabulously rent, upended, by his decision to leave Poland alone in 1930. He'd cast off from Radzanów, the village of his birth, a true shtetl in steep decline, with all of history's calamities behind it—Polish insurrections, Russian pogroms farther east, the Bolshevik upheaval and war between the Poles and the Soviets in 1920, with more yet to come. An even more spectacular disaster was in the wings. No event is fated, and anything might have befallen Radzanów in the 1930s. Anything at all. Z tore himself—these are the words of family lore; no archive holds them—from a house full of wailing women. It was this departure, in early November 1930, that was the beginning of his masterpiece, his great act of will. Its first scene: the waiting horse cart, the rye fields arranged around pine forests, the waters of the still Wkra under leafless linden and acacia trees, the *Mlawer Gasse*, the street that led from the village toward the train station in Mława where one started for the coast. His masterwork. Let's start where he began.

Yehuda Yoseph Eisenstein was born in Radzanów in 1901. His father, Berel, is the only one of my four great-grandparents not born in Radzanów. He was from Drobin, a nearby town, remarkably similar in its makeup. Zaida Berel Eisenstein studied at Łomża Yeshiva, which, in its time, was among the finest in Poland. When he lived in Radzanów, he was known as the town's leading Talmud rabbi. Among traditional Polish Jews, this role combined the qualities of justice of the peace, marriage counsellor, lawyer-mediator, and constitutional law expert: disputes of all kinds among Jews were settled by men like my great-grandfather, who relied on Talmudic precedent and story to make each decision. The wife of Zaida Berel was called Henna. They had five boys, one of whom died young, and two girls.

When my grandfather, Yehuda Yoseph, was twelve, he was sent to study at the Gerrer *shtibel* in Mława. This reflected his parents' goal of placing him in the Chassidic context of rabbinical education. Although my grandfather's immediate family members were not adherents of any Chassidic court, they did have personal links to Chassidic figures in the area, including the Gerrer and Alexandrover Rebbes. Yehuda Yoseph was offered room and board at the house of a well-off family called Frank. This was in the lead-up to the First World War, and when war broke out he was taken home to Radzanów. Yehuda Yoseph was hesitant at first to heed the draft call for the Polish army. But when the government made loudspeaker announcements in the village that draft evaders, when caught, would be shot, he made himself known. His posting turned out to be a fortunate one. He served as the orderly to a Polish officer stationed in Warsaw.

From his teenage years, my grandfather pined after the daughter of Menachem Mendl and Chana Margulies, Chaya Dina. But the girl's parents did not see Yehuda Yoseph as a good match for their daughter. One reason might have been that, as a love match, made obvious by the romantic inclinations of my grandfather, the marriage would have been outside the usual matchmaking patterns of a traditional Polish Jewish community.

When my grandfather's father was dying of cancer in 1925, he called the mother of Chaya Dina Margulies—Baba Chana—to his bedside and told her in Yiddish *"Ich vil az undzer kind Yehuda zal areinkumen in eyer reshoit."* That is, "I want you to take our child, Yehuda, into your household." But even with Berel Eisenstein's death, Baba Chana Margulies was unmoved. It was only when Yehuda Yoseph's mother died a few years later that she relented. In 1928, my grandparents were married. The marriage took place not in a synagogue but in the home of my grandmother's half-sister, Mariam, in Mława. The rabbi who officiated was Segalovitch, often referred to as the last rabbi of Mława. The ceremony itself was undertaken without a civil marriage licence—against Polish law—since my grandfather planned to leave for Canada, emigrating alone and telling the Canadian government that he was single. The common-sense planning behind the decision not to apply for a marriage licence—one with which the rabbi was uncomfortable—can be found on Polish passports of the time. They are ecumenical documents; they do not categorize the holder by religion or race or origin or any further unnecessary term, considering that they are evidence, simply, of Polish nationality. The passports do highlight civil status—*żonaty*—Polish for a "married man." So my grandfather, with planning barely begun, avoided that mark on his official documents.

My grandparents lived during the first two years of their marriage in my grandmother's parents' home in Radzanów. The house was one of the low, hipped-roof, wooden buildings owned by Jews on the fringes of the market square. From there, they would have taken part in Polish Jewish village life at its most emblematic: market days in front of the houses, the rituals of Saturday prayer and high holidays in the nearby synagogue, animals in the back property honking and braying.

What did my grandfather do—a newly married man in his late twenties—to make a living? He was a grain merchant, buying grain from the farmers around the outskirts of Radzanów and selling it to the mill owners, many of whom used the Wkra River to power their mill wheels. He had a good relationship with a mill owner in Ciechanow, a larger place nearby, named Itcha Meir Petrokovsky, and it was through him that Yehuda Yoseph sold much of the grain supplied to him by Radzanów-area farmers.

Sometime in the late 1920s, my grandfather began to view his future in Poland with doubt. With three siblings abroad, and many others leaving Radzanów for North America and Palestine, this was not an unusual shift in outlook for a young person in the Polish countryside. Leaving was an act in keeping with the time.

LEAVING

Here we arrive at the kernel—is it more provocative to say ground zero?—of emigration activity: the decision to leave one's home for an unknown place. I can say reliably that for my grandfather this decision took place in the fall, most likely in 1928, during the Jewish holiday of Sukkot, when observant Jews eat and sit with their families in makeshift booths meant to recall the structures built by the wandering Israelites in the desert. The *sukkah* is a kind of tidy camp table with chairs under cover of branches set atop makeshift walls. What took place that Sukkot crystallized what must have been a lingering set of intentions, an ongoing discussion with his young wife, and letter writing to his brothers abroad about the possibility of leaving Poland. My grandfather would have been emboldened by the fact that three siblings had already left: his elder brother, Hiram, Chaim Issar as he'd been called in Radzanów, had settled in the American Midwest; his sister, Hadassah, had been sponsored by Chaim to enter the United States; and his younger brother, Israel, had travelled via the American west coast to settle in Vancouver in 1928. It would have been Izzy who aided his elder brother in securing a Canadian visa, and offering sponsorship, as required in the late 1920s to enter Canada. It was likely his advice, too, that because of Canadian interest in immigrant single men, my grandfather should apply as single and work out his family's travel once he was settled.

There is a further narrative strand to add in understanding the decision to leave, which is compelling and related to events in Poland. It went this way: in the last months of his Polish years, my grandfather continued to be active as a grain merchant, or middleman, arranging the sale of wheat from Polish farmers to the mill owners along the Wkra River near Radzanów. A son of one of his customers had joined the trend—just beginning but already trickling down to youngsters as local sport—of calling him some version of a dirty Jew. My grandfather pursued him and gave him hell, and news of this altercation made its way back to the kid's father, who put out the word that my grandfather would pay for what he'd done. For the first time, and in a general atmosphere of Jew-baiting in Polish life, a vague sense of personal threat haunted Yehuda Yoseph. But then there is another version, accounting for a turn in his mind, that is equally compelling. It went as follows. My grandfather was sitting with his family in the *sukkah*. I have no photograph to show how the rural Jewish bourgeois family's *sukkah* might have looked in the late 1920s, but behind the houses around the square in Radzanów there was a good deal of back property on the way down to the marshy bank of the Wkra River. Maybe the *sukkah* was prepared there of boards and branches. Nearby were horses in their stable and geese by the marshy riverside. While the family sat in the *sukkah*, a rock was thrown inside. The same expression of wilful abuse as that offered by the long-time customer's son. My grandfather's response to this was to say "I can't live with these people anymore." Or, as he would have said in Yiddish, "*Ich ken mit zei mer nisht lebn.*" It's good to hear some of these things in the language in which they took place. In this incident, the spoken words evoke the moment of decision with clarity and purpose.

So there it is—the kernel, as I like to call it—of my grandfather's migration story. The moment of crystallization, followed by some lost correspondence with his brother who lived on Vancouver's Victoria Drive on the city's east side. It was surrounded by other momentous events in a young man's life: his marriage just over a year before, without a licence and thus illegal, and then his departure, alone. By 1930, the Canadian immigration regime had tightened up dramatically, but a single man could attain a visa with a brother's sponsorship. My grandfather's visa attested to his unmarried status, as did his brother's sponsorship papers. The illegality of it all would come back to haunt Yehuda Yoseph in complicated ways.

❀ ❀ ❀

Poland in the late 1920s was an open book. What would happen in the new nation was anyone's guess, for much of Europe, in the post–First World War era, remained upside down. Years of Soviet brutality on the eastern border included, for Poland, a hard-fought war *after the end* of the First World War. The rest of Europe was not a comforting alternative. Fascism and street fighting were the Roman status quo. Militias, their financing for new uniforms and spiffy vehicles coming from mysterious sources, were on view in Vienna and in supposedly demilitarized Germany. A right-wing insurgent nationalist movement under the misleading moniker Endek, or National Democracy, challenged the Polish leader and military hero, Józef Piłsudski, who had the overwhelming support of Poland's Jews. The outflux of Eastern European Jews was an established trend that rose and fell, in part promoted by the increasing appeal of Zionism among young people.

❀ ❀ ❀

In Canada, what was shaping up in the years when my grandfather made his plans to emigrate? In this book, I aim to paint a detailed picture of the time and place, with careful attention to Western Canada, where he went. A telling artifact of the time is a school history book, used by Western Canadian students in the 1920s, though published at the country's centre in Toronto. Titled *The Story of the Canadian People*, it is bound in red cloth. Its frontispiece shows not the prime minister of the country but the king of England, George V, with his flowing moustache and one hand on a sword at his waist. A late chapter, titled "The Canada of To-Day," proclaims that "the progress of education and Christianity has kept pace with industrial growth," an odd link between the economy and social and religious life yet one that flies the flag of key Canadian values. Canada, the textbook tells us, is "too young a country to lay claim to a literature of her own," while in "art, also, Canada has made . . . a beginning."[1]

Canada in the late 1920s. We're all kindergartners, forget the high school curriculum, when it comes to knowing the place in 1928–30. *Who knows Canada in 1928?* It's the kind of tough question that a teacher might ask her students. No one beyond a few historians knows 1928. In that year, two years before my grandfather's arrival at Quebec City, immigration was an all-consuming topic of discussion. The newspapers of the time reveal that the topic just wouldn't go away. Ideas, policies, and popular opinions were in flux. The federal government, under Liberal William Lyon Mackenzie King, was under pressure from its opposition, who looked forward to fighting an election on the topic. In Saskatchewan, Premier James Garfield Gardiner, a Liberal, would be unseated in the coming year by a Conservative, James Anderson. The debates over immigration were not as overtly nasty as they are today, especially as they play out in the United States; still, as the federal election of 1930 came over the horizon, there was no doubt that a spectre was haunting Canada, and its name was *Continental Immigration*. That pairing of words, so common in the 1920s and 1930s, underwrites a long story as it relates to Jews arriving in the country.

A roughly fifty-year period of substantial immigration numbers was being reviewed by commentators on all sides. Robert England, the continental superintendent of the Canadian National Railways Colonization Department, was one of the balanced voices, aiming, as he wrote in 1928, "to avoid controversial treatment of the subject, seeking rather to deal with it objectively and without bias."[2] Still, when his book *The Central European Immigrant in Canada* appeared in 1929, he acknowledged that many Canadians sought a substantial change in the status quo. According to England, between 1881 and the end of the 1920s, Canadian immigration numbers looked like this:

FROM THE BRITISH ISLES 2,148,164

FROM THE UNITED STATES 2,161,078

CHIEFLY FROM CONTINENTAL EUROPE 1,457,730[3]

The trends were clear. Through the 1920s, the number of those arriving from Britain was on a steady downward curve, whereas the number of those arriving from Continental Europe remained steady. England framed his discussion of "the central European immigrant" with these facts, but he wrote to calm the minds of those Canadians who found these numbers terrifying or simply not to their taste. His way of softening the blow—of confirming that Canada was changing unavoidably in the direction of a more multi-ethnic society—was to focus on a project run by the Masonic Order of Saskatchewan, which offered scholarships to young teachers willing to work for at least a year "in the more backward non-English speaking districts" of rural northern Saskatchewan.[4] Fifty-one teachers were sent to oversee what England called "an experiment in racial co-operation" never before seen in the Dominion.[5] As part of their assignment, they were expected to report back—as amateur sociologists or statisticians—on the states of family life, communal activity, and assimilation among the new non–Anglo Saxon Canadians of the Prairies. This they did by using "chain letters"[6] and by filling out detailed questionnaires on their work and its outcomes, which sought basic data ("How many pupils are registered in each grade?") and posed policy-oriented queries whose answers could only rise to the level of personal opinion ("Should Immigration from non-English speaking countries be restricted until our present population is more thoroughly assimilated?").[7]

Assimilability was the byword of the late 1920s. At an Ottawa conference on immigration and labour, the federal finance minister, James Robb, expressed a common view: "One good newcomer who has a good racial backing and who fits into our Canadian life is worth 1000 unassimilables."[8] We can only guess who the minister had in mind in his invocation of "1000 unassimilables," but perhaps he conjured up for himself and his audience the 376 "Asiatics" aboard the *Komagata Maru* who had been sent back to the Punjab. Earlier in the year, a parliamentary committee on immigration was said to have been "impressed with the need for more settlers of the British breed, and practically all declare that the bars must be raised against Southern Europeans and Polish Jews."[9]

These prominent voices on immigration issues in 1928 were responding, indirectly, to an actual "controversy" over immigration that year. Although Canadians and their elected representatives might have had opinions about what it meant to have Punjabis, Southern Europeans, or Polish Jews as neighbours, the uproar in Parliament that year was over reported immigration permit trafficking in Ottawa, Montreal, and farther afield, in Regina. A Regina alderman was pulled before the committee following his claim to "know who sold them. At least some of the members of parliament have sold" visa permits.[10] The going price was said to be $100 apiece, but when the alderman appeared before the parliamentary committee his facts changed, his knowledge becoming increasingly vague. An investigation was launched by C.H. Cahan, Montreal Conservative MP and, later in his career, member of Prime Minister R.B. Bennett's Privy Council. Immigration scaremongering would play an increasingly effective role back home, as Cahan likely knew. (As with so many names in the general discussions regarding immigration in this period, Cahan's will recur in regard to my grandfather's own immigration efforts.)

One wonders who read England's book about the fifty-one teachers who fanned out across Saskatchewan to bring small-town new Canadians properly into the fold. His work had precedents, and we can see it as part of what must have been a minority trend among a certain kind of forward-thinking post–First World War Canadian. An early contribution to this trend was J.T.M. Anderson's *The Education of the New-Canadian: A Treatise on Canada's Greatest Educational Problem*. Published in 1918 when its author was the inspector of schools in Yorkton, Saskatchewan, it is focused, too, on how education, in particular in rural contexts, can include the new Canadian in institutions that promote mainstream identity. Anderson—the Conservative premier of Saskatchewan between 1929 and 1934—acknowledged a "great problem," but his tenor was upbeat and idealistic, lacking the rancour and demagoguery of the federal government's finance minister's fantasy of "1000 unassimilables."[11]

Anderson's treatise presented a detailed and sympathetic account of Canada's Jews, an account absent in the work of his compatriots, and perhaps his hands-on experience as a school superintendent in Saskatchewan made him both knowledgeable and sympathetic (Jews received hardly a mention in England's book, as if they were an overly pungent ingredient that might spoil the ethnic ragout that England hoped to sell to his readers). Anderson supplied an overview of the major groups of new Canadians: Scandinavians, Mennonites, and "Our Slavic Fellow-Citizens," among whom we find Poles and

"Ruthenians," the term of choice for Ukrainians at the time. In a turn that reads as a response to the tendency to decry Southern Europeans and Jews as poor immigrant stock, he asserted that the "Italian and Hebrew immigrants are better known to us, because we are more familiar with their history; we know something of their home life and racial characteristics."[12] He described Jewish new Canadians in a tenor unheard of among railway managers, immigration agents, bureaucrats, and academics at the time:

> The manner in which the Russian Jews are coming to the front in educational circles throughout Western Canada seems to substantiate the above statements. Many are winning enviable reputations in the medical and legal professions, and at least one recent Rhodes scholar from the West was of Jewish parentage. They are good linguists, and quickly gain a knowledge of our language. There is every reason to believe that the latent intellectual strength of this much-oppressed people will find a free outlet in this land of freedom, and it is to be expected that in time many of their noblest national qualities will be incorporated in our Canadian life. There is "an innate racial superiority" which manifests itself in the almost marvellous work done by young, adolescent Jews in our colleges and universities.[13]

At the end of this quotation, Anderson larded his argument with the language of a leading Canadian educational theorist of his time, Peter Sandiford, who relied on racial categories to support his educational theories. Although no eugenicist work is cited in Sandiford's 1928 study, "The Mental Capacity of Southern Ontario Indians," one finds in it the academic focus of the time on the "comparative intelligence of races," which made use of a battery of tests to arrive at the conclusion that the "more white blood the Indian pupils have the higher their intelligence."[14]

Anderson wrote from his experience as a school superintendent in his own prairie community of Yorkton. One wishes that he was more specific about his encounter with "the almost marvellous work" of Jewish students and "their home life." It is unsettling to find his claims for Jewish assimilability based upon ideas of "racial superiority," even if Anderson meant this as a compliment. Still, he presented an opposing voice to the likes of Cahan and Robb, whose parliamentary speeches nakedly sought a populist response back home. Anderson's views were part of the uniqueness of 1930s Saskatchewan. They were shaped by his intimacy with communities in his home province and by his comfort with their still growing and varying ethnic complexity. The lack of serious mention of Jews in much writing of the period, and the government's propensity, in census data and landing documents, to list Jewish numbers using the archaic moniker *Hebrew*—almost as if to avoid saying the word *Jew*—were contrasted by Anderson's forthrightness: "No description of the foreign nationalities of Canada would be complete," Anderson wrote, "without reference to the Jews, who are found in every part of our country."[15] His treatise provided a rare corrective to the slur that Jews always shifted toward the city.

Anderson's and England's books on the Continental European stand as bookends at either end of the post–First World War decade. By 1928, with widespread controversy and a parliamentary inquiry reviewing Canada's immigration policies, it's no surprise that government bureaucracy and regulation were undergoing change. In 1928, a new system of medical inspection was put in place that assured Canadians that "*all* prospective immigrants prior to leaving their home" would be seen by Canadian medical officers.[16] This system, developed over a number of years, placed twenty-seven doctors at major ports and centres in Europe and the United Kingdom, including Liverpool, Bristol, Birmingham, Glasgow, Aberdeen, Belfast, Riga, Danzig, Hamburg, Paris, and Antwerp.[17] Canadian medical officers were expected, as well, to travel to nearby towns, with advance notice going out from booking agents to prospective immigrants that an immigration doctor would be in their area.

Not long after my grandfather's departure from Gdynia, the modern port near Danzig (the city that Poles knew as Gdańsk), Canada's chief medical officer of the Overseas Immigration Service, H.B. Jeffs, described the new medical examinations this way:

Complete personal and family histories are obtained with particular reference to insanity, epilepsy, mental deficiency, tuberculosis, accidents, injuries, and illnesses of any kind. All applicants are required to strip to the waist and remove shoes and stockings. The examination of men is carried further by dropping the trousers to the ankles, but women are not more completely undressed unless there is some indication of the necessity for further investigation. Careful examination for diseases of the central nervous system, lungs, heart, blood vessels, skin, and special senses is done. Particular attention is paid to the presence of physical defects, special care being taken with the feet and legs.[18]

My grandfather's shipboard travel documents reveal a trace of this undertaking, with the notation above his name "Copy on Fyle No. 530775." This was his file number with the Department of Immigration in 1930 and remained so throughout his efforts to bring his family after him. The "CANADIAN GOVERNMENT RETURN" document for his ship's sailing is a remarkable artifact.[19] Such things were once probably difficult for descendants to access, but they are now freely available through any number of websites, including records digitized at Library and Archives Canada, as well as at the archive and museum attached to Pier 21, the long-time immigration reception site in Halifax. The original pages were wide and long, with as many as thirty settlers accounted for on a sheet. The information for each traveller runs in a line from left to right, with many columns duly filled in and checked off. First a set of handwritten numbers; then the traveller's family and given names, transliterated into English in unpredictable ways (my grandfather as Ajzensztejn Juda Josef); a column dubbed "Relationship," referring to his being the brother of his Canadian sponsor; sex and age (my grandfather was twenty-nine); country and place of birth (Poland, Radzanów). Next come two vexed columns that must be returned to at greater length but here in short are "Nationality" and "Race or People." In both cases, the information for my grandfather in these columns was overwritten, reconsidered, semi-readable. Someone initially typed "PO" under his nationality, but this was overwritten by hand. In the case of his "Race or People," one must look to the neighbouring travel columns to try to decide what might have been meant here, as distinct from nationality. Others with Polish nationality had their "Race or People" noted as "RUSSIAN" or "UKRAIN," which seems to suggest ethnicity, though certainly in 1930 "RUSSIAN" was also a nationality. So one would have to say that the "Race or People" column is a stumbling block—the information that it offers is suspect, ambiguous, while also revealing, in ways that might not be entirely forthright. In my grandfather's case, as one might guess, his "Race or People" was confirmed, in cursive handwriting, as "Hebrew"—this over the crossed-out typed letters begun as "PO." Of his shipmates with names alphabetically near his, my grandfather was the lone traveller with a handwritten emendation in this column. Further columns report whether the traveller has been in Canada before, has been refused entry or deported, intends to reside in Canada, is capable of reading; for my grandfather, the answers were no, no, no, yes, yes. "What Language" the next column asserts. Again my grandfather's information stood out: he had two languages, Jewish and Polish. The immigration clerks got beyond themselves. My grandfather had two *Jewish* languages, Yiddish and Hebrew, in addition to Polish. And, finally, who paid his passage? "SELF."

So let's say that there are oddities and revealing particularities on his "CANADIAN GOVERNMENT RETURN" form. The line of typed and handwritten information irks us; it calls out for careful interpretation but resists it since we lack the mindsets of the immigration officials and clerks who filled it out. Just one of his shipmates listed bore the "Copy on Fyle" notation, so for these two an account had circulated with Canadian immigration officers, possibly in Poland, either through their passport applications or through arrangements made by sponsors in Canada. Maybe this bureaucratic designation spared my grandfather some of the hullabaloo associated with the physical inspection at Gdynia described by Jeffs, the chief overseas medical officer. This mark of official sanction rode with my grandfather through Southampton, where the shipping agent for the CNR would have noted it, and to his arrival at Quebec City. His way, at least in the early stage of his Canadian foray, was clear.

The confusion around categories such as "Race or People" was not a Made-in-Canada problem. Anti-immigration elements in the United States had aimed to add similar designations to the American census in 1910. There it was the category "Color or Race," which was debated in Congress as a possible designation but not yet among the questions asked of ship-bound newcomers to the country. Among its proponents was Edward F. McSweeney, the assistant commissioner of immigration at the Port of New York. In his promotion of this idea, he was indiscriminate in his use of the terms "race," "people," "stock," and "nationality." Pushback against such categories of immigration and citizenship came from the American Jewish Committee, which argued that the proposed "schedule of races is a purely arbitrary one and will not be supported by any anthropologists."[20] Resisting such categories, Colorado Senator Solomon Guggenheim asserted that "I was born in Philadelphia. Under this census bill they put me down as a Hebrew, not as an American."[21] So it was with my grandfather aboard the SS *Ascania* on its way to Quebec.

The ship was set to arrive at port on November 10. What did he eat, I wonder, on the ten-day crossing of the Atlantic, on the first days of his life devoted to the New World? It turns out that on a more storied Polish ship, the *Batory*, a well-known Vilna-based restaurant owner maintained a kosher kitchen for travellers.[22] Cunard line ships like the *Ascania* had kosher menu service, including for third-class travellers; at Southampton, the butchers were kept busy supplying meat for the travel trade.[23] For lunch, *omelette Portugaise*; for dinner, boiled fresh salmon and creamed potato and celery soup.[24] The cabin was likely one of the newly dubbed "Tourist Third" cabins, with a pair of narrow bunks on one side of the room, a day bed on the other, and a sink with a mirror in between.[25]

On the second sheet of the Return form, the trade of my grandfather in his "own country" is listed incorrectly as "TEACHER," and the same is there for the trade that he would "FOLLOW IN CANADA." This must be seen as part of his sponsor's—his brother's—advice on how best to present himself. His brother's address on Victoria Drive, on the east side of Vancouver, is listed, followed by his nearest relative at home, and this detail tells its own story: Yehudah Yoseph's sister, Chana, no longer resided in Radzanów but had moved to a nearby town listed as Raciat, which, more properly, should be called Racoinz, in the county of Sierpc. My grandfather was issued three "NOS" in answer to whether he was physically or mentally defective or tubercular. His passport, the landing form tells us, was issued at Mława, its number noted. He claimed five dollars in his possession (others listed on his page of the Return form also claimed only five or ten dollars, but a few did admit to carrying more). The CNR would take him west, giving him his first view of the country as a "LANDED Immigrant."

When the Return form is looked at not for personal details but for overall accounting, one gets another array of information. The *Ascania* sailed from Southampton, a major emigration transit point at the time, on November 1, 1930. Because ships of this kind attract fans and aficionados, it's easy to discover that the *Ascania* was a Cunard liner, a great deal more sizable and suitably accoutred than the *Komagata Maru*. Its tonnage was roughly three times that of the latter ship, and it sported a good deal of upscale first-class finery—a smoking room in the style of an old Italian palazzo, viewing decks, and a nursery with its own chocolate shop—to which I assume my grandfather's ticket did not give him access. Among the third-class travellers, my grandfather was kindred in some way to the bulk of travellers on board the *Komagata Maru*, though he certainly travelled with fewer discomforts and no crowding, and the *Ascania* was expected at port and duly received upon arrival at Quebec.

Anyone with sailing experience or interest in ship life and business will recognize in the Return form a version of the traditional ship's manifest—the legal document by which the ship's ownership, route, cargo, and soundness are confirmed. In the case of the Canadian Government Return form, immigration laws were extended and applied to the ship's human cargo. As one was taken on at Southampton, the terms of travel included a sponsor, a bill of health, a destination upon landing, and the more troubling designation of "Race or People." These prerequisites responded to terms set out in immigration regulations of the time, some of them created and confirmed in orders-in-council signed off by the Privy Council of the Liberal King government and, by the time of my grandfather's arrival, the new Conservative cabinet of R.B. Bennett. In this context, orders-in-council were cabinet-level legislative instruments requiring no parliamentary overview. Each one went before cabinet at the recommendation of ministers and was given legal effect by the signature of the governor general or his deputy.

What else should we know about the 1920s and early 1930s in Canada to appreciate the country's view of itself in relation to its immigrants? We know, with hindsight, that Canadians in these years were heading for troubled times, capped by the collapse of the New York Stock Exchange and Depression, drought on the Prairies, the spectacle of Canadians in work camps, and discontented unemployed men riding the rails. But the country inherited, too, from the pre–First World War years, a strong set of voices arguing that Canadian immigration policy was dangerously laissez-faire. In 1911, pre-eminent Canadian humourist and McGill University political economy professor Stephen Leacock, a model elite voice of his time, quipped that Canada recruited its immigrants from "the least educated and most illiterate of the European peoples."[26] Under both Liberal and Conservative federal governments in the following years, policy reflected an increasingly suspicious or, one might say, contradictory view of immigration and the pursuit of regulations that would maintain the cultural status quo that was already a myth. A variety of voices influenced this discussion. The Federal Bureau of Statistics gauged population shifts using the census, requiring those filling out their forms to acknowledge their "racial origin," even though there was no consensus on the meaning of this type of "origin." The question that lurked behind the gathering of such statistics was when could one rightfully call oneself a citizen of "Canadian origin"? At what point was one bathed in the right stuff so that prior "origins" had been washed away? This sort of mind-bending question remained a point of contention through the early decades of the twentieth century.

Robert Hamilton Coats, the country's long-time Dominion statistician and controller of the census, asked the same question using different terms: "How can the assimilation of foreign stocks be measured?"[27] His background resembled those of many other government officials of this period, born in Ontario to Scots parents. Coats studied at the University of Toronto's University College. Early in the century, he edited the *Labour Gazette*, a government publication devoted to the statistical study of the labour market. In 1912, Coats sat on a commission that proposed the foundation of a "centralized statistical agency," and he became the director of the Canadian Census and Statistics Office in 1916 with a staff of fifty. The tabulation of data, by the early 1930s, was done via a machine with "extensive circuits" reading the information as it was tabulated on punch cards.[28] The work of Coats points to the importance of economic concerns, associated with labour competition among countries, price increases, and movements of workers in early Canadian statistical research. Some students of his accomplishments assert the "impartiality and disinterestedness of the statistician, his independence of people's wishes and interests, even those of his own employer."[29] This suggests an impartial stance by the statistics gatherers. But this is a tall order for any bureaucrat, however disinterested the fact-gathering methods. It's true that Coats expressed himself on subjects such as population growth—inevitably linked to immigration—in a way that did not directly promote ideological views. Writing in 1923 of the settlement of Canada's "last best West," Coats accounted for the movement of people across the U.S.-Canada border, and Canada's "relative" population gain compared with Australia and New Zealand, acknowledging the relevance of "racial distribution and assimilation."[30] Canadians move about in his study, travelling here and there, from rural to urban locales, increasingly to Toronto, Montreal, and Winnipeg. But something more direct is on offer in a book that Coats published in 1929 based upon the 1921 census. Titled *Origin, Birthplace, Nationality and Language of the Canadian People (A Census Study Based on the Census of 1921 and Supplementary Data)*, it was a government document published in Ottawa by the "Printer to the King's Most Excellent Majesty," though it does not present itself as government policy. Rather, it proposes to be "analytical of the data on population collected by the census."[31] Between the lines of its argument, and sometimes overtly, one sees an interwar Canadian point of view in line with the views of Liberal and Conservative federal governments of the 1920s and 1930s.

The core of *Origin, Birthplace, Nationality* is a collection of 139 tables. They range over subjects such as origins of newcomers to Canada, distribution of people between urban and rural places, literacy, and rates of incarceration. A recurrent question that Coats raises is how to categorize someone of Canadian origin versus an "alien" (foreign-born) person. This goes to the root of the question of when a newcomer becomes a "new Canadian." Coats is not comfortable with the term "race" and dispenses with it, saying that its meaning is "neither definite nor free from confusion. . . . Most modern national groups are composed of widely varying racial strains." In this he counters race-based nationalism and eugenicist trends of his time. He proposes, instead, for the purposes of the census, the term "origin," which in his view addresses a person's biological, cultural, and geographical makeup.[32] The official indecision on such ideas is reflected on the Return form, acting as the ship's manifest on my grandfather's cross-Atlantic travel, in which both terms—"race" and "origin"—are used and thus in some way cancel each other. Although Coats avoids some of the worst ideas associated with race, national groups, and nation building that asserted themselves in the 1920s, his proposed link between "biological" and "cultural" makeup does not entirely jettison these ideas. The willingness to categorize people maintains its reflexive pull, as do ideas about the "assimilability" of different groups.

It is telling how Canada's sixth census, in 1921, categorized Jewish newcomers and citizens. In his analysis of the census, Coats cites the "relevant instructions to enumerators," which included the requirement that a "foreign-born" person not yet a "naturalized citizen" be "classed by nationality or citizenship according to the country of birth, or the country to which he or she professes to owe allegiance."[33] It's worthwhile to read that direction twice because certain groups were never or almost never categorized in this way. Their identities were severed from the places to which they "profess" or "owe allegiance." They included

"Hindus," "Negroes," and "Hebrews" (the term typically used to refer to Jews in the tables in *Origin, Birthplace, Nationality*). These people couldn't take shape in the census takers' data (or imaginations) as people of fixed national origins, leaving them vulnerable to peculiar and arbitrary treatment. This pattern is evident in the overwritten information on the immigration landing form for my grandfather. When he departed from the Polish port of Gdynia on the Baltic coast, and in turn from Southampton, where he boarded the *Ascania*, he carried a Polish passport (his citizenship in that country having been asserted through his service in the Polish army). Yet his Canadian immigration travel document categorizes him as Hebrew, not Polish. There is even the clear indication that a clerk or immigration agent marked him down at first as Polish and then retracted that, inscribing him on the manifest, the contract between the shipping line and the Canadian Department of Immigration, as Hebrew. This, too, is how the tables in the book by Coats designate Canada's Jewish inhabitants. In a few rare cases in the tables, the term "Jewish" is substituted for the archaic term "Hebrew," but there is no logic to this substitution. It is, to the steadfast statistician's embarrassment, an inadvertent slip in terminology.

What do we learn from the census takers' measure of Canada's "Hebrew" population circa 1921? They were a large component of the Canadian population—roughly 125,000—putting them sixth in line in the "Numerical Strength of Stocks in Canada," led by the English, then the French, Scotch, Irish, and German.[34] "Hebrews" were shown to have among the lowest rates of intermarriage and relatively high rates of English-language literacy.[35] These two markers contributed to the appraisal of their ability to "assimilate fairly rapidly in Canada's 'melting pot.'"[36] Yet Coats reasons that low rates of Jewish intermarriage with non-Jewish Canadians could be taken as resistance to assimilation. Still, from our perspective today, if one is acquiring English at a high rate, that signals the opposite tendency. Although his logic on the matter is contradictory, no doubt the census itself, and his analysis of it, aim to measure processes of assimilation. Coats acknowledges this directly: "Certain stocks assimilate fairly rapidly in Canada's 'melting pot'; others more slowly, while many appear to be practically inassimilable. It is a matter of indifference whether foreign people fail to marry with the British and French stocks because of aversion on their own part or on the part of the British and French. The result is the same so far as Canada's population structure is concerned."[37] Coats states that "Orientals, Hebrews and certain of the Slavic peoples ... are practically inassimilable by marriage."[38] This, of course, is what the immigration commissioners in Ottawa and on the country's coasts thought, and they were likely glad to see the census and the country's head statistician backing this supposition.

❀ ❀ ❀

To men like Coats, assimilation was linked directly to nation building, and for them there was a consistent fear that what they thought of as "racial mixing" would ensure a "permanent deterioration in the species."[39] Immigration numbers in the 1920s stoked this fear: if English immigration to Canada was decreasing, then which sort of people should fill the gap? More to the point, how many non–Anglo Saxon newcomers should be allowed into the country without diluting the status quo? These discussions were heightened by the influence of eugenicist thought on politicians as well as the experts who oversaw Canada's census takers. Racialist ideas were on the rise in the United States and Europe before the establishment of the Canadian National Committee for Mental Hygiene in 1918 and the Eugenics Society of Canada in 1930.

These discussions motivated essays published in the late 1920s with titles like "The Case for a Quota" and "Is There a Canadian Race?" by W. Burton Hurd, an influential interwar demographer and expert on "origin statistics." Trained in political economy and sociology, Hurd was an economic adviser to the federal government. One of his areas of study focused on the difficulty that his Canadian contemporaries had in their efforts to agree on what was meant by an individual's "origins," revealing the shakiness of the terminology applied in the census. Hurd and others wrote prolifically on how the Dominion Bureau of Statistics (DBS) ought to merge geographical, cultural, and "racial" components in a way that might characterize reliably a newcomer's "origin." However careful such arguments aimed to be, much of what was said was circuitous, even illogical, since issues of cultural and "racial" background proved to be impossible to define. Hurd applied one rule of thumb confidently, and his approach was reflected in "Instructions to Commissioners and Enumerators" put forward by the DBS: "Except in the case of the Hebrews, the term 'origin' always connotes the original geographical habitat of a population group, usually implies a distinct culture, and often a definite biological strain."[40] This tangle of would-be logic and categorization echoed other writing on this subject in the 1920s and 1930s. "Usually" and "often" were not terms of confidence in outlining the enumerator's task. Worse, the confidence with which the "Hebrew" was placed outside this area of definable background derived from which position—scientific or sociological? It must have followed from some childhood notion of the "Wandering Jew," or the related canard, beloved of 1920s Fascists, who organized their own sense of identity in contradiction to "rootless Jewish cosmopolitanism." In fact, the Eisensteins had inhabited the Polish plains longer than the Hurds had dwelt in the Brockville area. And most of them surely would have continued to do so, with satisfied and increasingly assimilated Polish character and culture if not for the breakdown of Polish democratic society and, much more darkly, the arrival of the Wehrmacht on a fine day early in September 1939. So, *origin*, who gets to name it? And how do a country's laws, bureaucrats, and border clerks assert such naming?

It is a pleasant surprise to learn that Coats had a Jewish counterpart, a Polish-born bean counter whose work responded to the government's tried and true Scotsman. Just as Coats was at the cutting edge of sociological and statistical measurement in 1920s Canada, so too Louis Rosenberg's demographic work on Canada's Jews set a unique standard for the 1930s. Educated in Leeds, England, Rosenberg emigrated to Canada in 1914. From 1915 to 1919, he worked as a teacher at the Lipton farm colony in Saskatchewan. From 1919 to 1940, he directed the Jewish Colonization Association's prairie farm colonies from its Regina office, aiding in settlement and maintaining these communities (in this role, he would correspond with my grandfather). It was in this period that Rosenberg began his "systematic statistical studies of Canadian Jewish life." Upon moving to Montreal, he took up the position of national research director for the Bureau of Social and Economic Research for the Canadian Jewish Congress. Sociologist Mort Weinfeld tells us that the bureau was in fact a one-man band without staff or funds to support Rosenberg's far-reaching work.[41] We can view Rosenberg's 1939 publication, *Canada's Jews: A Social and Economic Study of Jews in Canada*, as the countertext to the study of the 1921 census by Coats. Rosenberg's goal, based upon census data from 1931, was a "social and economic study of Canada's Jewish population" that would avoid "apologetics" and "special pleading." Rosenberg hoped that his work would "serve to sweep away the mass of ignorance and misleading half-truths which exist in Canada concerning its Jewish population." His data-gathering methods included regular letters to the Dominion Bureau of Statistics "requesting a certain tabulation or bit of information," in response to which statistics officials would, when "feasible, supply him with the needed data."[42]

What do we learn from Rosenberg's demographic work that is not made clear by Coats in his analysis of the DBS census? The short answer is everything. Census data in Coats's tabulations cause Jews to disappear, not just behind the obfuscating rubric of "Hebrew" but also behind a few key diminishing abstractions—they will not intermarry, they are overly prone to dwell in cities, they are numerous, and they are "to an abnormal extent . . . very often found in quarters or wards," a "tendency" that is "significant from the standpoint of assimilation."[43] One point in their favour: they have a low rate of ignorance of either French or English. On this point, Rosenberg offers a knowledgeable and nuanced view of the data. Alongside English-language literacy, he finds a high retention of Yiddish as the mother tongue, crediting the idea, ahead of its time, that assimilation to the mainstream language of workplace and social interaction does not "necessarily involve the abandonment of other languages." Rosenberg was guided by what we might call a proto-multicultural ideal, which the census takers did not consider. And, though Rosenberg takes note, like Coats, of low rates of Jewish intermarriage, he suggests that there are other ways, beyond intermarriage, for a group to attain "language and cultural assimilation."[44] Demography, for Rosenberg, should work to counter stereotype or what he calls "prevalent impression." One of these stereotypes was the notion that "Jewish women become mothers at an earlier age than women of Anglo-Saxon origin in Canada," which census data disproved.[45]

Rosenberg characterizes changes made to Canada's immigration regulations in the 1920s as being based upon "'racial' theories similar in many respects to those subsequently adopted by Hitler and his Nazi

Party."[46] He is even careful to place the word *racial* in quotation marks since in his mind it had no basis in science or social policy as applied in Hitler's Germany. Here, too, Rosenberg hits on an explanation for why, in *Origin, Birthplace, Nationality*, as well as in the census data, Polish Jews were placed in the semi-mythical category of "Hebrews," a people who have no nationality to claim for themselves. New categories for immigrants, introduced by the Liberal government in 1923, did not use overt racial terminology but relied on racialist ideals to differentiate between "Preferred" and "Non-Preferred" countries of origin. This hierarchy followed contemporary notions of racial desirability: the "Preferred Class" of newcomers consisted of Northern Europeans; the "Non-Preferred Class" was made up of Central and Eastern Europeans from Austria, Hungary, Russia, Poland, and the Baltic States; finally, a "Special Permit Class," which trailed even the "Non-Preferred Class" in desirability, could gain entrance only by way of an order-in-council. Lumped into this class were applicants from Italy, Greece, Bulgaria, Syria, and Turkey, all countries with low numbers of emigration to Canada. But there, too, were the Jews, regardless of their places of birth. In this context, each file could be looked at by immigration commissioners and their cabinet allies in response to a perceived overflow of Jewish newcomers in the country.[47]

Those from "Non-Preferred" countries could gain access to Canada officially only if they were farmers with means, farm labourers, domestic workers, or wives and minor children of Canadian residents. But railway and steamship agents were told *not to include* Jewish applicants in this "Non-Preferred" group, whether they met these labour expectations or held Polish, Romanian, or any other passport from the "Non-Preferred" or "Preferred" countries of origin. Rather, Jews would be considered not by national status but as requiring a "Special Permit," to be decided by the Department of Immigration on a case-by-case basis and in many instances by an order-in-council. Rosenberg characterizes this development this way: "the Canadian government did not extend to all bearers of a passport issued by the Polish, Roumanian, Lithuanian, Austrian or other Government the same treatment and regulations, but made a distinction between the Jewish and non-Jewish subjects of those countries."[48] Here the period and its bureaucratic machinations come into focus. I liken such immigration strategies to the dressing down that a military officer once received in a trial for treason—the breaking of a sword over a knee or some other such demotion of a person's identity. Just so, my grandfather's nationality—his citizenship guaranteed by his passport from Rzeczpospolita Polska—was replaced by a made-up, not-understood category chosen by the federal bureaucracy, its immigration department, census takers, and transport clerks. He was branded on his way out to cattle country with a scarlet H.

"PURE RUSSIAN, JEW, GERMAN"

Coats, the census, and ever-tightening immigration regulations might represent key mainstream Canadian ideas of the nation in the 1920s, but it is possible to find contrary views. Such views represent alternative trends, more forward-looking, less conservative approaches to nation building and identity. On this side of the equation are personalities worth recalling who have fallen entirely by the historical wayside and whose views of Canada are rarely considered.

Ironically, the railways, so central to colonization and western settlement, acted as enthusiastic promoters and facilitators of a heterogeneous population. For the Canadian Pacific Railway (CPR), the lead promoter and believer in its potential as a transporter of new Canadians was John Murray Gibbon. His background—unlike other influential contemporaries—might have prepared him for this work. Born in Ceylon to Scottish parents, Gibbon studied at Oxford University and in Germany. His literary interests led him to write for the London-based weekly *Black and White*. In 1907, he was a publicity manager for the CPR, and in 1913 he became the railway's chief publicity agent, working out of its Montreal office.[1] Gibbon was a cultural impresario on many fronts. His most impressive undertaking was a series of Folksong and Handicraft Festivals that he mounted at the railway's showpiece hotels. Between the spring of 1927 and the summer of 1931, there were sixteen festivals staged in the Prairies, the Rockies, Toronto, Quebec, and the BC coast. They were usually three-day events highlighting fare as varied as the "Canadian Folk Song" and "Old English Yuletide" music. The guidebook for the 1928 "New Canadian Folksong and Handicraft Festival" asserted that a country was "enriched more quickly by assimilating and absorbing the ideas of other races which may be neighbours or may be invaders or may be immigrant refugees." As proof of this, the Winnipeg festival highlighted the "fine culture brought to this country from Continental Europe by newcomers of other races—particularly Scandinavian, Romance, Slav Magyar and Teutonic."[2]

These views ran counter to many of the political and legislative undertakings of the period. Through his festivals, Gibbon was an early supporter of the idea of a Canadian "mosaic," a term that he acknowledged borrowing from Kate Foster's 1926 book *Our Canadian Mosaic*.[3] Foster's book, published by the social activist Dominion Council of the Young Women's Christian Associations of Canada, was based upon her cross-country travels. It included a foreword by James Coyne—the president of the Royal Society of Canada—who insisted that there was a "general consensus of opinion . . . that only the readily assimilable races should be admitted" as immigrants to Canada.[4] This was the usual upper-crust boilerplate on immigration, but Foster presented a more open-ended set of possibilities, ending a chapter titled "Our Provinces: Of Interest to Newcomers" with "Pointed Questions," including "is assimilation of certain peoples impossible? . . . Would it involve a complete acceptance of the culture of the new environment and a complete abandonment of the old? Would this be good for the immigrant?"[5] The willingness to ask the last question separated Foster from many of her contemporaries.

Foster speaks for the status quo when she acknowledges that "Canada has never sought colonists from Asia," noting that "no Chinese were admitted to the country as immigrants" in 1925.[6] But she announces her faith in "Our Canadian Mosaic" in her concluding chapters, in which she proposes an assimilationist ethic that would see "each race contributing something of value and so slowly but surely evolving a new people enriched by the diversity of its origin." This proposition set her apart from many of her influential contemporaries. In a chapter titled "A Near View of Our New Canadians," Foster presents a catalogue of the "Foreign-Born" who have made their way to Canada.[7] There are the Armenians ("very ancient"), the Bulgarians ("found in Toronto"), the Chinese, none of whom was welcome in 1925, and on through the alphabetically ordered catalogue, past the Doukhobors, prohibited because of their "peculiar customs," and the Jews. Foster's willingness to use the term "Jews" and not the odder, ancient moniker "Hebrew" seems to be a good sign. She is actually referring to people one might meet on a Toronto street rather than biblical archetypes. But she begins her section on one of the largest immigrant groups in the country with a proposition better suited to stand-up comedy than an effort at sociological clear-sightedness: "One thing is certain Jews are readily identified the world over by their distinctive facial characteristics." Having stepped on one slippery banana peel, she wipes out on another: "Very few Jews are on the land, in Canada or elsewhere."[8] Careful investigation along rail lines throughout Saskatchewan, with an eye for merchants in small towns, or homesteaders on the sections fanning out from the rail lines, would have offered evidence contrary to this claim.

A sense of Jews not seen, or not comprehended when seen, is a good guiding principle by which to consider the Canadian mainstream of the 1920s and early 1930s. Gibbon's New Canadian Folksong and Handicraft Festivals—even as they paraded the West's ethnic mix—were arenas of not seeing. For each festival, a hand-sized pamphlet was printed to serve not only as a program but also as a kind of map that would provide attendees with an appreciation of the cultures on view. At the Winnipeg festival, the Manitoba Branch of the Canadian Handicraft Guild acknowledged that in Western Canada "so much of the native art of older lands has been transplanted to our soil" that the branch organized a competition among dedicated artisans to highlight this handiwork.[9] In Calgary, in 1930, prizes of five dollars were offered for basketry and rush work, lace work, pottery, quilting, and woodworking.[10] Alongside the guild's handicraft displays and competitions, the CPR presented a main-stage show of folksong concerts and dance programs. They included Don Cossacks alongside acts from Poland, Iceland, Denmark, Sweden, Norway, Holland, Hungary, Ukraine, the Schwarzwald, Finland, and, as the festival guide has it, Czecho-Slovakia, Roumania, and Jugo-Slavia. Among the Swedish folk dancers at Calgary were thirty child performers. The Don Cossacks mounted a "Musical Quartette with Balalajka, Mandolina and Guitarre"; the

Hungarians employed "gypsy arrangements"; the Czecho-Slovaks sang a song to the memory of the fourteenth-century religious martyr "Master, John Huss."[11]

Festivals in prairie cities had a multi-ethnic flavour and exhibited a kind of proto-multiculturalism or at least a whiff of the Canadian mosaic before Canadians thought of it as being part of their national identity. The pamphlet advertising the events at the Palliser Hotel in Calgary in 1930 could be mistaken for an album of ethnographic photography: Highlander dancers in quilts; Welsh in stovepipe hats; Danish folk dancers in lace caps and aprons; "Kossak" dancers in peaked Persian lamb hats, their sabres raised; a "Hungarian Cowboy" alongside a "Jugo-Slav Bagpipe player." The pamphlet's preface highlights song and craft with an eye to nation building. The "main idea" of the festival, its writer tells us, is "to help Canadians to realise the priceless heritage they possess in the traditional melodies which have been brought to this country by immigrants, and some cases have been composed in this country by early settlers." The dances, music, and costumes on show at the Palliser are said to be "centuries old and yet . . . still as fresh and delightful as if they had been invented in our own day."[12]

The CPR festivals were an unusual merger between folk or ethnic culture and elite figures and institutions. In Quebec City in 1927 and 1928, the National Museum, National Gallery, and Public Archives of Canada contributed to presentations alongside folk singers and craftspeople from rural Quebec. In the day, woodcarvers displayed the art of church decoration, and the final evening of the festival included a "Folk and Canadian Historical Costume Ball" hosted by the wife of the premier, Mme L.A. Taschereau. "Folk costumes" were available to rent through Holt Renfrew & Company for a fee of five dollars.[13]

The Calgary festival took place in early summer 1930. My grandfather's trip west was on a CNR train, so in November the train would have pulled up at the sandstone station in the city's "Rouleauville" district, where early French Catholic settlers from Quebec had staked out a missionary village, building a church and parish hall, the latter of which was sold to the CNR and repurposed as its depot. Had his brother written to him to explain the trip, that on his way to the coast, passing towns and wheat fields, he would soon come upon the fantastic vision of the Rockies and then the western slope down to the water, his new home waiting for him on Victoria Drive? If my grandfather had time to step onto the CNR station boardwalk, then he would have seen Tin

Lizzies parked at an angle. November in Calgary is grey. The CPR festival's folk-dancing and folk-singing ethnics would have been long gone. But someone might well have been waiting on the platform for another Jewish traveller from out east. An acknowledgement under the eaves of the platform would have led to a back-and-forth in Yiddish, maybe to the local's mention of the pack of "Kossak" dancers who'd passed through town. In Radzanów, in the not-too-distant past, Cossacks had rolled through on horseback. My grandfather might have regaled his Calgarian pal with his Polish army doings and the Russian cavalry's presence in the Radzanów area on their way down from Sierpc.

This is fun to imagine, but the activities of the New Canadian Folksong and Handicraft Festivals also present a sobering picture. Among the early, important groups immigrating to the Prairies and invited to the festivals, there was a notable absence: Jews. In his 1936 study, *The Colonization of Western Canada: A Study of Contemporary Land Settlement (1896–1934)*, Robert England reminds us that "it is not commonly recognized that Jewish settlers were amongst the early settlers of Western Canada and that their settlement predates the German, Ukrainian, Doukhobor, Russian and Hungarian settlements."[14] England adds a few words about the early Jewish farming colonies at Moosomin and Wapella, Lipton and Hirsch, Sonnenfeld and Edenbridge, but he does so in the context of a chapter titled "Hungarian and Other Communities," a title that, like Foster's entrée into a discussion of Jewish newcomers, sounds a bit like the opening of a comedy routine.

What can we say about the Jewish absence at the Calgary festival and its counterparts? One could not argue that all of the invited groups represented their native countries, since two—the Don "Kossaks" and the Schwarzwalders—represented an ethnic or regional culture rather than a national identity. We might hope that the Poles brought with them a hint of Jewish music, for the two traditions enlivened each other through the nineteenth century and early twentieth century. However, if one listens to contemporary versions of the songs chosen by the Polish contingent invited to play in 1930 at the Palliser (they included "Pod bialem orlem" or "Under the White Eagle"), there is no hint of klezmer or even gypsy influence on the Polish *kapela*. The Don "Kossaks" with their "Mandolina Quartette" are another group ripe for investigation of possible overlap with Jewish culture. Mandolin orchestras proliferated among Jewish groups on the Canadian Prairies in the early decades of the twentieth century.

Calgary's Glenbow Museum archives hold a remarkable photo-graph that is not related directly to the folksong festival in 1930 but overlaps with it in uncanny ways. Dated 1929, the photo is titled "Peretz School Orchestra, Calgary, Alberta." Its black background is punctuated by thirteen figures, standing and seated, holding stringed instruments. Among them is a teacher—Mrs. Smith—and the rest are young people aged from ten to their middle teens. They hold mando-lins of various shapes and sizes, a guitar, and, in the case of one young female performer, a tiny banjo.

The female performers wear silk dresses with long fringes, their dark hair glossy. In one case, a youthful forehead is decorated by a neatly curled lock of hair, Josephine Baker–style. The orchestra players look seriously at their photographer. The Glenbow Museum lists the names of those pictured: Ida Robinsky, Anne Levine (who holds the tiny banjo), Max Eisenstadt, Morris Estrin. . . . The photograph would not look out of place among those collected in the pamphlet for the festival in 1930 in Calgary, with its "Czecho-Slovak Dancers from Saskatche-wan" and its "Irish Jig Dancers (Pupils of Alice Murdoch, Calgary)."[15]

The mandolin was a ubiquitous folk instrument in Eastern Europe, unique to no cultural locale. Around Radzanów, it was played by Poles and Jews, and Jewish musical influence was ever present as young men hired themselves out for weddings and weekend dances, sometimes at the local noble's manor. Immigrant Jews brought mandolin music with them to Western Canada, and it was associated with secular Yiddish schools where folk culture was promoted, like the Calgary Peretz School. The mandolin orchestra was a rare venue available to young women who yearned to perform. A commonly played piece was the "Polonez" (Yiddish for "Polonaise"), whose title highlights the cross-over potential between Jewish and Polish "folk" music. In 1930, Mrs. Smith, Anne Levine, and her pals were all living a few blocks from the Palliser, almost in its shadow. Based upon their photo, they were rarin' to go had they received an invitation to perform.

Jewish absence in the festivals was interrupted once but not with the goal of highlighting Jewish "national" or "folk" culture's place in "Our Canadian Mosaic." Rather, the occasion was the performances at the Quebec City festivals of 1927 and 1928 of the Toronto-based Hart House String Quartet. In 1928, the year that the quartet gave a prize-winning performance of a composition based upon Canadian folk melodies, its members were Milton Blackstone (viola), Harry Adaskin (second violin), Boris Hambourg (cello), and Geza de Kresz (first violin).[16] Historian Claude Bissell states the obvious about the Hart House String Quartet, that "at any stage in its long existence, the majority of its members were Jews."[17] Hambourg, the son of a student of Arthur Rubinstein, was born in Yaroslav, Russia. Adaskin's family left an observant Jewish upbringing behind in Riga in 1903. With their European ancestry, training, and peripatetic careers straddling North America and Eastern Europe, the men of the quartet were representative of a host of folk and immigrant cultures and their musical traditions. The quartet's prize at the 1928 New Canadian Folksong and Handicraft Festival did not reflect this; instead, it highlighted what might be called their skill at passing via their ability to translate a set of local motifs and melodies. When they were not playing at Hart House, they were sent abroad by the CNR and the CBC as ambassadors of Canadian musical culture. In most of the historical material devoted to them, their Jewish background is not mentioned.

If non-Jewish Canadians typically were *not seeing* Jews, what were they thinking about them in those years? In Canadian government circles, increasingly, bureaucrats and elected officials were thinking about keeping Jews, along with a host of other undesirables, out of the country. In the case of Jews, immigration numbers point to their success in this effort. In 1930–31, my grandfather's year of arrival,

3,421 Jews entered Canada; in the following year, the number dropped to 649, where it would stay more or less until the outbreak of war.[18] Foster thought that they didn't like to farm. England, writing in 1936, knew that they were settled early on the southern Saskatchewan prairie. When it came to Gibbon's spectacles, with their depth and cultural variety and willingness to highlight the cultures of new Canadians, Jews did not appear. The great Yiddish word for this is *farshvundn*. They "disappeared."

All the while, Eastern European Jews were riding the rails from ports inland. Many stayed put in central Canadian cities, whereas others were part of the railways' much-sought-after westbound business, which began with ticket agents in European ports, connected with steamship line marketing efforts, before arriving at an eastern port. In the middle and late 1920s, these travellers were officially in the hands of the CPR and CNR, following the terms of the federal government's Railway Agreement, which in 1925 passed responsibility to the rail companies for attracting and conveying Continental European agriculturalists. This responsibility included the ability to "select, transport and settle agriculturalists, agricultural workers and domestic servants from 'non-preferred countries.'"[19] The epithet "Continental European" showed up in these years as a euphemism, seemingly at times as a neutral way of referring to people from countries of Southern and Eastern Europe that Canadian immigration regulations characterized as Non-Preferred. The willingness to seek them in the middle 1920s reflected an upturn in the economy and labour needs, though not all Canadians agreed with this approach. Communal organizations, including the Canadian Legion of the British Empire Service League, wrote to Robert Forke, the Liberal minister of immigration, to express their displeasure that immigrants from Central and Southeastern Europe were taking jobs that they did not deserve to have.

People from these places wanted to come to Canada, making up a large contingent of the 800,000 who came between 1925 and 1930.[20] The CNR, as an arm of the federal government, went to great efforts to document the progress of these newcomers to prove the success and profitability of their settlement efforts. One remarkable outcome of this documentation was the railway's creation of a dossier of photos taken at the Quebec City and Halifax immigration reception centres and more dramatically, from the standpoint of our view of 1920s Canada, on homesteads. Albums are devoted to each western province and to various settlement "schemes." They look like large, old-fashioned family photo albums. Each page shows a rectangular black-and-white photo, set into adhesive corners, picturing the settler or "Head of Family" with wife and children. In a few cases, it's the "Mrs." alone, holding a child before a log-and-mud house, birch trees in the background. Beneath these pictures, one finds the date of arrival in Canada, the steamship line, and the settlers' "European Address" and "Nationality." The information in this latter category, a bit like the "Race or People" rubric aboard the ship, offers a varied set of details—"Ukrainian, Orthodox," "Polish, Roman Catholic"—and in this way presents a shifting portrait of identity as it relates to homeland and religious affiliation. The settlers' "Present Address" is genuinely moving, placed as it often is in a far-flung settlement in northern Saskatchewan— Paddockwood, Parkside, Henribourg—along with the number of acres under cultivation. On each page is a summary of the settling family's progress and homesteading efforts. Of Mrs. Brodacki, whose Polish address is so detailed and tangled that one wonders whether it could be found on a map, the CNR notes the settler's "comfortable little house. Since buying the farm, Brodacki has cleared and broken up some land and has also taken advantage of the good wages offering during the harvest time."[21] Sometimes the summary highlights the settlement "scheme" responsible for sending the settlers west, how much money they brought with them, their direct investments in newly bought farmland, and the number of children they brought from Europe.[22]

Photos from this dossier found their way into newspapers and magazines as part of an ongoing discussion about the place of immigrants in national culture. CNR office correspondence about the photos is revealing. In 1929, the railway's superintendent of land settlement wrote to a colleague: "The photographs are generally excellent. We would suggest, however, that in the future it would be a good idea to have the women remove the head shawls before taking the photographs. Mode of dress is responsible for much of the criticism of newcomers as 'foreigners' and in our photographs it is well to have them look as 'Canadian' as possible."[23] This proviso reverberates in Quebec today, with efforts by the provincial government to ban varieties of religious or cultural dress said to clash with "Quebec values" or the society's expressed "secular" character. A commonly invoked canard suggests that, because Quebecers —traumatized by their colonialist Catholic heritage—threw off their links with an inherited religious culture, they cannot bear to see

CANADIAN NATIONAL RAILWAYS

Head of Family: Michal Brodacki
European Address: Ziemia Siodlecka,Wajow,
                       Lubielski, Bieta,Podliaska
                       Lomasy,Wies Hluszcza,Poland.
Nationality: Polish, Roman Catholic,
Arrived Canada: July 22,1929,ex.s.s.REGINA
Steamship Line: White Star
Presnet Address: Paddockwood, Sask.
Land Location: S.W.¼ 22-52-25-W/2nd.

This family were located by the Canadian National Ra ilways
in the Paddockwood district in Northern Saskatchewan where
Brodacki purchased a partially improved farm of 160 acres
at a price of $9.00 per acre, paying $500.00 in cash, the
balance being spread over 12 years. In the above photograph
Mrs. Brodacki is shown standing in front of their comfortable
little house. Since buying the farm, Brodacki has cleared
and broken up some land and has also taken advantage of the
good wages offering during the harvest time.

                              (Scheme A - 2229-893)

such religious expression in newcomers to the province. NDP leader Jagmeet Singh received the same message when he was approached while campaigning and told that he should remove his turban to look more Canadian. The opinion of the CNR's superintendent seems to be, nearly 100 years after it was set down, a perfectly contemporary expression of social engineering. Some ideas, however demeaning, simply don't go away.

I wonder how my grandfather was dressed when he met with Canadian immigration officers, first at the port of Gdynia in Poland, where he would have been examined by a Canadian medical officer, and then at Quebec City. I have only a few pictures of him at the time of his travel to Canada. In a photo taken around the time of his marriage in 1928, two years before he set out, he is the picture of cosmopolitan suaveness in a tailored suit, dark striped tie, high white collar with collar pin, and white pocket square, his face smoothly shaved and his head uncovered. He went with the object of his romantic energy, Chaya Dina, to Mława's old market square, to Zygmunt Lipszyc's busy photo studio. The photo has the studio's name on its back. Chaya Dina wears a dress that one would describe as modern: a wide scoop neck, dark material with widely spaced white stripes, and a black silk bow at her hip. The couple are the picture of the Polonizing cosmopolitan twentieth-century culture that would be destroyed utterly by the Germans in a decade.

Once active as a *shoichet*, a teacher and religious leader on the Canadian Prairies, my grandfather would change his comportment: his head would be covered, his beard neatly trimmed. At his departure, to complement whatever decisions he made regarding clothing, there was the distinctively cosmopolitan German name Eisenstein. This meant, though family lore carried no details, that his forebears on his father's side had come to Poland from the Prussian west, and certainly this would have accounted for his light hair and blue eyes.

❀ ❀ ❀

Germans. Let me say a few words about them, for they play an interesting role in what I have set down so far. Whether one were to read the minutes of meetings in the parliamentary Privy Council chamber, or to overhear the chatter in a smoking car full of CNR immigration agents as they considered their hard-won photo dossier, Germans were thought to be the best catch if one could not get the desired numbers from the United Kingdom and United States. Evidence of this preference appears in a photograph taken in 1908 by John Woodruff, hired by the Department of the Interior to photograph newcomers at immigration ports in Quebec City and Saint John, New Brunswick. Often he gathered three types or, in the lingo of the time, three examples of different national stock. In the photo, three men stand with their backs to a wooden door, possibly that of an outbuilding at the Quebec port. Its descriptive title, "Pure Russian, Jew, German," aims to name the three figures pictured.[24] (In comparing it to other Woodruff pictures of the time, one gets a sense of the genre that the Department of the Interior was pursuing: trios of men of working age wearing their characteristic "costumes"—jacket modestly buttoned, headgear distinctive.)

What can we say about the Russian, Jew, and German? They are men of roughly the same age and height, each wearing a hat and heeled boots. All three have facial hair, though the Jew has the most, a dark beard trimmed to a point that covers the bottom half of his face. The cap on the head of the Russian is a bit sportier than that of the Jew, and he has a stolid stance, whereas the Jew presents himself diffidently, standing a bit behind the other two, less casually. Only he has his back against the wooden outbuilding.

The German demands detailed comment. His hat is a gentleman's bowler. His jacket is matched with a buttoned-up vest, and his overcoat rests lightly over his arm. The white of his shirt is prominent. He stands with his feet apart, a cigarette in one hand, the picture of insouciant but casual confidence. He is the one among the three who might be described as an up-and-comer. A casting agent calling for a Canadian of his time surely would spot him as the right man. Remarkably, like the documentation on my grandfather's landing form, the Jew in Woodruff's photograph has been stripped of his nationality. He is a Nobody from Nowhereville, a figure of lore and medieval legend, the Wandering Jew. He is one degree more real than the Canadian census taker's version, the Hebrew. One wonders whether the Department of the Interior was aware of the intricate code behind the message of the photo, or whether these ideas were simply in the air that people breathed in the early decades of the twentieth century and Woodruff was not concerned about the camera's editorial gaze.

There is a revealing popular context in which this photograph was used. In a 1910 article in the *Canadian Courier*, a "national weekly" magazine published in Toronto, the three figures appear as cutouts in a group of twelve "Types" of "New-Comers" from "Photographs Taken at Quebec and Halifax." These exemplars are presented in two of six rows. The top row is headed by the "English" type. He is the trimmest and, we must assume, the best suited to Canadian life. The "Pure Russian" from the Quebec trio is dubbed an "honest plodder" by the magazine's editors. The "German" receives a vote of confidence: "In Ontario, Thousands; in the West, Tens of Thousands." The "Jew," looking lost without his wooden door to stand against, is fleshed out a bit and called a "Russian Jew." He is last in line in the bottom row, tagged with an insult, a kind of classroom bully epithet: "Not anxious to farm—a dweller in cities."[25] We hear, in this willingness to sling dirt, the railway superintendents, the photographer for hire, and the magazine editor as they join the team of identity makers, all willing to rely on stereotypes and faux categories. It is as if the CNR photos were meant as templates rather than as pictures of real people. "Jew." "Russian Jew." "Russian." The terms shifting and arbitrary. In Canadian cities, around cabinet tables and university lecterns, bureaucrats and social scientists mused about the meaning of cultural origin, ethnicity, race, and peoplehood, and they took part in discussions of eugenic theories that contributed to worldwide disasters.

My grandfather's landing document; Woodruff's portraits for the Department of the Interior; the folksong festival in Calgary in 1930; the forgotten Peretz School mandoliners; each reflects the shifting and unsure role of Jews in early Canadian imagination and public life. In some unquiet way, all four point to what Canadians thought about Jews. In each case, it seems, they thought rather little, and if anything their ideas were askew, based upon confused notions and stereotypes that led up blind alleys. I have no photograph of my grandfather upon his arrival at Quebec City. I do not have his Polish passport of the early 1930s in which his nationality was made clear. Of his travels across the country toward the coast, I can only daydream. In Polish photos of the late 1920s, he is a young man, bright faced, at ease. Make of him what you will.

OH, OTTAWA

I f this were a silent film, then the next part of the story would open with an iris-in shot—the tiny black circle expanding to reveal a silver-and-white scenario that includes my grandfather aboard a train travelling toward his point of departure on Poland's Baltic coast, the ship setting out for the New World at Southampton, his CNR train departing for the west at Quebec City as he considers the tin of sardines that he's been given sans key to wind back its top.

Set these views aside for a bit. They await us, these immigrant scenarios that blend heartache and a slapstick kind of unheeding movement forward. They're fun. And scary too. But the black circle expands first on a Canadian setting before those above could take place.

The setting is Ottawa. The year 1926, before the Depression and directly between the world wars. Close in on characters worthy of a dramatic scenario, like nothing showing at the time on a Canadian stage. Our stage is the country's Parliament, with its Gothic byways and towers. All of the players are men, though one woman lurks, off-stage. As in a Shakespearean tragedy, there are two bitterly opposed sides. On one side are figures of Canadian authority—parliamentary ministers, deputy ministers, immigration commissioners, some wearing high wing-tip collars and waistcoats and sporting fulsome moustaches. Arrayed against them are men less prone to the moustache but well tailored all the same (one is a manufacturer of suits in Montreal, another the owner of the biggest department store in Ottawa). These men are representatives of the Canadian Jewish community, leaders of social welfare organizations, success stories from the Montreal and Ottawa business communities. If, at the time, there was a Jewish Canadian aristocracy—however tiny—these were its male representatives.

Before these actors appear, we are entertained by a folksinger, a troubadour, the parliamentary fool. I'll tell you what he sounds like, no matter how anachronistic it might seem. He sounds like Johnny Cash. More specifically, he sings and plays in the style of recordings that Cash made at the end of his career—country songs, murder ballads, covers of popular songs in a style not out of place in the 1920s. This scenario is best set to his baritone, its grimly humorous existential rumble, like a physical presence in your head. It's this music that allows us to feel properly the spirit of Canada in 1926.

The scene opens on Parliament Hill, under the Gothic rooftops, which sit high above the river. What are the Jews doing in Ottawa? The Jews are begging. That's putting it bluntly because they comport themselves like dignified callers on professional equals. But begging is what they've come to do. We know this because one of the beggars, Simon Belkin, a veteran worker in Canadian Jewish immigration and settlement organizations, has appointed himself the beggars' note taker. In his notes, he calls the Jews' efforts that December day a "general conference on Jewish immigration between the Government and the Jews of Canada."[1] The date of this conference might be auspicious: in mid-December, the new Liberal government has just settled into power.

Belkin acknowledges the two-sided nature of this "conference" with admirable directness. The Jews have come to meet the new immigration minister, Robert Forke, an MP from Manitoba and the leader of the short-lived Liberal-Progressive Party. Prime Minister King remains offstage, allowing his ministers and deputies to represent his government.

The Jews who have come to beg along with Belkin are an interesting bunch. There's Lyon Cohen (soon to be Leonard's grandfather), a clothing manufacturer and key figure in an array of Montreal community organizations. With him are two crossover figures, Jews whose parliamentary seats—A.A. Heaps from Winnipeg and S.W. Jacobs from Montreal—place them close to power. Morris Abraham Gray is there too. He is a long-time Jewish Immigrant Aid Society manager and Winnipeg alderman from the city's Jewish North End, and he would become a helpmate of my grandfather a few years later. Belkin's companions include, as well, representatives and executive directors of Jewish immigration aid agencies.

The immigration minister, Forke, is new to his job. Who might be cast in his role? We would need an actor sporting a full greying moustache, and the costume department would have to find a high white collar. Forke has with him a deputy minister, W.J. Egan, as well as the immigration commissioners A.L. Jolliffe and F.C. Blair, department bureaucrats who will outlast governments, each of them skilled at watching the political winds change from their bureaucratic roosts. Jolliffe was on the job in Vancouver when the *Komagata Maru*'s future was being debated in court, and in later years he would pen dark missives to my grandfather's representatives at the Jewish Immigrant Aid Society. If immigration commissioners are remembered, and most often they are not, then Jolliffe will be remembered forever for guarding the door to "White Canada." His word to the undesirables, whenever possible, was *no*.

The Jews, especially Cohen, cry out for human recognition, for an appreciation of the destruction wrought in European Jewish communities by the First World War, the Soviet upheaval, Ukrainian nationalist extremists, and the Russian Civil War, all of which have rolled across the eastern Polish borderlands and communities deeper into Soviet lands. Cohen points out that Jewish refugees and immigrants will be taken care of by their own community's support network. This is where men like Belkin come in, as resource workers able to settle newcomers on the Prairies, fund them through difficult crop years, issue aid, and renegotiate mortgage loans. Cohen, not afraid to play the officials' game, argues for immigration as an economic engine. The country's "railways need more income. The national debt of Canada is a heavy burden on the small population. We must, therefore, allow to come into Canada all those desirable immigrants who would be an asset to the country." Jews, he insists, are "easily absorbed into Canadian life, and establish themselves quickly in the country of their adoption." Jewish organizations are ready to aid the Department of Immigration in meeting the semi-official "Jewish quota."[2]

The minister expresses sympathy but is noncommittal.

The heavy in the government group is Blair, assistant to the deputy minister. To play him, we need a white-haired, smooth-faced man in a Sunday School teacher's rimless spectacles, with a jaw on hinges like a *Howdy Doody* puppet. It would be fun to cast a puppet, with clacking teeth on a puppeteer's knee, as the grim-minded Blair. He disagrees with each argument that the Jews muster. He counters that the recent years of unofficial "quotas" for entry of Jews into Canada—steady at around 3,000 annually—are in fact illegal, his implication being that even this small favour that the government has been allowing could be swept away. But before the disagreements get out of hand, Minister Forke interrupts and suggests that a smaller committee of begging Jews return soon to Ottawa for further discussions. To this suggestion everyone agrees.

When the Jews return in mid-December, Belkin, the note taker, is with them, as is Cohen. Joining the group this time is A.J. (Archie) Freiman, an Ottawa counterpart to Cohen, a successful businessman, active in many Jewish causes, whose contacts reach all the way up to Prime Minister King. Here, by way of a dissolve, the PM makes a ghostly appearance. He floats above the action, seated at his writing desk in Laurier House, not far from Freiman's big Victorian home on Somerset Street. King almost sings "I was dreaming of Sir Wilfrid Laurier this morning" but then shifts to a plain-spoken voice. Looking straight ahead, he describes how he has just been to the big Ottawa synagogue at the invitation of the Freimans. "I felt much more at home than in a Roman Catholic Church & in complete sympathy with the entire service," he announces. "It was simple & dignified & the customs and traditions of 3,000 years being followed brought one into close touch with the remote past. . . . I felt the nearness of the worship of the one God."[3] At this point, his voice stutters and breaks up, and King and his desk dissolve like a puff of cigar smoke.

The brute drama retakes the stage as Forke, Blair, Egan, and Jolliffe listen to Cohen's "guarantee that no immigrant will become a public charge." Freiman, not used to being talked down to, puts it to them straight. He insists that the government should recall the orders-in-council demanding a continuous journey and an up-to-date passport. "These regulations," he tells the bureaucrats, "have been passed by you to hinder Jewish immigration to Canada, and if you cancel them now, it would be of great help to us."[4]

Here Blair steps up as the henchman, the little, bespectacled Eichmann of this scenario. Not for the Jews, these rules! For the Hindus! As if this will placate his begging Jews. Remember the *Komagata Maru*, he seems to say. Forget your German refugee boats. Although sometimes, he knows, they do overlap.

Then the unpleasantness breaks out, as it tends to do in meetings joined by people with diametrically opposed goals. Blair leads the way. His is the masterful bureaucratic voice in response to Cohen's businessman's complaint. The blood runs cold to hear Blair direct his lawyerly criticism at the status quo on Jewish immigration while offering nothing new, stonewalling any option that might replace what is already in place. It must be said: he is the well-raised Canadian boy, with his peculiarly obsessive way of asserting rules, regulations, and orders from higher up, proclaiming past methods "illegal" when doing so suits him, and suggesting that the record shows that "the Jews have utilized the opportunity and, when occasion has arisen, have taken advantage of the political situation."[5]

Blair makes way for Egan, the deputy minister, who accuses the Jewish Immigrant Aid Society of neglecting to investigate its applications carefully while charging outsized fees to its applicants. Someone has briefed Egan, for this issue is a sore spot, a point of contention in the mid-1920s on the editorial pages of the Montreal Yiddish press. "*Dos schwindlerishe arbet muz oifhern*," the editors of the Montreal *Keneder Adler* announced ("The Activities of the Swindlers Must Cease").[6] Egan's accusation, rather than relating to the issues that the Jews have brought to the Ottawa meeting, insinuates that the Jewish Immigrant Aid Society operates as a confidence outfit, making money on the backs of its applicants. Egan proposes no changes to the status quo and promotes the idea that MPs should continue to submit recommendations to his department for individual consideration. Belkin confirms in his notes that the deputy minister has acknowledged the government's future plan: "A small unwritten quota" of roughly 3,000 "was thus established arbitrarily for the Jews."[7]

It's the note taker, Belkin, who preserves the details so that the scene can take shape before us. It would be "illegal," Blair facetiously claims, for the government to help any one group while not helping all of the others. After lunch, two Jewish representatives do not return. One of them is the Ottawa businessman Freiman, who has told his companion that Jews must not be forced to beg for access to the country's ports. He's had enough of that work for the day. A quiet chat with the prime minister is likely what he has in mind in response to the stonewalling and bluster of men like Egan and Blair. He might even send his super-competent and influential other half, Lillian Freiman, into the fray. She knows how to deal with such men. Egan is beneath her, but she'll wash the floor with Blair. Lillian is this chapter's *deus ex machina*—her force from outside unstoppable, almost inexplicable, and her doings will come to the fore in my grandfather's efforts too. But for now, she remains offstage.

At a break for lunch, in an empty parliamentary office, let the Fool step out and sing a long ballad—with many verses—that details just one of a thousand examples of Lillian's work. In the fall of 1921—not so long before our winter meeting in Ottawa—a ship called the *Saxonia* arrives at the Halifax harbour, carrying 156 Jews, all of whom are promptly interned and deemed unacceptable, either for lacking the proper "in the pocket" funds or for having violated the continuous journey provision. They are all ordered deported back to their homelands. The Jewish Immigrant Aid Society puts in a call to Mrs. Freiman, who raises the possibility that they might be admitted to Cuba. With this in the works, the deportation order is stayed. Freiman attains a "special permit" from the Department of Immigration to visit the detainees at the Halifax harbour, where she tells them, in her inimitable way, that if Cuba is their destination she will travel there with them. But time is on their side. The oncoming election—as is often the case—puts the government in a forgiving mood, and on the eve of the election the detained passengers of the *Saxonia* are permitted to land.[8]

Belkin's "Conference on Jewish Immigration" is about to go over a cliff. No change will be made to official or semi-official policy, and the only way that a Jew will enter the country will be by way of recommendation by someone of influence, which will lead to a special permit being considered by the Department of Immigration and an order-in-council. This backroom approach to permits will come back to haunt the government. Leaving access to the country to private recommenders with the ears of MPs and deputy ministers looks less like a policy than a confidence game. General suspicion of this approach contributed to the creation of a parliamentary immigration inquiry in early 1928. Egan, who hammered at the Jews visiting Ottawa to plead their human cause, was forced to admit the number of "special permits" that his department had issued. Ontario member of Parliament W.D. Euler topped the list of influential recommenders, having secured 208 immigrants in response to his overtures to the Department of Immigration. The Jewish MPs, Heaps and Jacobs, had done admirably under the circumstances, gaining 85 and 143 permits respectively. The only other recommender with a Jewish constituency was A.J. Freiman. And Belkin expected that, among the 33 successful permits in response to his interventions, some were likely sponsored and forced over the goal line by Lillian Freiman.[9]

I have not risen to the challenge that I set for myself at the outset of my little drama. No great monologue—the closest being Archie Freiman's advice regarding the government's disingenuous abuse of orders-in-council. No all-out battle between the benign and the malign. No punchouts around the cabinet table or bit players thrown from the window to the ground below. One member of the group abandons the field in disgust. The prime minister dreams of Laurier and lets his underlings do the heavy lifting with the begging Jews. What we get are parries and feints. Then the players exit and head home. Iris out.

But consider what Belkin, the humble note taker, helps us to glimpse: the Big Boys in action. How often do we get such a view? To the people's Parliament come community leaders who face the wall of official refusal, snide ad hominem argument, whatever you want to call it. These scenes are among the clearest that I can convey of where Canadian Jews stood, as a community, as individuals, in relation to their government in the period before Yehuda Yosef Eisenstein got on board the *Ascania* at Southampton. They might as well have stood in their doorways and wept, which some of them likely did. Belkin does not hesitate to convey his own anguish, along with that of his compatriots, in response to the failures that he has witnessed.

And what of the folksinger? The Fool. The empty screen allows for haunting background music, let's say this silent movie's theme song, played on a hobo guitar. It's called "I Hung My Head." It's a devastating song about a man who goes with his brother's rifle to an outcropping from which he sees a man riding a horse. He fires the gun, killing the rider for no reason. He is hunted down and caught. It is cowboy Kafka. When the killer is asked what went through his mind, the Fool must do his best to imitate Johnny Cash, whose voice best conveys the meaningless act, the empty willingness to orphan children and widow wives. There's more humanity in the song's confession than in anything offered in Blair's rhetoric or in Egan's aggressiveness. Still, the song is a perfect backdrop for the theatrical rendering of a December day in 1926 in Ottawa. Men arrive at the office in vests and ties. They cite regulation to assert their authority. At the end of the day, they step onto Wellington Street, having plied their executioner's trade before heading home through the snow.

GO WEST, SLOWLY WEST,
KNOWING NOTHING AT ALL

My grandfather arrived in Canada at Quebec City, then crossed the country by train to join his brother in Vancouver. There he stayed through the end of 1931, when he returned by train to the Prairies, to his first Canadian job and prairie home, at Dysart, in south-central Saskatchewan, just north of the Qu'Appelle Valley and the old Hudson's Bay Company outpost at Fort Qu'Appelle. As I better understood his story, I was increasingly haunted by my inability to appreciate what he knew about his new home.

His arrival, as part of the Canadian project of sending European newcomers west, was belated. The big numbers of west-travelling newcomers had come, many of them moving on, either to the United States or to bigger Canadian centres. Some had been tempted west by promotional offers in Europe, which included steamship passage, train travel, and farmland at $2.50 per acre with friendly repayment arrangements on mortgage loans. Canadian immigration representatives appeared at regional exhibitions in the United States and Great Britain, and the government oversaw a worldwide network of as many as 300 settlement agents and subagents who received a commission for each settler whom they successfully brought over (three dollars per man, two dollars per woman, one dollar per child).[1] Steamship companies were "bonused" for promoting immigration to Canada, and the CPR undertook its own program of appealing to emigrants.

Steamship ticket hucksters plied their trade in Hamburg and London. Some of the offers made in European ports turned out to be more fast talk than the real deal upon arrival at a Canadian port, for terms promised on one side of the Atlantic vanished by the time of arrival on the other side. Such fiascos in European emigration had a long history and played like practice sessions for the *Komagata Maru* Incident. In 1900, two ships carrying 2,000 Romanian refugees, with many Jews among them, were held at port in Montreal while officials decided whether to allow them into the country. A landing fee of ten dollars, meant to prove that they were "non-paupers," was deemed unduly low while the ship was in transit to Montreal. The requirement upon arrival was raised to twenty-five dollars per person, making many of the Jews "paupers" and in danger of an immediate return trip.[2] In this period, Jews from Romania still found their way in substantial numbers to Montreal. Romanian Jews were on the move by the thousands following a pogrom in 1899. These *fusgeyers* ("foot travellers") "trekked on foot" to Hamburg. Young men and women trained for months before departing. Each group carried "personal belongings, water supplies, and tents, often sporting a special group uniform. Some even had their own press . . . and published their own poems."[3]

Once on the way from the eastern ports to their prescribed homesteads or new hometowns, newcomers like my grandfather travelled in the railways' "colonist cars." One wonders, based upon photographs and drawings of them, if they were a feature or a kind of demotion, somewhere below third-class travel but above cattle-car fare. The railways had fleets of them, serving immigrants heading west from the ports at Quebec City and Halifax. They were in use beginning in the mid-nineteenth century and through the heavy immigration years of the early twentieth century. In photographs and drawings—usually presenting cars empty of the people they were meant to carry—they are bare bones in terms of comfort. Wide, straight-backed benches on each side of the centre aisle sat three people apiece. A pair of windows overlooked each bench, with pull-down canvas blinds. The beds, or "berths," were pull-down affairs, too, and resembled oversized versions of the rounded overhead cabin baggage containers on a modern airplane. A ladder served each car's seventy would-be sleepers for getting into their upper berths. Unseen in these depictions is the kitchen that the travellers shared to cook their own food on the way west. I don't know if my grandfather rode in one of these cars. Perhaps because his travel was not part of any larger settlement program— he was not brought over as part of the many "schemes," nor was his travel supported by the Canadian Jewish Immigrant Aid Society—he simply travelled in whatever was available for bottom-of-the-rung cross-country travellers.

At this late stage of the settlement of the "Last Best West," the federal government pretended to follow independent-minded policies even though they were tied routinely to those of Great Britain. Increasingly xenophobic immigration policies in the United States provided Canada with cover to change its own policies, though it remained open to British and American newcomers. While the European situation became ever more chaotic, immigration numbers to Canada shrank—though not for the shortage of willing newcomers. The 1920s confirmed the Canadian government's radical turn, first under Liberal leadership, then for the first half of the 1930s under Bennett's Conservatives, toward strict limitations, focused on agriculturalists and the family members of Canadian citizens. As regulations tightened, following a number of related orders-in-council, immigration commissioners retained their independence to oversee the outcomes of applications to enter the country. It was an era of hands-on bureaucracy, of paper files, of typewritten and type-copied correspondence. Letters of polite rejection went out on letterhead bearing the impressive crest of the nation above the request that the correspondent "kindly . . . not write on more than one subject in any one letter."[4]

The situation of Jews aspiring to enter Canada became increasingly difficult, though Jews did continue to enter at Canadian ports, sometimes with the intention of departing for the United States. It is this fact that lends an obscure character to the damning and in many ways telling phrase "none is too many." If it *wasn't none*, then what of those who did get in?

※ ※ ※

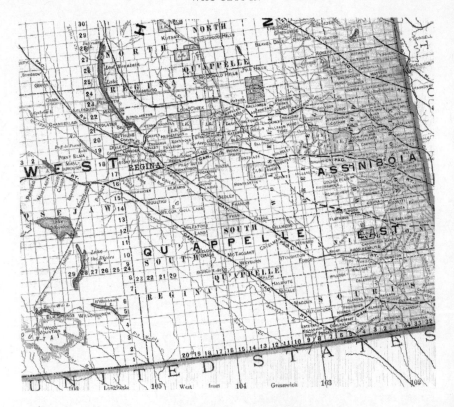

The dark turn in the 1920s—it has to be viewed this way; how could it not be?—must be understood as the last stage of early decades of settlement on the Prairies, of the impact of the railways, which crossed the country to their western ends in the last decades of the nineteenth century. Alongside these developments went unformed ideas among Canadians about what their country was and what it should become. This early history helps us to comprehend the better-known narrative laid out in Irving Abella and Harold Troper's *None Is Too Many: Canada and the Jews of Europe 1933–1948* as well as my grandfather's story.

To understand westward immigration in twentieth-century Canada, and in what we now call Saskatchewan, we should go all the way back to the earliest incursions of the European traders, trappers, and settlers who went west to the southern prairies and beyond. What they began my grandfather finished as he took part in the final stage of settlement. Their arrival had a devastating impact on Indigenous patterns of daily life.

This part of the country was, and to some remains, *terra incognita*. Throughout its exploration and settlement, early Canada was established in acts of war, trade, homesteading, and technological change. South-central Saskatchewan's landscape is largely predictable, often flat and treeless, though its major river valleys—the Qu'Appelle, north of Regina, and the Souris, down south, crossing over the American border before re-entering Canada in southwestern Manitoba—are striking exceptions. Trails running through this area were early Cree and then Métis trade routes along which, eventually, fur traders found an entrée into the established Indigenous economy. In this area lived the Rabbit Skin, Calling River, and Touchwood Hills peoples. The long-standing Indigenous populations in this part of the country were mobile. Along the Souris River in the south lived Cree, Assiniboine, and Ojibway. Sioux tribes moved up from the Dakota territories as the U.S. Army pursued them and took away their land rights.[5] Competition among local groups for lands and resources was complicated by the arrival in the early 1670s of the British, who had established their first outposts around Hudson Bay. French fur traders later competed for access to furs and for the trust of Indigenous communities by venturing farther and farther inland. Indigenous people obtained many types of European goods in exchange for furs and, for their allegiance, received arms. The Sioux fought on the side of the British during the American Revolution and again in the War of 1812.[6] And a little later, not far from the settlements that would be named Hirsch and Bienfait in the late nineteenth century, Indigenous groups fought over what each viewed as sacred ground—in particular a hoodoo pierced by a hole that stood out from the porous sandstone riverbank. Dubbed Roche Percée by settlers arriving from the east, the rock surrounding it was marked by petroglyphs, carvings of men and animals, their age unknown, as part of group devotion and ritual.

While the Hudson's Bay Company initially clung to its outposts on Hudson Bay, the French made their way into the interior of what was then known as Rupert's Land first via the St. Lawrence River from Montreal and then the Great Lakes, Lake of the Woods, and trade routes established by Indigenous peoples, both on water and on land. In the 1730s, the Trois-Rivières-born explorer and trader La Vérendrye authorized the establishment of trading posts in what is now Manitoba, among them one at the confluence of the Red and Assiniboine Rivers at what is now Winnipeg (Fort Rouge) and another where the city of Portage la Prairie now stands (Fort la Reine). Beaver pelts were a major part of the early fur trade; 100 years later bison hide robes also began to become popular and were a major reason for the near demise of that animal. The great American writer Wallace Stegner, who spent his formative childhood years in Eastend, Saskatchewan, remarked on how the huge herds of these early years travelled like a "blackness" on the land. Alongside them one found the "red-tawny shadows of antelope bands."[7] Elsewhere one reads of the broad range of fur-bearing animals whose skins fed the burgeoning trade: beaver, lynx, and mink. Much of southern Saskatchewan was dry, treeless, bald, a cactus-ridden moonscape suited to limited breeds. But in the southeast rise the Moose Mountain uplands, and in the southwestern corner of the province, in the Cypress Hills rising up to the west and north of Stegner's Eastend, one finds "a lush ecological island." In the Cypress Hills stood forests of pine and spruce unlike any in the rest of the territory.[8]

In 1793, the Hudson's Bay Company built a trading post at the junction of the Souris and Assiniboine Rivers, in what is now Manitoba.[9] Still, the old plains frontier had seventy or so years to run its own course before European settlement and political and economic activity destroyed age-old patterns of daily life.

Change was the status quo. Settlement on American territory and cavalry activity drove numerous Indigenous bands over what was known as the "medicine line," the territorial divide between the United States and British colonial lands to the north. At Roche Percée, Sioux and Assiniboine fought skirmishes over access to the hoodoo that each community viewed as sacred. This kind of competition increased in the nineteenth century as greater numbers wanted to "make their homes in the Great Mother's country."[10] Upon arrival on the northern side of the medicine line, bands were met by representatives of the North West Mounted Police, who gave what amounted to a lecture on the rules of order of the Great Mother's country.

Through the late 1700s and into the next century, smallpox ravaged Indigenous populations. At the same time, the fur trade, linked with trading forts extending farther and farther west, transformed the plains economy. The bison hunt was transformed from a "means of subsistence and small-scale trade into a system of resource extraction for a large trade economy." Through the 1830s and 1840s, companies moved as many as 80,000 bison robes a year.[11] Prior to a full-scale fur trade, Indigenous bands in the southeastern Souris River Valley sustained themselves with bison meat, using the animal in a hundred ways to answer daily needs. The bison stomach was fashioned into cooking pots; the sinew was used as thread; the hide was useful for making not only clothing but also teepees, saddle bags, and drum skins; the hooves were boiled to make glue; and the bison chips made good fuel for fires in hard times.[12] By the early 1880s, the large-scale killing and trading of bison had collapsed. The boom had guaranteed its own bust. Travellers on the Prairies kept an eye out for bison—once having had to let a herd pass the way traffic might on Fifth Avenue—and wouldn't see one. With this drastic reduction came a dramatic increase in destitution among the Indigenous communities. In 1881, Sitting Bull, the legendary leader of resistance to American incursions in the Black Hills, surrendered to the American Army at Fort Buford, Dakota Territory.[13]

Smallpox. Bison nearly wiped out. Economic and social collapse. What next? Well, the Canadian Pacific Railway, of course. The first train arrived in Calgary in 1883, and another train reached the west coast terminus at Port Moody, British Columbia, in 1886. In these years, there was an uncanny contrast, one might say a coincidence, between events on the southwestern prairies and events that transformed Jewish life in Eastern Europe and the Russian Empire. In 1881, reformist Czar Alexander II was assassinated by revolutionaries, initiating decades of calamities in Russian lands. The dead czar's son, Alexander III, instigated the anti-Semitic May Laws, which limited where Jews could live as well as their economic livelihood and access to educational institutions. Jewish flight from Russian lands, including the parts of Poland under Russian rule, increased year by year, with many choosing North America as their new home. The great wave of immigration to Canada was beginning.

The borderline between America and what would become Canada was a matter of great importance in the 1850s and 1860s, and both the British imperial and the Canadian colonial governments sent survey parties to the North-West Territories to prepare for border negotiations with the Americans. The British government sought to improve communications across its territorial possessions in North America; gold had been found in British Columbia, and increased settlement in the interior was an obvious response to ongoing American expansionist rhetoric.[14] A British expedition went west in 1857 under the leadership of John Palliser, whose name haunts a southern section of the province, the Palliser Triangle, which the expedition found unsuited to agricultural settlement.

The expedition sent out by the Canadian colonial government in 1857 and 1858 travelled in three groups, or parties, as historians like to call them. One of these parties pursued a "topographical and geological expedition west of the Red River."[15] The travelling company, led by Henry Youle Hind, a professor of chemistry and geology at Trinity College in Toronto, consisted of fourteen men, among them "six Cree half-breeds, . . . one Blackfoot half-breed, one Ojibway half-breed, and one French Canadian."[16] Hind made no comment on this diverse mix, but he admitted in his report that the "half-breeds" did the heavy lifting, getting the expedition's five Red River carts loaded up when it was time to move on.

With this party travelled Humphrey Lloyd Hime, responsible, among other duties, for an impressive stock of photographic equipment brought along to create a record of the expedition's tour of the Prairies. This equipment included a supply of glass plates, a sturdy wooden tripod, and a darkroom tent. For long periods of the expedition, Hime took no photographs. On one river crossing, his negatives, wrapped and stored aboard a Red River cart, were soaked. But impressive plates from his travels survive and depict the area where the Souris meets the Assiniboine in what is now far western Manitoba. The expedition was camped just three kilometres from the international boundary, in a territory that had burned the previous year in what the expedition report called a "vast conflagration extending for one thousand miles in length and several hundreds in breadth."[17] While his companions set out to look for the elusive bison, Hime set up his camera. Prints from these photographic plates have a smoky, unreal quality; they are like dream images but perfectly framed and focused dreams. A plate titled "Valley of the Souris" looks from a rocky outcropping to a bend in the river valley, with its scattering of trees and the horizon line expertly set at the midpoint of the image. In another plate, titled "Encampment—Little Souris," Hime captures the expedition's wooden-spoked Red River carts, its high white tents on the flat grassy prairie, and his colleagues, standing small against the massive white horizon line, with not a cloud in sight. Another remarkable plate taken farther along in the expedition shows a Métis or Indigenous youth with long dark hair and wearing a loose-sleeved peasant blouse.

A week after Hime took this photo at Fort Ellice, almost over the border into what would become Saskatchewan, he and his compatriots arrived at the Church of England missionary post in the Qu'Appelle Valley. Hime's photos of the Qu'Appelle Valley provide a ghostly impression of soft hills, the wooded lake shoreline, a range of hills beneath a glowing, blank July sky. The Qu'Appelle Valley photos are made more hauntingly strange by their water-stained condition. In a notebook that Hime kept, he describes how they got that way:

> The first cart upset in the rapid + I had the satisfaction of seeing my Photographic Apparatus, my gun, my clothes and all my Penates submerged, fortunately they were tied tight and did not get out of the cart—After about 10 minuits struggling the horse was loosed from the cart + swam down the River while the cart was dragged ashore. . . . Stopped to dry the things which although soaked were not much damaged.[18]

In Hime's proofs and prints, the land on which my grandfather would first settle, at Dysart, thirty-three kilometres from Fort Qu'Appelle, is seen through "Canadian eyes" for the first time, via Hime's camera and the chemistry of "wet-plate photography," which Hime practised in the open, using chemicals and water gathered from the prairie streams and rivers that he passed.[19]

The report of the Canadian government's expedition was printed in London and published in 1860. It is a remarkable record of the landscapes where my grandfather's first Canadian sojourn played out. And it includes, of course, no inkling that such a man could materialize in the territories, with his European middle-class dress and urban experience, his two Jewish languages, along with Polish, and his ancient but newly learned technique for slaughtering animals based upon the rules laid out in the Hebrew Bible's Book of Leviticus.

Hind's *Preliminary and General Report, on the Assinniboine and Saskatchewan Exploring Expedition*, presented as it was to "both Houses of Parliament," is a record of Canada's coming into being. Canada was doing so (under the careful eye of the imperial power) through the project of taking a fuller measure of its "North-West territory," with attention paid to "the natural features of the country" to construct "a map as complete as possible" and to produce a photographic record of more than three months of travel. To ready his reader for the travels that he means to describe, Hind begins with a didactic but useful discussion of the word *prairie*, whose multiplicity and unpredictability he aims to convey: "Prairies, or plains, may be level, rich, and dry, sustaining luxuriant grasses, and affording splendid pasturage; they may be marshy and wet, or undulating and stony, or sandy and barren, or salt and herbless, or arid and consequently sterile."[20] Hind's report takes account of river valleys, aspen forests, and long chains of lake and stream, but at bottom it is a divination of the possibility of the Great Plains as an integral part of a nation ruled from far away.

For the purposes of thinking about twentieth-century Saskatchewan and my grandfather's progress there, it's helpful to look at the part of the expedition that took place between late June and mid-July. This was when the company of men, animals, and Red River carts passed through the Souris River Valley and continued up to an outpost on what is now the Saskatchewan-Manitoba border before turning due west to follow the Qu'Appelle River to the Anglican Mission in the Qu'Appelle Valley. This part of their tour covered ground close to where my grandfather's "circuit" first took shape in the early 1930s. The Anglican Mission was founded in 1854. When Hind's expedition came through, it was overseen by "Charles Pratt, the catechist," about whom Hind says little in his report. It was his supporting missionary, a Swampy Cree called Reverend James Settee, who made the greatest impression. On the Sunday of the expedition's encampment at the mission, Settee preached a sermon in English, as well as in Ojibway, and led a hymn in Cree.[21] Hind and his crew moved on the following day, into a land of turkey buzzards, ravens, barking crows, and black terns.[22] On their way, they learned how to make pemmican and killed their "first buffalo bull." Vast numbers of pigeons flew overhead, and grasshoppers recalled "the devastating ravages of the Egyptian scourges."[23] As the expedition travelled, it became, if not a group of Saskatchewanians or Manitobans, then a group of North-West Territory Men. They ate Cree food and encountered Sioux death sites, the corpses wrapped and set high above their heads on poles, as if in offering to the sky. The bison were not yet gone, but their time was short. This was the beginning of an end time.

❀ ❀ ❀

Settling the West required bodies. The challenge of attracting homesteaders to little-known territory changed over time. In the late nineteenth century, the American West was the most popular destination, with its large population and, in certain locales, better agricultural climate. The first decade of the twentieth century was the decade of the "immigrant settler." Between 1900 and 1913, 2,521,144 immigrants came to Canada, some 870,000 of them from the United States.[24] Big numbers—Jews among them—went west. In this period, too, the geographical landmass called the North-West Territories gained

definition. From it, in 1905, were made the provinces of Saskatchewan and Alberta. The Canadian Pacific Railway moved through the
territory in the early 1880s, receiving for its efforts a grant of 25 million acres of land for which it was to seek settlers.[25] In this endeavour,
the Dominion government and the CPR, itself created in 1881 by an
act of Parliament, worked in tandem to fashion Canada as a new
continental territory.

But the question that arose from the outset and never quite went
away was who would be the new Western Canadian? An early answer
to this question was the Immigration Act of 1906, which introduced
new prohibitions—entry would be denied to epileptics, the blind, the
deaf, and the destitute. And, in a new power arrangement, the "Governor in Council," represented by the ruling government's cabinet, could
prohibit "any class of immigrants" that it considered undesirable.[26]
The "Chinaman" and the black were targeted for non-inclusion. The
Chinese "head tax" that followed the completion of work on the CPR
was meant to end the immigration of Chinese workers who had filled
the railway's labour needs. In 1885, with the railway almost complete,
the head tax was $50; by 1903, it was raised to a prohibitive $500.[27]
Similarly, Italians and Jews routinely received bureaucratic distinction
as undesirable newcomers. So, though Jews came to Canada in big
numbers in the first decade and a half of the twentieth century, they
did so in the shadow of mainstream views coloured by "Anglo-Saxon"
or "Christian" presuppositions held by the country's elites, intellectuals,
parliamentarians, and civil servants.

In 1912, in an American magazine, one would have found an essay
with the title "Jew and Chinaman." Its author aimed to address the
acceptability and adaptability of both groups to Canadian society.
The essay's somewhat ominous catchline was "the Chinaman is the
coming Jew."[28] But the writer was doubtful about racialist views and
debates with nativists and eugenicists whose claims for national goals
he viewed with suspicion. One of his rhetorical targets was Canadian
Chief Medical Officer of the Department of Immigration P.H. Bryce,
who expressed in his writings a fear of "the continual juxtaposition
of two races" leading inevitably to a weakened "intermixture of the
two."[29] The argument in "Chinaman and Jew" ran counter to such
fears, but the debates that the author addressed would intensify in the
coming years. It was in this atmosphere that economic, political, and

fraudulent scientific considerations contributed to a sharpening, in the minds of intellectuals and government officials, of the meaning of Canadian identity.

It's common to say that a new kind of independent Canadian identity was formed through the experience of the First World War. But it's less commonly acknowledged that it was in the postwar context that the desire intensified to ensure that the "country should remain primarily British in the make-up of its population."[30] The early 1920s saw increased efforts to entice British and American immigrants to the Canadian West as well as the creation of an increasingly hierarchical and ultimately exclusionary set of categories for immigrants. The federal government devoted itself to publishing more than 300 pamphlets aimed at English-language audiences (the CPR went farther afield, publishing translated promotional materials in Danish, Dutch, Finnish, and German). It was on the covers of these pamphlets that some of the richly coloured images associated with the pleasures of Canadian immigration first appeared, along with a welcome to contemplate the "Last Best West" and its "Homes for Millions."[31]

Border laws in the 1920s allowed Americans to enter Canada at crossings without a passport, whereas a 1921 order-in-council insisted that Continental Europeans travel with a passport that had been visaed by a British passport official since Canada lacked such officials in European ports.[32] The government, railways, and private colonization associations solicited British immigrants by offering highly subsidized steamship fares.[33] After the First World War, ex-service men and women travelled free. Free third-class travel was available for anyone who had secured employment before departure or "took up land under any of the Land Schemes" on offer at the time. An example in the mid-1920s was the "3,000 Family Scheme," which offered British homesteaders a $1,500 advance from the British government for stock and equipment.[34]

W.J. Egan, the deputy minister of immigration, busied himself with department land schemes, as settlement programs were called. In the autumn of 1928, he travelled to London to confer with the king, as the *Toronto Star* told it, about the possibility of moving 2 million "Britishers" to Canada (this pursuit of them took place not long after Egan and others haggled at length with Jewish leaders over allowing a few thousand Jewish newcomers to Canada per year). The reality, however, was that Britishers were coming to Canada in smaller and smaller numbers by the early 1930s.[35] A parliamentary committee on immigration tabled its report, downplaying rumours of permit peddling. Instead, it promoted the importance of "securing . . . British settlers" as well as the timeliness of cancelling the previous Liberal government's Railways Agreement, which had contributed to "thousands of Europeans" finding their way into the country.[36]

When Deputy Minister Egan wasn't browbeating Lyon Cohen or genuflecting before King George V, he was populating New Brunswick with Yorkshiremen, Scotsmen, and Welshmen, like the family of Morgan Walters from Regium House, Cross Hands, Carmarthernshire, Wales. The Walters, including their "fifteen robust and good-looking boys and girls," arrived as part of the New Brunswick Family Scheme, launched in 1927 as a partnership between the British and Canadian governments.[37] The plan was to send 500 British families over five years to farm in New Brunswick. The Department of Immigration toasted their accomplishments with a series of booklets, one of which, published in 1929, was a homey alternative to John Woodruff's Department of the Interior mug shots taken in front of immigration barns at ports in Quebec City and Saint John. It's unclear who authored the booklet, though its title page informs the reader that it has been issued by the

Canadian Government Department of Immigration and Colonization
Honourable Robert Forke, Minister
W.J. Egan, Deputy Minister
1929

This was the last gasp of the Liberal government of the late 1920s, which gave way to the Bennett approach to immigration. The booklet has the feel of something carefully vetted by actuaries, with its explanation of settlers' mortgage amortization and assurance that settlement was backed by the British government's subvention, from which the farming families could draw for "capital investment" on their farms, almost like a student loan. It evokes goodwill on all sides of the immigration challenge, with none of the usual anxiety about "Canadianizing" the newcomer. Yorkshiremen and Welshmen are viewed as ready-made Canadians, even though almost all of them must "acquire local farm experience," making their existential challenges on the land no different from those faced by some Continental Europeans out West.[38]

The families who settled in the Saint John River Valley and at Woodstock, not far from Fredericton, appear in photographs before their farmhouses, out "tending" the cows, exhibiting prize livestock, and "pulling" a crop of beans.[39] The grown-ups are introduced by name—Mr. White, Mr. Harry Brown—and the children are gathered together in the style of a family portrait, girls in skirts and boys in newsboy caps. The pamphlet closes with a list of family successes, the last of which is the farm taken up by Alfred Marks, "from Aylesbury, Buckinghamshire," whose wife agrees that the "farm was all right, and as for the winter, she did not mind it at all."[40] The department's willingness to attend to these people's needs is highlighted in the booklet. In one case, its writer is back on a farm near Sackville for a return visit. The family there receives a stamp of approval: there is "no question as to their ability to make good."[41]

A related pamphlet, issued the same year under the names of Forke and Egan, was titled *Winning Through: Stories of Life on Canadian Farms Told by New British Settlers*. It highlights a partnership between the Canadian and British governments, the aforementioned 3,000 Family Scheme, a Liberal undertaking that offered financing for farm purchase, assistance in settling, and practical instruction in agricultural methods. *Winning Through* is a collection of essays written by new farmers for a contest held through newspapers in British Columbia, Alberta, and Saskatchewan. Alberta farmers—eighty-six submitted their writing—competed for a first prize of twenty-five dollars. The fifth prize was five dollars. In Saskatchewan, sixty-four farmers wrote to the Regina *Morning Leader* and the Saskatoon *Star-Phoenix*. A rare entry from a farmer's wife—Mrs. J. Osborne, newly of Moosomin—describes farm life in the far southeastern corner of the province. She acknowledges the Farm Settlement Board's help in buying livestock and in enlarging their house while admitting to hard luck along the way: the need for charity from neighbours during the first winter, the loss of a flock of chicks after a "whole summer's work" raising them when storms wiped out the poultry stock. Still, she and her husband "are determined to get on and if we persevere I know we shall." They "are happy," she writes, "in the Great Land of our Adoption."[42] Mrs. Osborne's is a tale of work and woe and an acknowledgement of goodwill derived from a government program bent on making rural settlement succeed.

When these schemes did not attract the desired numbers, Canadian immigration policy set out a host of "Preferred," mostly northern European, nations from which to gather immigrants. These countries included Norway, Sweden, Denmark, Finland, Germany, Switzerland, Holland, Belgium, and France. They stood above the countries dubbed "Non-Preferred," which included Poland, Austria, Lithuania, Romania, and Czechoslovakia. For these nations, which one cannot help noticing were the sources of much Jewish immigration, entrance was offered only to agricultural and domestic workers as well as "those of a prescribed relationship to persons already admitted" into Canada.[43] No special ship rates or inducements were made available to these people, and no snappy pamphlets rolled off the presses with drawings of boys happily waving the yam their father had just drawn from the earth.

The most scrupulously adjudicated category—the special permit class—also appeared in this period, allowing immigration commissioners, the minister, and even the prime minister to make unique or independent decisions regarding particular files. This was where, increasingly, applications by Jews were likely rejected. Egan confirmed this way of doing business in his "conference" with Jewish leaders in 1926, but the trend, confirmed by cabinet-level orders-in-council, started in 1923, with additional restrictions added in 1930 and 1931 that shut Jewish immigration out of all regulated avenues beyond the special permit category. For the most part, by the spring of 1931, admissible immigrants were limited to American and British subjects, agriculturalists with means, and the wives and minor children of Canadian residents, whereas everyone else who entered the country came by way of an order-in-council. A leftover effect of the *Komagata Maru* events was in play in the order's final line: "The provisions of this Order in Council shall not apply to immigrants of any Asiatic race," placing the Indian subjects of Britain outside the pale of any consideration.[44] These developments in policy and immigration file management were reflected in demographic outcomes from the 1920s. The last notable influx of Jews into Canada took place in 1913. From there the numbers fell away.[45]

COMING FORWARD, FROM RADZANÓW

My grandfather travelled to Vancouver in November 1930. However hopeful he might have been that he would find work as a *shoichet* there, this hope was quashed by the dominant figure in that field in the city, Reverend N.M. Pastinsky, who happened to be on the board of the Pacific Division of the Jewish Immigrant Aid Society (JIAS) and thus was someone with whom one might not want to tangle. While Pastinsky was engaged with my grandfather, training him to slaughter cattle at the kosher abattoir in east Vancouver, Pastinsky was tasked by the JIAS to congratulate S.W. Jacobs of Montreal on his re-election to his parliamentary seat.[1] Pastinsky was willing to advance the skills of my grandfather as long as he agreed not to become a competitor in the local market for kosher meat.

My grandfather reversed his route and headed back to the Prairies. His initiation into Canadian Jewish life, and Canadian life more broadly, was shaped by rural small-town experience. This is not an often told set of experiences. Rather, it is a neglected part of Canadian Jewish history, made up of forgotten communities and little-thought-of men and women whose lives were every bit as interesting as those lived on the immigrant corridors of Spadina Avenue in Toronto, St. Lawrence

Boulevard in Montreal, and Aberdeen Avenue and Salter Street in Winnipeg. The thing hidden provides a telling story. And why, one wonders, was it hidden in the first place?

How to imagine the first train trip out of central Canada to the West? The lower quadrant of Saskatchewan was traversed by a set of rail lines that came west from Winnipeg, at that time the capital city of western economic and social growth. My grandfather's Canadian Government Return form for his trip on the *Ascania* lists his booking to travel "inland" on the CNR. In the 1920s and early 1930s, the Canadian Pacific and Canadian National Railways competed for cross-prairie business. The CPR dominated, with rail depots in Saskatchewan placed between ten and sixteen kilometres apart. Even as the Depression hit in 1929, both companies continued to build substantial branch lines in the province as well as in southern Alberta. As my grandfather went across the border between Manitoba and Saskatchewan on his first CNR route west, he would have passed through tiny place after tiny place such as Spy Hill and Bangor, small cities such as Melville and Saskatoon, and more archetypal prairie towns such as Biggar and Coleville before passing over the border into Alberta.[2] Those who travelled via the CPR watched a different, more southern, set of small farming centres roll by, with whistle stops at Moosomin, Whitewood, Broadview, Grenfell, Wolseley, Sintaluta, and on through Indian Head. In 1930, Indian Head was a prodigious centre of wheat production. There travellers crossing the Prairies for the first time saw a complete set of prairie infrastructure—a church, a hotel, a flour mill, and grain elevators, ten or more lined up like prairie skyscrapers.[3] After Indian Head on the CPR line came Qu'Appelle.

My grandfather would have seen, as he travelled, a great array of small and smaller-than-small places. A trusted recorder of these small places was Louis Rosenberg, both in his role as office manager for the Jewish Colonization Association (JCA) and then as demographer for the Canadian Jewish Congress. It's true that Jewish Canadians, in the 1920s, were an overwhelmingly urban group, but there was an exception on the Prairies, especially in Saskatchewan. Rosenberg tells us that in 1931 there were 5,116 Jews in the province, with 21 percent of them living rurally. One table counts seventy-five "Rural Municipalities Parishes or Townships Having Jewish Residents." Then he turns to a subject that he knew from personal experience: the four rural districts with

Jewish farm settlements whose populations exceeded seventy-five. As a JCA manager in the 1920s, Rosenberg visited them on horseback. They were Sonnenfeld (236 Jewish residents in 1931), Edenbridge (185), Hirsch (147), and Lipton Colony (93).[4]

Rosenberg's supplementary tables present a detailed account of Jewish populations in communities with more than 19 and fewer than 30 Jews, those with fewer than 20, fewer than 10, fewer than 5, all the way down to places in rural Saskatchewan that *once had Jews but no longer* (this was a remarkable reading; Rosenberg was the only student of this phenomenon, de-Jewed Canadian small towns and villages). He introduces us to a host of little rural places: Aylesbury. Blaine Lake. Broadview. Hazenmore. Imperial. Insinger. Leask. They all had eight Jews apiece in 1931. Plunkett, Semans, Shellbrook, and Truax had nine apiece.[5] The names of these places provide a litany, a tone poem recalling places that the American author Wallace Stegner artfully refers to as capitals "of an unremembered past."[6] Such are the places listed with loving care in Rosenberg's tables. We know little of the lives lived in them. Each one—including my grandfather's first prairie home at Dysart or nearby Cupar and Markinch, even Lipton with its rail depot, its synagogue, and its farming colony—compete to take the crown as Capital of an Unremembered Past.

Stegner, best known for his work on the American West, spent a part of his childhood in southwestern Saskatchewan, where his family lived during the summer on their homestead on the bald prairie along the Montana border and wintered in the town of Eastend, some sixty-four kilometres north on the eastern flank of the Cypress Hills. There he experienced what he calls "the last years of the Plains frontier."[7] For Stegner, this meant watching ways of life being swept aside by the rapid changes of the early twentieth century. In the tone poem of forgotten places, Eastend is among twenty-one other places whose general populations numbered between 135 and 1,305, each of which had six Jews living in them in 1931.[8] Eastend had a population of 545, so its six Jews might have been a single family or a family of five plus a loner. Stegner remembers an Eastender known as Jew Meyer. When his family's homesteading was at its most desperate, Jew Meyer, the town's storekeeper, cut off the Stegners' credit. For a while in 1916, the family "literally had difficulty getting enough to eat. We blamed his Jewishness, naturally."[9] But Stegner recognizes the Jewish shopkeeper as part of Eastend's diversity: "As elsewhere, too, the town's found-ers were of every stripe and spot—farmers, shopmen, sharpies, *métis* squatters, Texas cowboys, Syrian and Jewish peddlers, and Cockneys straight out of London's East End. It was a far from unanimous town."[10]

On both railways' lines, the first thing that a traveller saw on the horizon as the train pulled into town was a grain elevator, or a row of them, and then the depot. Many were CPR depots, but the other railways built their share. The village of Dysart, where my grandfather first settled after his start in Vancouver, began to develop with the construction of the CPR line through the area from the east in 1905. Rail access to the region was further improved with the completion of the Grand Trunk Pacific Railway's line from Melville through Fort Qu'Appelle and on to Regina in 1911.

Even the most far-flung stations—wooden outposts along recently laid branch lines—had a certain architectural flair and familiarity. Mirroring the length of track that they served, typically they were a good deal wider in front than they were deep, with a suite of paned windows out front and along the sides. They sported a sloped roof and overhanging eaves that Frank Lloyd Wright would make familiar in his "prairie style" houses. Many had dormers in their roof lines that faced the railway tracks and a brick chimney or two extending from the roof's centre point. On the side slopes, at either end of the roof, facing in the direction of arrival and departure, the locale's name was displayed in large white block letters: LIPTON. DYSART. HIRSCH. Sometimes the post office was housed in the depot, as it was at Hirsch, along with a telegraph office. Out front, separating the building from the rails, was a broad plank boardwalk. Behind all this hung a big sky. Settlers were picked up by a farmer with a horse and wagon. As one rode away from the train depot, it could be said that time moved in reverse. This was certainly true for my grandfather. His time in the Polish Army, his work for a Polish officer in cosmopolitan Warsaw, his ocean passage and then his time in Vancouver at the tail end of what was an Edwardian-era boom—all of this fell away as his new compatriots took him toward Dysart to show him the schoolhouse-cum-synagogue building, a modest thing of planed boards surrounded by rough fence posts. The Union Jack flying out front. A veritable dead end. The moon man is swept up in dust and chaff. Fade out. Fin.

DYSART, SASKATCHEWAN, CAPITAL OF THE FORGOTTEN WEST

t's the start of a vaudeville routine: a man is on his way across an endless country by train. He can communicate only with people from his own part of the world, and often they are unfindable. Many others speak only one language: the King's English, as yet unknown. Although Canada liked to blow its own horn abroad—big gay posters and fat glossy pamphlets of yam-wielding farmers—there was no tutorial or gratis language instruction for the newcomers from Continental Europe in 1931. The CNR promoted itself and Canada via its own radio broadcasts, available over headphones in the trains' radio cars. If the man managed to find his way there, he might have heard a smorgasbord of Canadian cultural output, some of it appreciable, such as a performance of the Hart House Quartet, and some of it incomprehensible, such as a poetry reading by the part-Mohawk celebrity E. Pauline Johnson, known to put her birchbark canoe in Vancouver's Lost Lagoon.[1]

The traveller left a troubled continent but found his way into the midst of Saskatchewan's troubles, which preceded the 1930s. The first of a number of drought years occurred in 1929. The area of the province where my grandfather settled was not spared. Drought brought dust storms so dark that one had to light a kerosene lamp in the daytime.

Farmers who'd known good years saw the price of grain plummet. The difficulty of maintaining a kitchen garden in these circumstances led to developments of which no one was proud. The provincial government of J.T.M. Anderson set up a relief commission, to which hard-bitten men and women applied for everything from underwear to grain seed. Other provinces sent food by train, the least happily received being the dried Maritime cod, which Saskatchewanians didn't like. The ever-present field rodent, the gopher, was stewed and canned, baked into pies, pickled, and smoked. Nobody had ever seen such a downturn in the basic features of daily life. Families fled the province. Census records for 1931 counted 5,183 abandoned farms.[2]

It was into this general state of disaster that my grandfather headed in 1931 as he went toward the job awaiting him in Dysart, roughly thirty kilometres northwest of old Fort Qu'Appelle and about 100 kilometres northeast of Regina. There he joined a phenomenon about which he would have heard talk in Vancouver: the settlement of Jews on farming colonies as well as the movement by Jews to small towns to become retailers, entrepreneurs of all kinds, cattle traders, the prairie version of the kind of middleman that my grandfather had fashioned himself to be in Poland as he bought wheat from farmers in order to deliver it to mill owners. Some of these Western Canadian Jews lived in small communities or colonies that were wholly Jewish—as was the case at Hirsch and Lipton and at Edenbridge in central Saskatchewan. Others became the lone Jewish family, or part of a tiny community of a few families, as in Markinch and Cupar, whose Jews my grandfather served along with those in Dysart. His lead role, the one for which he'd trained and become certified, was that of *shoichet*, that is, ritual slaughterer, but his responsibilities included teaching the farmers' children, marrying, burying, and leading synagogue services on the Sabbath and holidays.

Although my grandfather was not yet a part of the larger system of support for these places, organized by the Jewish Colonization Association, he worked alongside other functionaries who received JCA salaries at the farming colonies at neighbouring Lipton and at faraway Hirsch, down near the southern border. In late 1933, my grandfather would find his way to Hirsch—among the earliest of the Jewish prairie colonies—but first he paid his dues at Dysart. Jews had settled there, among the Doukhobors, Swedes, and Ukrainian farmers, and had built up a makeshift communal network linked to nearby Markinch, Cupar, and Lipton. Jewish Dysart has entirely vanished, whether on the ground or in archival sources. Nothing seems to remain, though whenever I think that this is the case about some aspect of my grand-father's story, if I take things slowly, and abide by a kind of hit-and-miss process of research, something emerges.

❀ ❀ ❀

It's almost impossible to recover Dysart. So much of importance hap-pened in its environs—events and calamities central to the outcome of Canada as a country—yet who knows Dysart? It's farther away and stranger than the moons of Jupiter, floating out in the ether. But that's too easy. Dysart sits at the centre of the early Canadian project that followed Confederation. It became a test case, a proving ground, that the country would populate its far reaches and live up to its motto of existing from sea to sea. And it was at the heart of the wheat economy that had driven Canadian prosperity into the 1920s.

You have to keep returning to the map to orient yourself on the first question. Where? Where is the lower southeast quadrant of what, until 1905, was called the North-West Territories and after that the province of Saskatchewan? In the nineteenth century, official Canadian author-ity and economic influence came via North West Mounted Police out-posts and Hudson's Bay Company trading posts and forts, scattered across the landscape. Fort Qu'Appelle in the rolling river valley is close to the village of Dysart, around which a host of churches established a dizzying array of missions and schools.

This area is recognizable on a map by two major land formations, the Qu'Appelle Valley and, to the northwest, the Touchwood Hills. The Qu'Appelle Valley holds a certain romance for those who know Saskatchewan, though most Canadians likely have not heard of it. Its uniqueness in the midst of rolling prairie provides some of its charm. The valley is nearly 480 kilometres long, running east to west. At certain points, it is over 137 metres deep and over a kilometre and a half wide. Its name is linked to a legend, often told with embarrassed irony, of an Indigenous canoer who, upon hearing his name called out, answered "Qu'appelle?" The story is a jumble of mixed cultural messages, but the name holds its own.[3] An Anglican missionary post appeared in the valley in 1854, overseen by Charles Pratt, who believed that the locals were the descendants of the Ten Lost Tribes of the Hebrew Bible. To support this fiction, he instructed his would-be converts in the Jewish Bible before he began the rudiments of Christianity. It was at a mounted police post at Wood Mountain to the southwest that Sitting Bull presented himself, having left the American territory, and asked for sanctuary for his band. The beginnings of European settlement in southern Saskatchewan coincided with the defeat of one of the great leaders of the Indigenous prairie peoples.

The vast plains around the valley and surrounding hills were bison country into the 1850s and 1860s. Cree, Saulteaux, and Assiniboine made up the large and mobile population, sometimes cooperating and intermarrying, other times raiding and competing with each other for land and food resources.[4] Life in this part of the country had been in flux for some time. An eighteenth-century transformation came with the arrival of the first horses, around 1730, which changed hunting methods and introduced a new resource and source of status to the Indigenous economy.

By the 1870s, Indigenous leaders recognized that, just as European settlers were appearing in numbers, the bison were no longer providing a reliable resource for food, clothing, and other needs that customarily had been filled by the hunt. Treaty negotiations initiated by the Canadian government in the early 1870s at first seemed to present an answer to the challenges of changing life on the Prairies, though on settlers' terms. The reserve system, as the treaties presented it, would assert a new order to ensure that settlers had access to available land, to guarantee the planned transcontinental rail lines, and to protect Indigenous access to fishing and hunting areas, along with the promise of annuities (outright payments) and access to implements, livestock, and housewares necessary to develop Western-style agriculture on the reserves. In exchange for these things, band leaders would agree to the "release and surrender" of Indigenous land rights and title (these legalistic manoeuvres haunt settler history on the Prairies, just as categories of race or origin trailed after my grandfather's arrival in Canada).[5] The appearance of surveyors who marked off reserve lands signalled the federal government's aim of ending the mobility so characteristic of plains life. The fact that the plains peoples did not farm in a way familiar to central Canadians, following instead long-standing patterns of food gathering, contributed to the logic of the Canadian government's claims on their lands.

With these efforts came a host of institutional and ideological efforts to assimilate—or disappear—the "Indian." Under the Indian Act of 1876, whose goal, as John A. Macdonald put it, was to "assimilate the Indian people in all respects," the government oversaw schools set up by a variety of Christian missionary organizations. A substantial and well-known institution of this kind took shape some thirty kilometres east of Dysart. It was named for another local feature of the landscape, the File Hills. The File Hills Indian Residential School was located north of Balcarres, where the Presbyterian Church owned 400 acres of land. A day school run by the Women's Missionary Society opened in 1889. Year after year, the school struggled to attract children from the nearby Peepeekisis, Okanese, Star Blanket, and Little Black Bear reserves. The church's goal, with the backing of the Department of Indian Affairs, was to Christianize and "civilize" the children, to remove them from their ancestral hunting society in favour of a settled farming economy. By 1924, the school taught eighty students.[6]

Alongside the school, the Indian agency founded a colony—a planned community—where graduates of the File Hills Indian Residential School were entitled to receive an eighty-acre farm. The colony at File Hills followed a larger policy shift by the Conservative government under Macdonald, which supported an "industrial school system" aimed at training Indigenous youth to draw them into the general prairie economy. The colony, established in 1901, staked out its goal as the prevention of what the Indian agent referred to as the "regression" of residential school students to their traditional ways of life on reserve lands. By 1915, there were thirty families farming at the colony.[7]

Both the File and Touchwood Hills areas were part of what surveyors had dubbed a "fertile belt," territory with good soil, a supply of timber, and reasonable amounts of rain. Conventional settlement in the area was given added momentum by the closing of the American frontier in the 1880s and the ongoing government policy of offering 160-acre plots in exchange for a ten-dollar fee. A typical settlement pattern followed, led by the usual Canadian potpourri of ethnic strivers from Ireland, Austria, Hungary, Ukraine, Germany, Romania, and Poland. The village of Dysart, between the villages of Cupar and Lipton, grew in the shadow of this activity. Its future looked promising in

1906 as a CPR branch line linked it with Lipton and then major centres farther afield. The train link was crucial since it allowed farmers to get their wheat, eggs, and livestock to market. In 1906, the first grain elevator was erected at Dysart.[8] The same year a wooden Romanian Orthodox church was completed, signalling the importance of that group's settlement in the area. Around this time, the Dysart Hotel opened, so the place, you might say, was making headway.

The tiny farming villages of Dysart, Cupar, and Markinch lay in an east-west line along what is now Highway 22 northeast of Regina. In them, some Jews farmed, whereas others established themselves as merchants in storefront businesses. When my grandfather was at Dysart, it had a Jewish population of twenty-nine, but its proximity to other Jewish communities, including the substantial colony at Lipton, ensured that there were plenty of ritual, educational, and devotional events to oversee. The distance from one village to the next was about sixteen kilometres. In the nearly two years that my grandfather spent along this rural spine, from the end of 1931 to November 1933, he would have travelled by horse cart, serving the communities in his various functions as a Jewish "ritual expert," "kosher slaughterer," or "religious functionary," whichever term you prefer.

The one domestic detail that I know about his time at Dysart is that my grandfather was accompanied there from Vancouver by his sister, Hadassah, who served briefly as his housekeeper. There are photographs of the Dysart train station. It was a low-hipped wooden building, with broad eaves, surrounded by plank boardwalks. I imagine the two of them disembarking in early winter. The prairie wild under early snow. A village like Dysart, in 1931, had a just-put-up quality, as if it had been built by film people to shoot a western. In a photo of nearby Cupar taken from a height—maybe from the top of a grain elevator—one sees a few streets of squared-off one- and two-storey plank buildings with a dirt roadway out front, the broad high line of the prairie horizon in the distance. High Noon country, the New World at its most barren.

The record of my grandfather's stay at Dysart is razor thin. General histories of the area say nothing about its Jewish population. Because my grandfather was not hired to serve the kind of communal colony funded and managed by a centralized philanthropic system, there is no archival record of his life south of the Touchwood Hills. The only thing that has lasted are the copies—on paper and in digital format—of the Winnipeg Yiddish newspaper, *Dos Yiddishe Vort*, which provided reports on the doings of small-town Jewish prairie life. The headline of these pieces in Yiddish read "Dizart, Sask." (דייזארט, סאסק). The articles varied in length from a paragraph to longer, more newsy pieces. Some were submitted by my grandfather to the Choshever Redaktor (Esteemed Editor), whereas others, written by members of his constituency, described his doings. In late 1932, my grandfather used the paper to report on his community's charity work as well as to request that the paper direct the $8.15 that he had gathered from the then ubiquitous blue Jewish National Fund *pushkes* or collection boxes. He sent a money order, care of *Dos Yiddishe Vort*, and listed the contributors as himself ($1.25) along with Naftali Fruman, Israel Viner, Abraham Silverman, Zvi Gibbs, and "Mr. Sangorski."[9] These names, inserted into what is an otherwise mundane report of Dysart doings, provide a record of the Jewish farming and business life in the village, a generation of pioneering characters of whom no record at all exists. In 1933, my grandfather sent news of a similar gathering, resulting in a money order for $30.25, this time on the occasion of Rosh Hashanah. He requested that the paper's editor direct funds to "*Idishe flichtlingen fun Deutschland*"—Jewish German refugees—while asserting the need to maintain a boycott against purchasing items made in "Hitler's Germany." To this, my grandfather affixed a kind of alias; he replaced his last name Eisenstein with its Hebrew equivalent, Evenbarzel, as if to assert that in the present context his German family name should be embargoed.[10]

In early 1933, my grandfather wrote to the Winnipeg editor providing an account of a prairie bar mitzvah that exemplified the active Jewish life in far-flung prairie villages like Dysart. Along with the young Meyer Silverman's presentation of a *sheynem maftir*, and his vow to "uphold the Torah's commandments," my grandfather described a group of fifty locals who gathered on the Sunday after the bar mitzvah for a *vetshere*, Yiddish for "supper," at the family home. A host of speeches were given, a rhetorical feast to go with the food. Young Meyer contributed one of them in what my grandfather called a *zaftikn Yiddish*—a "fulsome Yiddish"—followed by the bar mitzvah boy's brother, then a smattering of local social higher ups (Gibbs, Sangorski, and Jampolsky), and the author of the report, the *shoichet* and ritual inspector, Yehuda Yosef Eisenstein.[11]

These newsprint artifacts of the early 1930s—boasting of a *sheinem maftir*, and a prairie gathering of fifty, where the newly arrived *shoichet* joined community leaders in post-supper speechifying—reflect a spiritual and practical project of great pathos: against the backdrop of a Depression-era farming crisis, the Jews of Dysart and its surroundings recreated what they knew to be the Jewish template for an observant identity. This included an array of ancient rituals, *kashrut*, *mikvah*, bar mitzvah, and traditional marriage and burial. To maintain these rituals, one needed a ritual expert, such as my grandfather, whether with or without rabbinic ordination. This he did not have, though he was duly literate, experienced, an Old World personality who, as a young man, had studied with Gerrer Chassidim in Mława. He was competent at leading prayers, with all of this anchored in his familiarity with Polish Jewish ways. For this set of skills, his farmer pals paid a monthly salary of $100 by way of community collection, and they hoped that my grandfather would stick around for a few years, which he did. They would have heard, early on, of the personal crisis that he faced: his family left behind in Poland whom he had intended to follow him to Canada.

At outpost after outpost, a new kind of spiritual life took root on the Canadian Prairies.

At the same time, the Cree ways of spiritualizing the landscape and daily life were under calamitous pressure. Just as my grandfather settled in at Dysart, his monthly salary in hard-earned Depression dollars in return for maintaining religious custom and community, it was an end time for the Cree shaman, or medicine man, as the anthropologists who came to study local bands called him. Cree life in southern Saskatchewan is well documented in photographs from the 1880s through the early decades of the next century. Among these early photographers was Geraldine Moodie—the granddaughter of Ontario settler Susanna Moodie—who set up a photographic studio in 1895 in Battleford, the capital of the North-West Territories. Her husband's work as an RCMP inspector brought her from Ontario, but she established the first studio run by a woman in the territory. Moodie took conventional portraits of white settlers, but she also used her camera to capture the landscape and the Indigenous life of the plains. Her photos of the Sun

Dance gatherings of the late 1890s are among the best representations of Cree daily life in this period. She framed the Sun Dance lodge at a distance, with its centre pole rising into a cloudless sky, and in her Battleford studio she took portraits of Cree Shaman and Chief Kamiokisikwew or, as Moodie knew him, Fine Day. In his portrait, he wears his bison horn headdress, a leather belt traded by a local settler, and trim white moccasins, and he holds a long gun lightly in one hand. The studio's faux background—a vernal forest of birch and wildflowers—is rather like the false background against which my grandfather had been photographed in Warsaw, wearing his Polish Army uniform.[12]

In the mid-1930s, Fine Day offered himself as an informant to the visiting American anthropologist David G. Mandelbaum, who spent the summers of 1934 and 1935 gathering information for a PhD thesis on the Plains Cree. By this time, Fine Day was in his eighties and living at the File Hills Agency, near Dysart. The bison were just a memory. Muskrats and gophers were poor replacements for bison meat and skin. But the Sun Dance—a constant target of Indian Agency suppression—was being mounted, and Mandelbaum saw the dancers in the lodge in those summers.[13] Inside the lodge and on the surrounding grassland, he used his field notes to record the intricate workings of pipe offerings and the sweetgrass smudge, which called for long, dried, plaited grass to be laid on live coals to bring forth the precious aromatic smoke.[14]

Donald Cadzow, another American anthropologist, was drawn to the Plains Cree in these years, taking two extended driving trips in 1928 and 1929 across southern Saskatchewan. He had been through this landscape before, in 1925 when he visited the four reserves associated with the File Hills region: Little Black Bear, Okanese, Peepeekisis, and Star Blanket.[15] On the last reserve, he met a man whom he called "Keevisk" and based an article upon him, titled "The Vanishing American Indian Medicine-Man," that appeared in a 1929 issue of *Scientific American*. Cadzow describes Keevisk, known to his compatriots as Kīwisk, as "a Cree Indian, who makes his home at the File Hills reservation in the Province of Saskatchewan, Canada, is one of the last of the great medicine-men left in the West." Like Fine Day, Kīwisk was old. Among the things that anthropologists collected and bought from their Cree informants were "medicines" and ritual items falling out of traditional use. While Cadzow visited Kīwisk's teepee, a white man, "a rancher and an ex-Canadian soldier," appeared seeking medicine for a skin disease that no one else had been able to cure.[16] This kind of cultural crossing is difficult to find in the historical record. It signals aspects of prairie life outside the reach of church and government, wars and treaties; the meeting in the teepee was a real human exchange between the rancher and Kīwisk. I never stop looking for this kind of overlap between my grandfather's life on the plains and his Cree counterparts in the nearby File Hills. What were his medicines? In a soft bag, his "phylacteries"—*tefillin* in Hebrew—and a prayer shawl. A few religious books. A torah scroll, kept by a custodian of such things for the community.

❀ ❀ ❀

For a newcomer to the Canadian Prairies who knew a European capital and small cities, the isolation of villages and small towns must have hit hard. Compared with life in farming colonies like Lipton and Hirsch, Dysart and Cupar farmers lived isolated lives, kilometres apart. The largest Jewish community in the area was Lipton, a village with a synagogue and a school whose teacher was hired by the Jewish Colonization Association. In the early years of the Lipton colony, the farmers' children studied "Yiddish and Hebrew reading and writing, Hebrew translation, religion, Bible, recitation of prayers, singing of Yiddish and Hebrew songs, grammar and history."[17] This sounds remarkably like what Jewish kids at a big city parochial school would have been taught. My grandfather, in his Dysart days, and later at Hirsch to the south, was responsible for this kind of curriculum. The one ritual expectation that he could not fulfill was that of a *mohel*, the man who performs circumcisions. A son born to one of his farmer neighbours would have meant a visit from an even more specialized ritual expert.

But the Dysart-Lipton area was not wholly removed from the rest of the world. Romanian settlers of different types arrived there in the 1890s, and the Lipton Jews, mostly from the Bukovina area of Romania, continued to arrive throughout the early twentieth century. By the 1930s, some settler families had been on the land for three decades. They had young children as well as children old enough to leave the farm for education in Regina. There were widowers and widows.

The Jewish Colonization Association sent agents to make detailed reports on each homesteader under their management and to provide summaries of the colonies' progress. A summary document for Lipton's 1931 statistics looked like this:

1) *Population*
Number of Jewish Farmers - 25
of which   - 24 are resident

Resident Jewish Population consists of

> 23 men
> 16 women
> 28 sons
> 13 daughters
> 80

. . .

5) *Country of Origin of Lipton Jewish Farmers*

Rumania	14
Russia	5
Lithuania	3
Turkey	1
Canada	1
	24[18]

Of the total lands owned by the Lipton colony—13,831 acres—4,460 were under cultivation. The farmers' livestock included 201 horses, 87 milk cows, and 2,800 birds. The colony's farm machinery included 38 wagons, 14 buggies, 18 seed drills, and 2 threshing machines. The last two implements were the Rolls Royces among the rest, with a value in 1931 dollars of $520. For each farmer, the agent filled out a "Colonist Report," like the one done in 1931 for Mrs. Dora Schwartz. She was a widow with five children on the farm, her eldest twenty-three and her youngest eight. She had been on the land since 1902. She had twenty horses on the farm and sixteen head of beef cattle. Her liabilities totalled $5,320, most of it in the form of a mortgage on the farm.[19] The farm was rich in poultry. With 450 birds, Mrs. Schwartz was the chicken queen of Lipton. Perhaps the village had its ritual slaughtering covered, but it's possible, too, that my grandfather took a bird or two home in return for slaughtering a chicken for her on a busy Friday. This would have been a perk on top of his salary from the community at Dysart. Farmers like Dora Schwartz faced a series of highly inauspicious events by the end of the 1920s—calamity upon calamity, which presaged the bad decade to come. Cattle and grain prices collapsed, so the value of land and livestock was diminished. Drought was an intimate companion, wrecking crops from 1929 through 1937. New settler arrivals decreased in number, and people abandoned farms. But as some left, remaining homesteaders bought their land, increasing established farms' viability.

We should pause and consider the new Canadian, Yehuda Yosef Eisenstein, at his first position in the country. With his sister, he arrives near the winter-bound Qu'Appelle Valley to find his congregants, schoolchildren, and customers for kosher slaughter scattered along the rural byways. To see them, he must ride by horse cart, from schoolhouse to farmer's homestead, to Lipton or the Dysart train depot to collect mail, and back to his own place in Dysart. He has a scattered community of Eastern European Jews to mind, whose language and observance and cultural biases resemble his own. But so much of what was familiar has been left behind beyond the Atlantic's rough ride. The middle-class comfort of his in-laws' home in Mława. His father's status in Radzanów as a Talmud rabbi. His time serving a Polish officer in the army. Mława, with its many Jewish newspapers, businesses and political groups: Zionists, leftists, Chassidic adherents, Polonizing cosmopolites. In Poland, his life straddled a village and a small city, bringing together rural *heimishkeit* and a form of urban sophistication not so far removed from the country's modern capital. His own family and the one that he married into were well established in both places. While my grandfather spent the early 1930s in Canada, his first born, known by the Polish diminutive Berek, attended a Polish gymnasium where he was introduced to a modern Polish Jewish identity. He studied in Polish and wore a school uniform with a military style.

With all of this behind him, my grandfather stood on the inland sea that was the Saskatchewan wheat lands, writing in his head and then with a flowing fountain pen letters of woe and supplication to immigration service people, to government figures, to lawyers in Yorkton and Estevan, and ultimately to people of national influence. To bring his family after him. That became his life's work.

THE BENNETT YEARS

I n the commonly held narrative regarding Jewish immigration to Canada before the Second World War, men and women (children too) like my grandfather rarely exist. At the least, their stories are not part of the public narrative. Historians Harold Troper and Irving Abella interpret the mid-1920s shifts, under both Liberal and Conservative governments, to suggest that "by the onset of the Great Depression ... Jews had already been locked out."[1] Clearly, what the authors meant was that government regulations aimed to "close the door to all independent immigrants," at least as overt policy, but this is not a full description of the outcome of the immigration struggles of the first half of the 1930s. My grandfather's Canadian immigration landing documents of 1930 list his profession in Poland (incorrectly) as teacher and his expected profession in Canada to be the same. It was, of course, his brother's sponsorship that landed my grandfather a cross-Atlantic visa. As of 1930, he remained the kind of "first degree relative" that Canadian citizens could apply to sponsor. Ironically, he wound up living among "agriculturalists," the prized settlers of the West, as an all-purpose religious and ritual functionary and school-teacher. Prairie Jews needed men like him to make a go of things, and he found his way to them. Perhaps his dedication to them stood him in good stead as he embarked on his years of effort to bring his wife and children from their comfortable home in Mława, Poland, to the hardbitten Canadian West.

One of the cardinal realizations of my story is that my grandfather's years of struggle on his own in the early 1930s were lived in fact outside the "none is too many" narrative. The template offered there does not explain his predicament from outset to outcome. My grandfather launched his efforts at the federal Department of Immigration and Colonization, in which the notorious F.C. Blair was a commissioner but not yet the king of the hill that he would become under William Lyon Mackenzie King in the second half of the 1930s. The early years of that decade were Conservative federally, under the leadership of R.B. "Dick" Bennett, a New Brunswick–born millionaire who lit out for Calgary, where he joined the city's richest citizen, James Lougheed, in a law firm whose success helped to pave the road to a political career.

Of all the Big Boys who lurked in the background, sometimes moving to the foreground, who played a part in my grandfather's story, the biggest was Prime Minister Bennett. He is a largely forgotten figure. He is on no Canadian money. He is not the target of ideological shifts that call for statues to be removed from parks. His handling of the Depression, his East Coast roots transplanted to the Prairies, are of little interest to dominant narrators of Canadian history. Regardless of all this, he was the prime minister of my grandfather's story. His ministers became my grandfather's correspondents, as did provincial Conservatives, their compatriots in Saskatchewan, as well as in the immigration bureaucracy that the Conservatives oversaw. It was this realm in which my grandfather struggled to manoeuvre. Let's call it Bennettlandia or, if that seems silly, Early Thirties Time. Or more simply, and maybe provocatively, Conservative Canada. Whichever you prefer, the first half of the decade deserves its own distinctive name.

Bennett hovers in the wings of my grandfather's tale, a shadow player. I am partial to him in spite of my non-conservative tendencies. He was an oddball at a time when being an oddball in public life was not such a big deal. Like so many of the powerful men in the background or even the foreground of my grandfather's story, Bennett started out as a schoolteacher. In his case, in New Brunswick. A schoolteacher! In Poland, my grandfather would never have become one, but in Saskatchewan he did, supplying the Hebrew and Yiddish and religious learning that Jewish settlers wanted for their children when the public school board curriculum was over for the day. Bennett shifted to law and was lured out to Calgary in 1897 by Lougheed, a leading figure in what was still a horse town, a place of fewer than 5,000 inhabitants.[2] In legal practice together, the CPR was their main client. And a good client it was in those days.

Bennett acclimatized quickly to western ways, though it was generally agreed that he overdressed for his regular strolls through town. He lived first at the Alberta Hotel on 8th Avenue, holding court in the bar. For a time, one could find him in a rented flat in a wooden house overseen by two elderly ladies on 4th Avenue Southwest. In photos, it's a modest place, the kind of working man's house that once lined the city's streets. Bennett made a final move in 1924 to the Palliser Hotel, where he lived the rest of his years as a local MP. Through part of that time, his much younger sister lived in a neighbouring suite at the hotel and acted as a social consort for her bachelor brother, escorting him to ribbon cuttings and other official responsibilities as the member of Parliament for Calgary West.

Oddball? You bet.

By the time he arrived in Ottawa, Bennett was well-off, an entirely self-made man at a time when the average Canadian's economic fortune was shrinking or heading straight over a cliff. In one of the convoluted relationships that he had with widows, he inherited a pile of stock in the E.B. Eddy match and pulp and paper company. This was the final stroke that set him up as a millionaire, at a time when being one was big news and not a popular thing to be as leaders struggled to right the economy.

This portrait of Bennett is crucial to my story; however shadowy he remains in relationship to my grandfather's efforts, his ministers— especially Minister of Immigration Wesley Ashton Gordon—and the commissioners who acted on government policies and regulations are ever-present players. It doesn't hurt to remind ourselves that the "none is too many" story, the dominant narrative associated with Jewish immigration in the 1930s and early 1940s, is a story overseen by another prime minister, the Liberal King. He was an oddball in the grand style, though there was more to him than the common caricature foisted on us by writers who present him merely as a clown, a crackpot, and an anti-Semite. Bennett was a different sort, peculiar in his own New

Brunswick–turned–Alberta way, which, at least to me, is a breath of fresh air in contrast to King and his crystal ball, his mother worship, and his willingness to give prewar Hitler the benefit of the doubt.

Some work has been done to surmise Liberal Prime Minister King's personal view of Jews and Jewish immigration to Canada (though even Troper and Abella say less about this than we might expect them to). Little effort has been made to understand the role of the Conservative years under Bennett in this context. Biographies and historical studies of Bennett make no mention of the Conservatives' attitude toward Jews. It's as if what took place after the election of King's Liberals in the fall of 1935 was unrelated in any meaningful way to what went before.

There is one bit of Calgary lore, a piece of fancy, wholly undocumented, regarding Bennett and the Jews of Calgary. We know that he fielded a great many queries for help in the Depression years, personal requests from Canadians, to pay down a farm mortgage or to buy a child a pair of skates for the town festival. This resulted in a non-bureaucratic, independent, philanthropic project run out of the Prime Minister's Office. In many cases, Bennett's response to such a request was to tell one of his secretaries to send a gift of two or five dollars. His other gift of choice, for the staff at the Palliser Hotel or for colleagues, was chocolates. At Christmastime, Bennett gave out chocolates to the hotel staff who served him. And he had, the sources say, a "pound a day chocolate habit" himself.[3] Here the story goes in a surprising direction. His source for his fix—a bit like Lou Reed's trips up to Lexington to meet his man—was on the corner of 14th Avenue and 11th Street in a residential neighbourhood west of downtown Calgary. This was a good walk from his own digs at the Palliser and his habitual lunches at the Alberta Hotel on 8th Avenue. At 14th and 11th was Kesnick's Confectionery. In old-time Calgary, there were a great many confectioneries. An average year's *Calgary City Directory* might have included the addresses for sixty such businesses, from A B C Confectionery not too far from Kesnick's to Welcome Confectionery over on 1st Street West. The business names don't reveal it, but a good number of these small stores were owned by Jewish newcomers to the city, Russian and Polish men and women who'd arrived in the 1910s and 1920s, like my own paternal grandfather (the other grandfather, not the focus of all my work to this point), who makes his cameo in this story as the owner of "Mewata Grocery & Confectionery

513–519 9 St W M5253," as the directory had it.[4] Maybe the additional "Grocery" designated some kind of extra competitive level. Ice cream? Tea bags? Kesnick's special feature was that its owner, British-born Israel Kesnick, was a chocolate maker in addition to being a storekeeper.

Chocolates, the rumours say, brought Bennett to Kesnick's Confectionery often. But there was something more at the store of interest to the city's leading lawyer: Esther Kesnick, the wife of the chocolatier, Izzy, or, as we might call her in her own right, The Chocolate Lady. Bennett historians and biographers—anyone who's written on him in the past eighty years—say nothing about this. They are fascinated with the sister-as-escort scenario; they dwell on the widows with whom Bennett became close. Even the best-case-scenario specialist in this area, Harry Sanders, for a time Calgary's "Historian Laureate," has seen no source to verify the story of Calgary's leading lawyer-politician and the chocolatier's wife. "I've never heard this story," Sanders wrote in an email in response to my query. "I know of Israel Kesnick," he added, "because I researched the extant building that housed his confectionery where he made and sold chocolates." The one place where a suggestion of something more shows up is in a volume of local history called *Land of Promise: The Jewish Experience in Southern Alberta, 1889–1945*, produced by the Jewish Historical Society of Southern Alberta in 1996. There, in the notes describing the Kesnick family, we read that "Esther's close family relationship with R.B. Bennett dated well before the local lawyer became Prime Minister. Connections that Esther was able to make helped her obtain jobs for many Jewish persons."[5]

This certainly sounds like a historical detail worthy of a biographer's interest. And what do we make of the phrase "close family relationship"? It is both vague and mysterious, signalling something without actually saying anything. When Esther died "following a long illness" at forty-seven, she left a daughter, Victoria, and a record of having been an "active worker in Jewish and English activities."[6]

So what if the confirmed bachelor, Calgary's leading lawyer and political figure on the national stage, came to flirt with Izzy Kesnick's wife as he chose a pound of chocolates for himself alongside what he bought to give away to the staff at the Palliser Hotel? In certain circles, a "close family relationship" meant that Bennett had a love child with Mrs. Kesnick, a daughter raised by the Kesnicks as their own. *Land of Promise* does not go that far and provides only Kesnick "Family

History": "Izzy Kesnick, born in 1881, moved to Calgary from England in the early 1900's. He was a chocolate maker, and his excellent wares soon became well known. His store . . . was a favourite Calgary meeting place."[7]

What can we glean from this forgotten prairie narrative? If true, then the possibility of some personal interest, the meeting of Jew and non-Jew at a time when such intimacies were rare, in this case a man from the topmost crust of Calgary society intimate with a woman fully rooted in the city's ethnic working middle class. Esther Kesnick was buried in Calgary's Jewish cemetery early in 1935, the year that Bennett lost to King's Liberals, ending the Conservative prime minister's political career. Her story presents a surprising and sweet embellishment to the portrait that I present of the early 1930s, in contrast to the "none is too many" years under King. Bennett's attention to Calgary's Jews was not just one of private peccadilloes. In the summer of 1911, when the Jewish community laid the cornerstone for their new House of Jacob synagogue, Bennett was there to address the audience.[8] In his last days as leader of the opposition, and then in the early weeks of his new government, one finds correspondence between Bennett and the Dworkin family of Calgary, desperate to bring to Canada a family member from Danzig who has been prevented from sailing by the port's medical inspector. The documents include a hastily handwritten letter from Calgary whose tone suggests a constituent with some personal link with her member of Parliament. The file closes with a "night letter" from Bennett, sent by telegraph, expressing the prime minister's gladness "to be able advise you instructions have been issued allow your relative proceed to Canada."[9]

The Kesnick store was off Bennett's track, but there were other attractions on that side of the city, including the lofty sandstone house that Bennett's old colleague, Senator Lougheed, had built, surrounded by Victorian-style gardens. The senator was dead by 1925, but his widow lived on in the house till 1936. She was allowed to stay even after she could no longer foot the tax bill. Bennett was famously attentive to widows. It was Lougheed who'd brought him to Calgary in the first place, and Lady Lougheed had him to the house for dinner from time to time. So a little visit with the widow, and then over for some chocolates, where the locals hung out reading magazines off the rack. It was the kind of evening out that the prime-minister-to-be favoured.

❀ ❀ ❀

Bennett's Conservatives, like the Liberals they replaced in 1930, pursued a goal of ending large-scale immigration. In 1931, Canada allowed 88,000 immigrants; in 1932, 26,000; in 1936, 11,000.[10] Furthermore, in the first half of the 1930s, the status of the federal immigration bureaucracy was in flux. Prior to 1930, the Department of Immigration and Colonization was independent and focused its efforts on settling the West. In 1936, it became the Immigration Branch of the Department of Mines and Resources, losing its independent status.[11] Throughout the early 1930s, immigration policy was characterized by increased reliance on the deportation of immigrants to their native countries. One was most in danger of deportation if convicted of a crime, but destitution—or simply being out of work—could lead to the same outcome. Gaining access to the country by some prohibited subterfuge was, of course, a crime. In 1931, the year after my grandfather arrived, having lied about his marriage status, 7,000 immigrants were deported.[12] Lying about one's status on an immigration application remains a crime in Canada.

In the Bennett years, the immigration department's bureaucracy was headed by Wesley Ashton Gordon. His constituency was in Timiskaming, in northeastern Ontario, and by the time he held ministerial roles he was in his middle fifties, a senior presence among the other fresh Conservative MPs. He is somewhat of a cipher in the historical record, with no single location for his working records and almost no comment on him in historical and biographical works of the period. In this, ironically, he mirrors my grandfather's negligible imprint. In the early stages of Bennett's government, *Maclean's* ran a set of "Cabinet Portraits," including one of "Hon. Wesley Gordon, Minister of Immigration and Mines." Its author was M. Grattan O'Leary, an established parliamentary reporter who himself ran for the Conservative Party in 1925 in a federal seat in his home of Gaspé. O'Leary's portrait of Gordon highlights his small-town lawyering background and his involvement in the mining economy of northern Ontario. The most notable event in Gordon's pre-government career was his representation of the miners following the explosion at Hollinger's mine at Timmins, which killed thirty-nine men. O'Leary's portrait makes clear why Gordon was chosen to head up the ministry responsible for mines. It leaves his approach to immigration until last: "The minister," O'Leary writes, views his job as "not to let immigrants in, but actually to keep immigrants out." This, according to Gordon, has made him unpopular, even in the "ranks of his own political party." In contrast to the portrait of Gordon as hard-nosed doorkeeper, O'Leary adds that one "of the afflictions of the Immigration Department . . . was that Ministers and officials neglected the human equation, forgot that they were dealing with human beings." The cabinet portrait includes a headshot of Gordon in noirish shades. He is jowly, his hair receding on a wide forehead, the corners of his mouth turned down. O'Leary describes him as "genial, humorous, physically attractive," while his "large nose, firm mouth and firmer jaw, all tell of one who, once having made up his mind about principle or policy, will be prepared to fight for it."[13]

Gordon's ministerial appointments reflected Canadian political trends in the 1930s. As minister of mines and immigration and colonization, as well as labour from 1932 to 1935, his mixture of responsibilities reflected the government's focus on newcomers as key to the "colonization" of the West and on labourers as necessary for the country's resource economy. Newcomers in this period were thought of, to a large extent, as human *matériel* capable of meeting changing labour needs. Unless, of course, applicants were Anglo-Saxon, which meant that they arrived bearing cultural capital as more or less ready-made Canadians.

These are the broad strokes regarding Minister Gordon. One source in which we do encounter him is *Hansard*, the parliamentary record. There we encounter the voice of the minister of immigration and colonization as it shored up the official Canadian view of those who should gain access to the country. When he spoke in Parliament, Gordon spoke at length. He did not seem to hector his opponents. When asked a question, he answered it in detail.

In the summer of 1931, the minister read into the record an immigration order-in-council that dated from 1926. The point of this recap seems to have been to offer an account of immigration regulations as they stood and how they had changed under the Conservatives. Catchwords abound in the order-in-council, signalling government goals for immigration at the outset of the Depression. A "bona fide agriculturalist" with "sufficient means" was the prize to seek, and the country remained ready and willing to accept British subjects, notably those from "Great Britain or Ireland, Newfoundland, the United States of America. New Zealand, Australia or the Union of South Africa."[14] This list was stated in an almost offhand way, and one cannot miss its discounting of British subjects from India as potential immigrants. In this, the regulation of 1926 reiterated the stance against "Asiatics" set in law and practice while the *Komagata Maru* sat in the Vancouver harbour.

Gordon says that he has done away with a clause that allowed immigration access to any "person who has satisfied the minister that his labour or service is required in Canada." It is his opinion that this approach "gave rise to what was known as the permit system" in which members of Parliament were "importuned by certain of their electors with regard to the issuance of permits to bring in relatives and friends." Gordon is then challenged by opposition member J.S. Woodsworth: "Has that been absolutely done away with?" To which Gordon answers "Yes. Since I have been at the head of the department I have signed one permit, . . . that of a student coming to one of our universities." Perhaps Gordon is still getting his feet wet in a tricky official role, but more likely he is lying or at least obscuring how the pursuit of immigration permits worked in his department. At the time and in the coming years, the permit system, as he knew it (a back-channel array of discussions among everyone involved in immigration decisions, from the prime minister down to the lowly commissioners on the docks in the fog at the Halifax and Vancouver harbours), was a going concern. It accounted for most of the Jews who managed to enter the country in the Bennett years (420 "Hebrews" entered Canada in 1933 by the official government count, 577 the following year).[15]

The other source for Gordon's approach to immigration in the early 1930s is newspaper coverage of policy statements and public talks by the minister. A talk before Vancouver's Canadian Club in November 1930—my grandfather's time of arrival in the city—included the following:

"I have been criticized about the severity of some of the immigration laws which I have evoked," said Mr. Gordon. "I accept full responsibility for the course I am pursuing, and, along with every man in Canada who believes that this country must be kept clean, I have a common object. Our settlers must be chosen with the greatest care, and when we accept them they must be received in a spirit of friendliness and with a willingness to take them into our national life.

"We have every reason jea[l]ously to guard the traditions of our British ancestry," he said, "and we must build up our country by our British-Canadian strain. We must be strict in all matters referring to the complexion of our population."[16]

Early in 1931, back at the Canadian Club, Gordon asserted that "new peoples who have come into Canada have contributed largely to the displacing of Canadian-born people" and added that "the fact remains that they do replace our own people, and the undisciplined flow of immigrants has in a measure at least contributed to our own boys and our own girls going down to our big neighbor to the south. In so far as restricted immigration can cure that situation, I think we are very justified in restricting the flood of people into this country."[17]

In response to complaints regarding deportations, Gordon claimed that newspapers "unfriendly to the Government" circulated reports that "deportation proceedings are carried out by the Department of Immigration in an arbitrary, secret and ruthless manner, reference being made to the secret proceedings, Star Chamber methods, rushing people out of the country." The minister's statement in response to these claims insisted that deportees were "not denied the ordinary legal rights that any man is entitled to."[18] From these few sources, one gets a sense of the party line, the minister's way of conveying it, and a personal tone just short of strident, certainly confident, and willing to appeal to racialist arguments.

Under Gordon, immigration commissioners based in Ottawa, as well as at ports of entry, had substantial influence on decisions regarding immigration applications and permits. They were the judges, in effect, who applied the regulations set out by ministers and bureaucrats. The *bête noire* among them was F.C. Blair, about whom much has been written. In the early 1930s, Blair had the powerful and ambiguous role of "assistant deputy minister." The phrase "none is too many" is not ascribed to him directly, yet he embodied it in the history of Canada before the Second World War; with that phrase, we appreciate his entirely malign influence on Jewish immigration in the years before and during the war. Blair was the Canadian bureaucratic bogeyman, the church elder who expressed the idea in a department report, as late as 1941, that "Canada, in accordance with generally accepted practice, places greater emphasis on race than upon citizenship."[19] His ultimate rise to power took place in 1936 when he became the director of the Immigration Branch of the Department of Mines and Resources, a position that he held until 1943. But this bureaucratic ascent postdates my story. Everything that I have to tell with relation to settlement, European immigration to the country, and ideas of Canadians about the nation's identity predates his ascendancy in 1936. For Jews striving to enter Canada in the early 1930s, the days were already dark, but my grandfather's story predates the full bureaucratic calamity that took place under Blair, and not one letter or government document signals his involvement with my grandfather's file.

Central casting sends other figures to people my grandfather's early Canadian years. Among them is A.L. Jolliffe, who began his civil service career in 1913 as an immigration agent in Vancouver. There he played a role in the notorious handling of the *Komagata Maru*. A substantial memorial telling this story stands today on the seawall walk overlooking Vancouver's Coal Harbour, representing a kind of standing apology to the people sent back to India. Jolliffe's role in keeping the ship at bay, as well as in port decisions after this incident, is buried in the archives. Jolliffe was there in 1914 when Canadian attitudes toward immigrants were shifting, so one might think of the *Komagata Maru* Incident as an opening scene in developments that would shape Canadian life over the next twenty-five years. In the 1920s, Jolliffe was the commissioner of immigration overseeing the department's Vancouver office.

By the turn of the decade, he was in Ottawa, where he signed off on reports "of the Commissioner of Immigration." These were pamphlets commissioned and printed by Parliament, which reported on the recently ended "fiscal year," doing double duty as financial report and policy statement. The report for 1930–31 reveals the government's outlook at the time:

Since the publication of the last annual report conditions in Canada have materially changed, thus necessitating a revision of the Immigration Regulations to meet the existing situation. Such conditions necessitated a drastic curtailment of the flow of immigrants to Canada and, in August, 1930, the regulations were revised with this object in view. The new regulations did not affect British subjects coming to Canada from the British Isles and the Dominions, or United States citizens entering Canada from the United States. . . . The changes made restricted the admissible classes from other countries.[20]

In language befitting an accountant tasked with lowering one side of the balance sheet in favour of the other, Jolliffe was pleased to offer proof of the effectiveness of recent immigration regulations: a "reduction" in immigration numbers of "63 per cent was effected" between fiscal year-end 1930 and 1931.[21] The new regulations were confirmed by an order-in-council passed by Bennett's cabinet in March 1931. Under these rules, even American and British subjects were expected to have "sufficient means to maintain themselves until securing employment," as were agriculturalists who aimed to farm in Canada. "Immigrants of all other classes and occupations were explicitly prohibited."[22]

My grandfather's arrival in Canada coincided with these government accomplishments. Louis Rosenberg, working as the in-house demographer for the Canadian Jewish Congress at the time, tells the tale of the pre-Depression years this way: early in the twentieth century, Canada, after the United States and Palestine, was an important recipient of Eastern European Jewish immigrants. By the 1920s—well before the onset of the Depression—this changed. Between 1921 and 1931, 44,810 Jews entered Canada (over half this number left, in these years, for the United States). Things tightened further in the early 1930s, and in the "none is too many" years proper the number of Jews allowed into the country via ocean ports sank as low as 202 in 1931 and 655 in 1935.[23] All of this conveys how the first half of the 1930s was a period beset by complex, even convoluted, circumstances, a time of shifting status quo in government policy in the face of economic crisis, rising nativism, and an increasing number of out-of-work Canadians.

❀ ❀ ❀

In this context, Jews of my grandfather's era and trajectory—newcomers in the late 1920s and the first years of the 1930s—dwelt on the plains of the Dominion under a cloud of great misapprehension and doubt. As long as they did not exert themselves as labour organizers, or remain unemployed, or ask for relief, they were not expressly under threat, as their families back in Poland soon would be. And in this way Canada provided a haven. But they remained fundamentally unknown figures, and in important ways they played the role of bogeymen.

All of this, one could say, is like old-fashioned white noise behind my grandfather's arrival at Quebec City, his train trip west across the country to clasp hands with his brother on Victoria Drive in working-class east Vancouver, then, in late 1931, his arrival at Dysart, in the heart of the Canadian project to settle the Prairies, of which one outcome was the collapse of traditional Indigenous life. On the rails, on rutted wagon tracks, on city sidewalks, my grandfather was a player in the late stages of the massive undertaking to settle the "Last Best West." Crucial to his moment, integral to the national project, of which, I guess, he was oblivious.

As I consider the years in advance of his arrival, then the early 1930s, when he was alone on the southern prairie (like a Jewish Polish moon man setting his footprint on the wheat land), my grandfather represented an unquantifiable and unqualifiable presence in contrast to the shifting character of the country. What is the correct analogy? He was a container into which presumptions were poured. He was porous, like a net, so that any number of incorrect and vicious and vacuous theories might pass through him at any given time.

PART TWO

THE IMMIGRATION FILES:
THE HEART OF THE MATTER

At Dysart, my grandfather's great project began: to engage Jewish immigration organizations, lawyers, and government representatives with the issue of bringing his wife and children to Canada from Poland. I have not introduced them properly. Instead, I've portrayed my grandfather casting out alone and then heading west across the new country that he'd chosen. Here it is timely to introduce the objects of his project: his wife Chaya Dina and children Berel and Henna. Their photograph is the one that he used as a calling card as he embarked on his efforts, showing it as if it were the best hand that he held. I have it as a copy of the original. It tells its own story. It was taken at Zygmunt Lipszyc's studio in the Mława market square. The children—my mother and her older brother—are dressed like typical young Polish Jewish urbanites: little shoes, a ruffle at the boy's neck, and a tasselled crocheted head covering down to the eyes for the girl. My grandmother is demure in black, with a white lace collar, her hair dark, and just a hint of a smile on her face. With her husband abroad, she was being taken care of in the home of her half-sister in Mława.

Based upon what is contained in his archived documents, my grandfather wrote his first letters to the Winnipeg office of the Jewish Immigrant Aid Society not long after arriving at Dysart. It was the

closest JIAS office to him on the Prairies. Later he would divert his attention to head office on St. Laurence Boulevard in Montreal. His story could not be told if I hadn't stumbled upon his files, kept by the JIAS offices in these two cities, and later preserved in their original form in Jewish archives as well as in the files of the Department of Immigration, now held by Library and Archives Canada on Wellington Street, near Parliament Hill. I had tried on earlier occasions to learn about my grandfather's first Canadian years, but early searches offered up nothing. Some quirk in the searches, the way that I entered his name or how it had been written out in the archives, drew a blank. My first and most substantial archival find was the Montreal JIAS file preserved at the city's Jewish Congress Archives. It consists of a sheaf of paper originals roughly half an inch thick. This, in fact, was not the file on my grandfather—who had come to Canada without corresponding with the JIAS—but that of his family, opened when he began to look for avenues to bring them from Poland. On its title page, he is logged as "Surname Rabbi J. Eisenstein File No 17808."[1] Beneath that are the names of the family members he wished to bring from Poland, awkwardly transliterated in English as

Hae-Ding
Berek
Henna

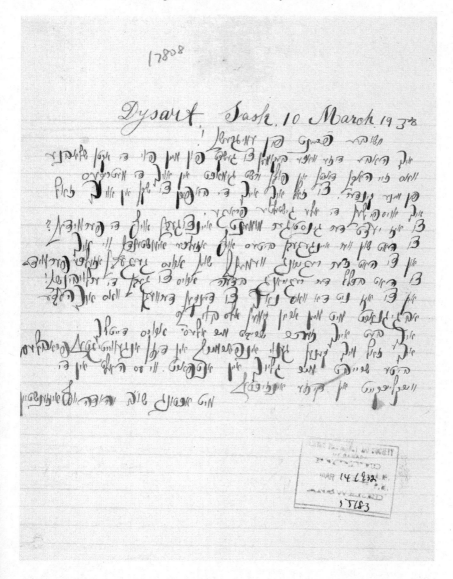

Although the children are properly represented—Berek being the Polish diminutive for the Yiddish Berel—the Hebrew name of my grandmother was Chaya Dina, or Sweet Life in Hebrew, since she was a survivor in a line of stillborn births.

My grandfather's Dysart letters are handwritten in Yiddish in blue fountain pen ink. This gives them a certain beauty as artifacts. The letters are substantial in length, often running to a second or third page. The lone English words on them are in their headings, such as

"Dysart Sask 25, January 1932." For the non-Yiddish reader, the only other decodable information is the stamp that a JIAS worker placed on each letter denoting receipt date and file number. Added to this, the JIAS office in the 1930s had a peculiar method of collecting material for a file—a spike of some sort that the handler would use to punch the corner of each sheet and then pile them, one after another. Every sheet bears the same puncture in the upper corner, which shows up on some photocopies as a blotch.

It's a commonplace today to note the ease with which we communicate with one another. It's a *Star Trek* world: "Beam me up, Scotty." And it's done. In the early 1930s, on the far-flung prairie, there was the mail, which arrived in sacks by train, and the telegraph. The latter is forgotten today, as are the blacksmith and the cowcatcher. Telegraph lines followed the railway tracks and first served the purposes of the railway companies and the North West Mounted Police. Sometimes telegraph lines followed established Indigenous trading and cart trails. When a telegraph office was built, it usually doubled as the operator's residence. The operator, in his or her spare time, might send weather observations back to Ottawa or post weather forecasts received from farther afield. For those who lived in a little rail-stop village like Dysart or Hirsch, telegrams arrived not at their settlement but at a larger place nearby with a telegraph office, where the telegram was then printed and put in the mail. For Hirsch, nearby telegraph offices were at Bienfait and Frobisher, to the west and east respectively. An early telegraph station near Dysart was set up at Fort Qu'Appelle.

Many things are missing from my picture. Where did my grandfather sit to write his long and often emotional letters? Where did he find an appropriate desk, or was a kitchen table the best he had? When he wrote, was there a window before him offering a view of the snowbound or parched landscape? Where did he get his fountain pen and ink? Was the pen a Polish one brought over with him or something bought in Estevan, at Mandel's store, when he was in town to meet his lawyer? A cineaste would make all this up, but I'm not allowed that freedom. What I tell is what there is.

The few envelopes saved in his file by an archive-minded secretary are the closest that we have to the technology of his information age. Pre-stamped envelopes—at least from Dysart—seem to have been common. Dysart had its own rubber postal stamp, which someone hammered into an ink tray and then onto an envelope. This was the village postmaster, who made sure that the mail got into the bag and onto the train.

My grandfather's early letters open with a formal salutation: "*Cho-sheve freint fun idishen immigrantn hilfs ferein fur Kanade*" (Esteemed friend of the Jewish Immigration Aid Society of Canada). Throughout 1932, my grandfather wrote to the JIAS office in Winnipeg. His early queries suggested a sense of hopefulness that, if the application process was done correctly, the outcome would be as desired. When the file was sent to the Montreal office, functionaries there seemed to encourage this hope, asking for documentation that my grandfather had to write to Poland to obtain: the birth dates of his wife and children and, more troublingly, a marriage certificate—not, the JIAS people told him, from a rabbi but from the *regirung*, Polish "officials." But then there was the suggestion that it was not the best time for the file to go forward to the immigration department. The JIAS hinted at some broader plan, not yet fully formed, for a permit like the one required by my grandfather's family. From the beginning, my grandfather was aware of and direct about having misled the immigration department upon his arrival. "Is there anything else to consider," he wrote, "regarding my illegal entry as a single person?"[2]

By the summer of 1932, he was following JIAS advice that he contact an MP to take up his case. This was the first overt sign of the curious character of Jewish access to immigration in Canada in this period: the backroom phenomenon of permit begging undertaken in private by MPs with the immigration department. My grandfather could not have seen this at the time as any kind of subterfuge, and not even as an open secret, since it was the way that Jews, few in number yet on an ongoing basis, entered the country. He wrote in return that he had "determined that the Liberal MP of his district," *Modervil* in Yiddish, would be approached. "Is there any difference," he asked his JIAS correspondent, considering that the Conservatives were in power in Ottawa, "whether the MP is Liberal or Conservative?" W.R. Motherwell was a federal opposition Liberal member in the early 1930s. His impressive fieldstone house near Abernethy, close to the Qu'Appelle Valley, was not far from my grandfather's outpost at Dysart. Motherwell was a pioneer of "scientific agriculture," which he promoted in bulletins in multiple languages focused on topics such as "summer fallowing, crop rotation, tree planting, farm diversification, co-operative associations, and dairying."[3]

In July 1932, my grandfather informed M.A. Gray, the JIAS general secretary in Winnipeg, that Motherwell had agreed to write to Minister of Immigration Gordon about his case and had assured him, in my grandfather's words, that he would "persuade the minister to forgive" him for his "sin of claiming" that he was single. Gray, a long-standing alderman in Winnipeg's Jewish North End, became an important correspondent and supporter. Like the executive director of the JIAS in Montreal, A.J. Paull, Gray made periodic visits to Ottawa in efforts to put particular files forward as "Special Permit" requests.

Responses to my grandfather's letters from the JIAS were typewritten in Yiddish. They were often lengthy themselves. Perhaps his case struck a specific chord with other community functionaries, even those far more influential, because in a sense—as a reverend, teacher, and kosher slaughterer—my grandfather was their co-worker, contributing to the maintenance of Jewish life in far-flung places. Soon enough the file included letters, typewritten in both Yiddish and English, between immigration representatives in Winnipeg and Montreal. In Montreal, Paull added an Esq. to his name in correspondence to give some flair. He had led a bifurcated life himself, having been sent to *cheder* in his native Russia but then acquiring a degree in social work once he came to North America.

In late 1932, my grandfather submitted his application materials to Gray's Winnipeg office, which officially activated his JIAS file. The form, headed "Application of Admission to Canada," shows up in the file as a single typewritten page in English, which must be a translated version of the information that my grandfather would have sent, handwritten in Yiddish. Even the "signature" on the form, "REV. J. EISENSTEIN," is typed. The application acknowledges that he was thirty-one years old and served "communities in Dysart, Cupar and Markwich at $100.00 per mon." It lists the "following Described Immigrants" whom the JIAS would promote for Special Permits to enter Canada. The proposed new Canadians were my grandmother, age twenty-eight, and the children, ages two and one. Their address is given as both the village of Radzanów and the city of Mława, and this correctly reflected my grandmother's habit of a life divided between village and city. My grandfather's occupation is listed as "Rabbi." His citizenship is given as Polish, contrary to that given by the clerks who minded his voyage across the ocean to Quebec City. JIAS bookkeepers had no reason to transform my grandfather and his family into mythical "Hebrews" of no fixed national locale, one of the *flichtlingen*, to borrow a term from his notes to the Winnipeg-based newspaper *Dos Yiddishe Vort*.

From the JIAS point of view, the application form represented information gathering covered in bureaucratic nicety, though these formalities had little effect on government bureaucracy or decision making. The application form represented front-end bookkeeping that provided cover for the background struggle over permits. Gray submitted the full application to the division commissioner, Department of Immigration, in Winnipeg. This step seems to be suspect, or at least to have been done in part as a formality to create a document trail, in order to open a file with materials that would be useful at some later date, at a much higher level of officialdom. In the Montreal JIAS file, there is no record of this stage beyond the prepared application form itself, supplied in triplicate. It is the Winnipeg file that includes a list of the supporting documents that Gray submitted: a statement by the Dysart community of willingness to maintain my grandfather's monthly salary of $100, the "Hon. Mr. Motherwell's letter" to Minister Gordon, and the minister's return letter to Motherwell. No copies of these documents found their way into the archives, but the package seems to be hopeful, at least, at the start of a long labour.

At the same time as the application was submitted at the end of 1932, the JIAS advised my grandfather to continue to pursue contacts with his MP. In response, he said that he was aware of other Jewish families like his who had been reunited with the help of Jewish members of Parliament and pursued contacts with both Liberal and Conservative elected members at the provincial and federal levels. He was writing for his life, not for political or ideological purity. The MPs whom he had heard about were likely A.A. Heaps of Winnipeg and S.W. Jacobs of Montreal. Both were long-time members: Heaps held his seat from 1925 to 1940; Jacobs held the Cartier riding in Montreal's Plateau district from 1917 to his death in 1938. Jacobs stood out in his willingness to provide unvarnished, outspoken complaints about the country's immigration policies, even when they were being overseen by his own Liberal Party. In a long discourse before other members, on a June night in 1922, he proposed to "criticize" his "own party in connection with its immigration policy," in particular new orders-in-council that heightened immigration restrictions. He cited those restrictions, just a month old at the time, which limited access to Canada to "bona fide" agriculturalists "entering Canada to farm," "bona fide" farm labourers with "assurance of employment," and "female domestic servants" with "reasonable assurance of employment." Added to these categories were the "wife and family of any person admitted to and resident in Canada" as well as any British subject or American citizen. Jacobs asked about the reasons for barring "every person who is not an English speaking person." He added to this a query about what he called the "submerged class" of UK newcomers prone to choosing Canada.[4] This was rare and provocative pushback to the long-standing offer of carte blanche entry to British newcomers. Jacobs noted the recent tightening of American quotas regarding particular nationalities and asserted that he had "heard it stated by a high official in the Immigration Department that it is only a question of time when they will put into force this American scheme of a certain percentage for a certain nationality, or a certain race."[5] He recognized the impact in Canada of British-first attitudes among varied proponents such as the Imperial Order of the Daughters of the Empire and the bishop of London, Ontario. And he raised the provocative statements of Agnes Macphail—first among female MPs—on what he called her "uncompromising" attitude toward immigration to Canada of what "she calls the inferior races from middle Europe."

Without saying the word *Jew*, Jacobs addressed the state of affairs in his home community in Montreal:

> We have in the city of Montreal to-day sixty or seventy thousand people who came to this country a few years ago, who were practically thrown on their own resources. They did not walk around the streets looking for work. Work was found for them by those of their people who came earlier. They engaged in the textile trade and if to-day the clothing industry is the third largest industry in the country, it is largely due to these foreigners who made that industry what it is, not only in Montreal but in Toronto and the other large cities.[6]

Jacobs finished his speech after midnight with a surprisingly strident attack on his own government's willingness—like that of the

Conservatives—to remake immigration regulations using orders-in-council out of view of Parliament and beyond public knowledge. And Jacobs insisted that the order-in-council that allowed for new restrictions should be reversed. My grandfather was correct in his appreciation of a decade's worth of effort by Jacobs on these fronts.

By the winter of 1932, my grandfather had corresponded with the Conservative MP for Regina, F.W. Turnbull. This shift reflected an effort to contact the right power base, wherever it might be found, and Turnbull, a member of the sitting federal government, was receptive. An Ontario-born lawyer, he was elected along with Bennett's other new representatives in 1930. There is evidence to suggest that he was a Klansman in an era when that organization experienced a short-lived resurgence, in part through its efforts to block French-language education and Catholic influence in Saskatchewan. And Turnbull, rumour had it, had the ear of Minister Gordon at the Department of Immigration and Colonization.

In a letter in late November 1932 to the Winnipeg JIAS office, my grandfather reported the strange outcome of Turnbull's encounter with Gordon in Ottawa. Turnbull, he told Gray, "has worked for me with Minister Gordon, regarding obtaining a permit. The answer I received was that I must immediately travel to Poland" and "in this way receive a permit. . . . My reply was that travelling to Poland was something I cannot do, and I have discontinued talking to Turnbull." The minister's advice was analogous to a maniac telling a child to jump in front of a bus in order to ensure himself a seat on public transit. My grandfather's imploring tone with the JIAS signalled his befuddlement: "Minister Gordon allows me to bring my family but only on the condition that I return to Poland to fetch them. I pose to you this question. Will I be able to receive the permits without travelling to Poland? What is the logic that makes travelling to Poland a koshering?"[7] Whatever the bizarre background of Gordon's suggestion—was it sheer flippancy?— my grandfather did not entertain it. Turnbull left the stage (though he would reappear a few years later, offering "representations" in my grandfather's favour).

In early 1933, some months after my grandfather submitted the "Application for Admission to Canada," Gray informed him that it had been rejected and, in my grandfather's words, that he would "not receive a permit to bring over" his "longed for family." In response, my

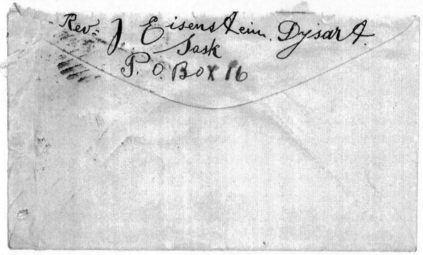

grandfather suggested that Gray himself write to Gordon, and then he turned his sights on Paull in Montreal.

An envelope survives for one of the letters posted to the JIAS in Montreal. In the archives, such envelopes are often without stamps, which have been cut away by some collector among the staff, but this one retains its postage. On the envelope, my grandfather inscribed the JIAS address on St. Laurence Boulevard beside the Dysart postmark. On the back flap, he designated himself as "Rev. J. Eisenstein."

What a lachrymose document of early immigrant life this is. The JIAS application file calls him "rabbi," and he was acting as one in his new prairie home, but my grandfather acknowledged in his correspondence that he was no such thing. Rather, he was a "reverend," a person who could offer spiritual leadership and ritual proficiency but had no rabbinical certification. The ability to begin his letter with some English-language information, alongside the inability to argue his case in English, is to be expected, and Jewish aid agencies of this period operated, fully bilingually (trilingually in Quebec) in Yiddish and English, for this reason.

❊ ❊ ❊

In early 1933, Paull reported to Gray of having visited the minister in Ottawa to discuss my grandfather's case. Gordon would soon be hearing about the "rabbi" from Dysart from a number of callers. Paull's access reflected an Old World Ottawa manner of doing business as well as the established backroom approach to Special Permit agreements. Paull wrote to Gray on February 3, 1933:

> I have returned to-day from Ottawa where I discussed the cases of Rev. J. Eisenstein ... and Meyer Low....
>
> The Minister refuses to revise his previous decision in the matter of men who came in as single men, and there is hardly anything that we can do at the present time to assist these people. I do know of some cases that were granted by the Minister when the applicant, who arrived as single, was five years in the country and produced Canadian citizen papers.[8]

In his report to Gray of his Ottawa visit, Paull veiled the vehemence of the response to his presentation on the two men's behalf from the immigration department. We find it quoted in a letter that Gray sent to Paull in early February. Gray quoted the immigration department decision, directed to him by C.E.S. Smith, the division commissioner for the Winnipeg Division of the Department of Immigration. Smith signed off as "Your obedient servant" even as he informed his correspondent that, if he could help it, what he had requested would never happen:

Referring to your letter of the 12th instant, regarding an application of Rabbi I.J. Eisenstein, of Dysart, for the admission to Canada of his wife and two children, I beg to advise that inasmuch as the applicant effected entry to Canada by flagrant misrepresentation, the Department is not prepared to take any action with a view of facilitating the movement to this country of his alleged wife and children and you may advise him accordingly.[9]

There is nothing here of Paull's conciliatory "at the present time" or a suggestion regarding men who have been naturalized as citizens making successful requests regarding their families. This is the official middle finger, the full shoulder block, whatever you want to call it. Admittedly, it was from the lower echelons of government power: the Winnipeg Division of the Department of Immigration. Still, it was a no, along with the backhanded implication of improper dealing. The insinuation regarding my grandfather's "alleged" family was motivated by his inability to produce a Polish marriage certificate, documentation that my grandfather chose not to apply for when he and his wife were married in Mława. But the response rings, too, of the kind of bullying that officials indulge in because they can, going beyond what is necessary in order to advance a veiled threat.

In an effort to combat these rhetorical assaults, JIAS representatives asked that my grandfather get copies of his children's birth certificates, as well as proof of his wife's birth date, for which he had to write to Poland. It does not seem that he was pressed for a wedding certificate, though the issue did come up in another context. From Dysart to the JIAS in Winnipeg in early 1933, he wrote that the "Montreal immigration office has suggested that my wife obtain legal marriage documents and send them to me."[10] The subject of a marriage certificate hardly comes up again, and there is nothing in the two JIAS or government immigration files to suggest that this was pursued.

It's interesting to compare my grandfather's doings with those of other men who had come to Canada as "single," only to proceed, at some later date, to bring their families from Poland. At around the same time, files in the JIAS archives in Montreal follow one of these men, with a wife and child left behind, who wrote to his hometown in Poland to receive an original certificate. It was supplied in Polish not by the *regirung* but via the town rabbi's communal office. It bore a single złoty duty stamp, much like a postage stamp. The translation of the Polish certificate of marriage referred to the "register records of marriage of Israelites in the Town," part of the civil record, so a record with *regirung* status. In an affidavit attached to the file, the applicant put forward that it was his sister who had applied for his entry to Canada at a time when she did not know that he was married.[11]

Recognizing the difficulty created by his actions, my grandfather queried the JIAS: "Has anyone, in similar circumstances, submitted a request? . . . Is there anything else to consider regarding my illegal entry as a single person?"[12] Here he revealed characteristics that he would maintain throughout his years of effort—an acknowledgement of the barriers before him and an unstinting willingness to consider them in order to decide what had to be done to succeed. There are repeated signs that the "single" men—misrepresenters, liars, however you dub them—trying to bring their families after them were a discrete category in the JIAS caseload.

By early 1933, my grandfather's letters reflected the range, and the undercurrent of desperation, of his efforts. He wrote to F.W. Turnbull in Regina, who agreed to approach Minister Gordon. His correspondence with Gray in Winnipeg, at this point, seemed to indicate a concrete outcome. But these efforts retained a strong element of the Kafkaesque. Usually, it was the JIAS people who reported, but sometimes letter writing and independent efforts by my grandfather generated developments that he reported to Paull or Gray. As his permit pursuit took on an increasingly complex, even incomprehensible, character, my grandfather wrote in early 1933 to the JIAS in Montreal with a piteous plea for help: "I beseech you and your esteemed friend, Mr. Paull, that you perform the great mitzvah of approaching Minister Gordon via letter and person that he should facilitate the bringing of my longed for family to me. . . . Cheer me with a favourable response as soon as possible."[13]

What becomes clear, as we follow this story, relying on what the archives offer, and recognizing how mainstream Canadian historiography misses stories like that of my grandfather, is that from his outpost near Fort Qu'Appelle, with hints here and access to knowledgeable professionals there, *he knew what he was doing*. He was listening to the experts, but even more importantly he was asking questions, some repeatedly, and following leads where he found them, which sometimes led him to guide the guiders and move in directions on his own. Part of the reason for this is that my grandfather would not take no for an answer. But add to this the fact that the system itself—the immigration regulations and the gatekeepers put in place to control people like him—was a tangle of sideroads, backrooms, contradictory viewpoints, leavened to an extent by the ability of those with some access to the gatekeepers to tweak it, to bend it, to make use of its soft spots, so that it might serve a particular purpose.

This is a Kafkaesque aspect of these Canadian decades rarely acknowledged: a system of authority, when called upon by an outsider to explain itself, cannot do so. Even more importantly, a system that seems to be an expression of total authority—cynical and unrelenting—is no such thing. It is always in danger of being undermined, some links weakened to the extent that the whole thing rattles apart. This is another point at which the "none is too many" rubric obscures the story that I want to tell. Even if he had heard of such a rule regarding Jews entering Canada from his homeland, my grandfather clearly did not heed it.

AT HIRSCH ON THE
SOUTHEASTERN BORDERLANDS

My grandfather's move from Dysart to Hirsch in late 1933 could be seen as a step up. The colony, one of the Jewish Colonization Association's oldest, was close to the U.S. border, to Estevan and the substantial coal mines of Bienfait, as well as to the Sonnenfeld Jewish farming colony at Hoffer. In Dysart, my grandfather had served scattered homesteaders and villagers, whereas Hirsch itself was a long-standing colony with thirty Jewish farming families, a constituency of 114 people.[1] The colony's position was less isolated than Dysart's and offered a certain degree of economic and social liveliness. At nearby North Portal, Saskatchewan, Americans hopped off the train from St. Paul to enter at the relatively freewheeling immigration gate to see how agricultural life looked on the Canadian "'El Dorado' of wheat and corn."[2]

❁ ❁ ❁

Jewish settlement in the North-West Territories began in the area surrounding Hirsch in the last decades of the nineteenth century. The Hirsch colony was facilitated by the JCA, the organization directly responsible for managing prairie settlements. Funded by the

Paris-based philanthropist Maurice de Hirsch, in a sometime part-nership with Montreal's Young Men's Hebrew Benevolent Society, the JCA lobbied government agencies, when they were willing to listen, and interacted with other Jewish immigration organizations to respond to the dramatic refugee crisis created by Czarist policies. Among its early accomplishments was the settlement at Hirsch, in 1892, of forty-nine Russian Jewish families who arrived via Hamburg.[3] The decision to settle them in the far south of the North-West Territories, in what was known as Palliser's Triangle, would prove to be imperfect. But the nearby CPR station provided crucial contact with surrounding communities and markets. Early years brought poor crops. But 1899 was a good year, with the settlement's agricultural territory covering roughly 12,500 acres.[4] That year, too, marked the arrival of twelve fam-ilies, including that of Marcus Berner, who would become a mainstay at Hirsch as the archetypal farmer-rabbi. JCA documents from these years are intact and detailed. The first group of Jewish pioneers to head west, the sizes of their families, those who had left family members behind in Russia, and the quarter sections to which they had been assigned are available to the interested researcher. Of these men and women who headed out in 1892—Zelickson, Emmes, Vineberg, and their cohort—sons and daughters were still farming when my grand-father arrived at Hirsch in November 1933. By way of the description of quarter section, township, and range, a prisoner of memory—and only such a one would go this far—could go stand by the roadside where one of the nine sons and daughters of farmer L. Herzcovitch said a *gut morgn* to my grandfather on any given day. On this list of early farm-ers, there is a hint of his immigration predicament: like him, five of the early homesteaders—Vineberg, Emmes, Hartenstein, Joshua, and Elkin—had left all or some of their family members in Russia.[5] What were the outcomes of those family stories? Maybe there was time, in the early years of the coming century, to work things out. But there were, of course, Jewish men who arrived at their new homes and went forward without much thought or effort with regard to the past. That was, for some, what the New World was for.

Much of the wind behind the backs of these early settlers was a Rus-sian-made refugee crisis, propelled by government-backed pogroms and the curtailment of rights. The beginnings of places like Hirsch and Lipton, up near Dysart, followed from events not unlike the ref-ugee crisis of 1930s Germany, the calamities brought on by the Syrian civil war, and the current Ukrainian disaster caused by the Russian invasion. In each case, social and political threats sent huge numbers in search of sanctuary. In the European 1880s, many refugees from Russian pogroms found their way to London, where the lord mayor set up a refugee fund in response to the influx. These events coincided with the Canadian government's goal of attracting settlers to its western territories, conveyed by Canada's high commissioner in London, Sir Alexander T. Galt. At the same time, in Montreal, an early Jewish communal agency, the Young Men's Hebrew and Benevolent Society, was investigating the idea of establishing a colonization society as part of its work with newly arrived immigrants from Eastern Europe. The leaders of the Benevolent Society were community leaders interested in social welfare, but they also found themselves dealing with an overwhelming influx of newcomers. One of their responses was to move some of them west to lessen social relief demands in the city.

A parallel development in the phenomenon of Jewish settlement in the Canadian West was the philanthropy of Baron Maurice de Hirsch, who built his fortune in banking and then undertook railway projects, including the Chemins de fer Orientaux linking Vienna and Istanbul. Hirsch supported the activities of the Young Men's Benevolent Society in Montreal. But a major target of his philanthropy in Canada was settling Jews on the land. In response to the Russian pogroms of the early 1880s, Hirsch founded the Jewish Colonization Association with its headquarters in Paris. Its first settlement projects were in Argentina, but early work was also directed at the Canadian Prairies.

The Hirsch colony, named for the baron, was laid out near Bienfait and the Souris River Valley, the territory that Hime photographed as the Canadian government expedition headed west. The JCA relied on local land agents to choose farmland. In a pattern that would repeat itself elsewhere, the Hirsch colony developed around two distinct areas, one of which sprang up close to the CPR depot. The village of Hirsch, near the station, had its own school, and another school and a synagogue were established in the northern part of the colony.[6] The settlement consecrated a single cemetery.

The train station, with its post office and nearby stores, was an active rural centre; the U.S. border was a few kilometres south; about ten kilometres away was the town of Bienfait with its coalfields. Into this context came men and women not unlike my grandfather's parents, Jews of late-nineteenth-century Eastern Europe. Some shared national backgrounds. They shared literacy with their fellow colonists, in Yiddish, Hebrew, and Slavic languages. They also shared religious goals, whether they represented strict observance or, more simply, a reliance on customs associated with synagogue attendance and holiday rituals. Their plans included Jewish education for their children and kosher slaughter. Institutional structures to support these goals were maintained by the settlers themselves, with the support of the JCA. My grandfather, upon entering this New World communal and religious infrastructure, remade himself. Although his father was a Talmud rabbi in Radzanów, and a religious upbringing prepared my grandfather religiously and intellectually, his own study was interrupted by his years in the Polish Army. His marriage itself was non-traditional—a love match, such that it was nearly prohibited by his would-be bride's family. In married life, in the late 1920s, my grandfather chose commercial pursuits as a grain merchant in the rural Polish economy. In the early twentieth century, and even today, established Canadians highlight the importance of assimilation for Canadian newcomers' success. In the first decades of the twentieth century, this was a central tenet. As non-English-speaking, non-Christian immigrants settled on the Prairies, the expectation was that they would accept and emulate Anglo-Canadian values. This expectation was given intellectual underpinnings by sociologists and government statisticians who followed the processes by which different groups let go of "attachments" to their home cultures in favour of New World ways.

Immigration to and settlement on the Prairies caused my grandfather to travel in the opposite direction. By emigrating to Canada, he was forced to refashion himself as a religious functionary and teacher. His labours in Dysart and Hirsch were focused on allowing the settler families to maintain their attachments to a traditional religious past. A modernizer in Poland, he became a preserver of tradition on the Saskatchewan prairie. Is it a rare paradox, or does his personal adaptation reveal how little we understand of the transformation of identity in the chaotic twentieth century?

❊ ❊ ❊

My grandfather's move to Hirsch in November 1933 presented another wintery arrival at a new prairie home. The JCA was his new boss, whereas at Dysart my grandfather had been paid by a collection from the complement of Jewish farmers in the area, a kind of community dole. In the fall of 1931, the Hirsch area was an important topic of discussion among Saskatchewan and Ottawa Conservative parliamentarians because of a dramatic miners' strike. One of the salient characteristics of the Souris River Valley, bordering the land where the Hirsch farmers toiled, was the lignite coal deposits not far below the ground. The centre of coal activity was at Bienfait (a name left over from French traders, which locals pronounced Bean-fate). It was one train station west of Hirsch on the way to Estevan, a larger town dubbed "The Power Centre" for its economic links with the coal mines. Although the late 1920s and early 1930s brought notable crop failures to the southeast corner of the province, the coal mining companies expanded, employing miners from Eastern Europe, notably the Ukraine. Among the many ethnic prairie enclaves of this period, Bienfait's population was almost one-quarter Ukrainian.[7]

Things heated up in the summer of 1931 as union organizers from Winnipeg came to town to organize the miners. RCMP investigators followed the activities and reported back to Regina and Ottawa. Among the informants, acting as a kind of back-channel representative for the coal mining bosses to Regina Conservatives, was Estevan lawyer W.W. "Wally" Lynd. His confidant in the provincial legislature was Thomas Molloy, the deputy minister of labour, who reported to Premier James Anderson. Provincial Conservatives kept Prime Minister Bennett up to date. Once a strike was declared, in September 1931, it was Lynd who stood for the mine owners in their discussions with representatives for the miners. Lynd, an inveterate insider, represented my grandfather in his immigration efforts once he arrived at Hirsch.[8]

The outcome of the strike was bad news for Bienfait and for union organizing in Canada. Facing a parade of miners in Estevan, RCMP and local police officers fired into the strikers and their supporters, killing three and wounding twenty. This was followed by the trial of miners in the spring of 1932, leading to the deportation of those characterized as communist agitators.[9] One of the ways that the government dealt with labour unrest was to provoke fears, which haunted the early Depression years, that immigrant agitators were undermining the country's economic future. Lawyer Lynd's role in these events was the subject at times of public scandal and strife. More important for my grandfather, though he might not have been fully aware of it, was Lynd's wide range of political connections. During the lead up to the strike at Bienfait, Lynd met with government officials in Regina as an informant of mine owners' goals.[10] His correspondence on other matters of interest to provincial and federal Conservatives was wide ranging. This included long letters to the prime minister regarding the party's prospects in local elections and an effort, in 1932 and 1933, to appeal directly to R.B. Bennett for an appointment to the Senate. In these letters, Lynd acknowledges, too, his collegial relationship with Arthur Meighen, the short-lived Conservative prime minister of the 1920s.[11]

My grandfather came to coal country a couple of years after the strike and its outcome. But the distance from Hirsch to Bienfait was about ten kilometres, a negligible trip on the prairies. Bienfait in 1931 had Jewish storekeepers (as did the majority of small Saskatchewan towns). They were Sol Adler, Jake Lishinsky, and Sam Lischinsky, all of who moved from Hirsch to Bienfait in the 1920s.[12] The nearby small city of Estevan had a community of eighty-eight Jews. When settlers from Hirsch and the other neighbouring Jewish colonies were passing through, they stayed at the Singer Boarding House, by the railway tracks, where one could count on a kosher meal. The Singer house was located near other "boarding" houses better known for their "ladies of easy virtue."[13] It could be that a stay at the Singers' led to some discussion about Lynd as a lawyer with influence among federal and provincial politicians. Or a visit to one of the Jewish-owned businesses in Bienfait. Whatever the source, its unlikely outcome was that the lawyer with connections all the way up to the premier and beyond took as a client the new *shoichet* and teacher of the Hirsch colony.

✿ ✿ ✿

For many years before my grandfather's arrival, Hirsch was overseen by the farmer-rabbi Marcus Berner, who came to Canada in 1899 from London, England. Like my grandfather, Berner was trained in kosher slaughter, led religious services, and taught schoolchildren. Fifteen years after his arrival at Hirsch, he had 360 acres of his own land under cultivation, growing wheat and oats; he kept twelve horses, three cows, and about a hundred poultry. On the farm with him were his wife Yetta and six children.[14] In 1920, the Russian Jewish journalist Vladimir

Grossman visited Canada to appraise the country's Jewish colonization projects. An editor of Russian-based magazines focused on emigration, he viewed himself as a freelancer in this undertaking—"I was
my own emissary," he wrote—and headed up to Edenbridge in central
Saskatchewan and to Hirsch in the south. In his account, *The Soil's
Calling,* Grossman depicts the difficulties of life in such settlements:
"For years the whole district—and not only the Hirsch settlement—
had been locust-ridden. Locusts were a curse." But Rabbi Berner of
Hirsch made a strong impression on him. "I was staying in the house
of a comfortable farmer," Grossman wrote, "a former Jewish cleric in
London and now the owner of a considerable estate."[15]

Between Berner and my grandfather was Reverend S. Polonsky. In
1933, the inaugural year for my grandfather at Hirsch, he was met by
a community of thirty farmers who, with their families, made up a
village of 114 souls. The complement of adults and children helps us
to imagine his duties in his two and a half years in the colony. Among
the Hirsch families were thirty-three sons and thirty daughters—a full
house of students in need of Jewish learning. Most of Hirsch's Jews
would also expect a well-run Sabbath and High Holiday service.

At Hirsch, there was a wooden synagogue, and the story of its
building is a good one. I can find no photograph of the building when
it was in use as a sanctuary. One amateur historian offers the following
record on his website dedicated to Saskatchewan heritage: "The Hirsch
Colony Synagogue was built around 1929 by the Jewish Colonization
Organization of Montreal. It was a white building with blue trim.
There were three windows on the east side of the main level. There was
a coal furnace in the basement and a brick chimney on the exterior of
the east wall. . . . There was a Mogen David on the west wall near the
top gable." He adds that the cornerstone was made of a tombstone, but
this part of his report would need some support for us to feel confident
about such a detail.[16] "Around 1929" is an almost accurate accounting,
since it was in 1928 that Rabbi Berner's efforts began in earnest to
convince the JCA in Montreal that his community needed a proper
synagogue building. His correspondence is preserved in the Canadian
Jewish Congress Archives as part of the larger JCA documentation of
the prairie colonies. In 1929, Berner wrote to the chairman of the JCA
in Montreal, who happened to be Lyon Cohen. We have met him as

he experienced a browbeating on the topic of Jewish immigrants from F.C. Blair under the eye of Minister Forke.

Berner, like my grandfather, would not take no for an answer. He addressed his correspondent as Lyon Cohen Esq. He used a fountain pen with flair. But London-raised Berner was a master of the English language. His lines on the page are ruler straight, while his handwriting leans hard and entirely legibly to the right. In the summer of 1928, Berner wrote to Cohen: "Your very welcome letter of the 21st ulto., in reply to my humble appeal for assistance in building a place of worship for the Jewish farmers of Hirsch, duly received, and contents fully noted." He was responding politely to the city people's rejection of his request to fund a synagogue. His response relied on a mixture of courtesy and the argument of a well-trained barrister: "Now my dear Mr. Cohen, your kind communication has rekindled in me the hope, which I and every Jewish citizen of this district have been entertaining for the last 36 years, since founding of the Colony, that we may yet see achieved this fond desire of ours." In Berner's English is a hint of Dickens, of awareness by a colourful character that he must play a role as much as state his own argument. Berner noted the absence in Hirsch of men like Cohen himself—businessmen with "all the necessary means" to "subscribe liberally" to the building of a place of worship. "There are," Berner told Cohen, "two Jewish storekeepers in Hirsch, and they consider themselves fortunate indeed to be able to pull through the year without a deficit." He then suggested that, with "the inauguration of the Wheat Pool, the position of the western farmers is tending to become more and more stable." The colony, he added, raised $500 toward the cause of the synagogue. Berner himself contributed fifty dollars to the building fund, the amount of choice among contributing farmers, though some came forward with ten or fifteen dollars. By the end of 1928, they had collected $740. Drawing Cohen into the intimate circle of those devoted to Jewish colonization on the Prairies, Berner wrote,

> Now, my dear Mr. Cohen, as the head of the Jewish colonies in Canada, for the last forty years, it devolves upon you, as well as upon myself and my neighbours, to put forth your best efforts in behalf of such a sacred cause.
> We must have a Synagogue at Hirsch!

Berner signed off this way:

> Believe me to be
> My Dear Mr. Cohen
> Most respectfully and faithfully Yours
> Marcus Berner[17]

Berner's plea bore fruit. By late 1929, Hirsch had a synagogue built of wood; the roof was shingled; the chimney was made of bricks; the foundation was made of cement (no small detail in a part of the country at a time when wooden buildings were towed from one place to another like boats on the land). The Northern Assurance Company of Winnipeg signed off on an insurance policy on it valued at $2,000. The company's application form contains a line that queries "Racial Extraction of Applicant," which in the case of the synagogue no one filled in.[18]

The synagogue was not four years old when my grandfather arrived to lead its congregants in regular worship. At the High Holidays, he would have blown the ram's horn, at least metaphorically, to open the gates of heaven, getting down on his knees and even farther, almost prostrate in a kind of Jewish sun salutation, in supplication to a divine overseer in favour of his congregants' goodwill and intentions in the coming year. And there you have it, an image of a true inner sanctum, European-style, on the southern Canadian Prairies. Berner was long gone, having moved up in life to take the position of rabbi for the venerable congregation in Victoria, British Columbia, where rabbinical work did not include minding livestock or worrying about locusts. My grandfather would not put in the years that Berner did. But there he stood, in the autumnal weather of 1934 and then 1935 (he arrived too late in 1933 to officiate at the High Holiday services), in a synagogue built in part by farmers' subscription, supported by Berner's expert lawyerly debate with the big men back in Montreal, capital of Jewish Canadian philanthropy.

This is the ecstatic version of Hirsch. It is the mundane most readily found in preserved JCA files on the colony. In 1933, the year of my grandfather's arrival, the summary prepared by JCA agents tells us that, before they'd turned into Canadian farmers, the denizens of Hirsch had been European housewives, merchants, barbers, millers, carpenters, and blacksmiths (my grandfather, we know, had been a grain merchant and an army officer's assistant). Nine among the farmers in that year (four were independent women) had been farmers in Europe. Their countries of origin included Russia, Poland, Galicia, and Lithuania, with two being born in Canada. Among their children over nineteen years of age were mechanics, merchants, and dressmakers, while four-teen remained on the farms.[19]

What were the Jews of the Hirsch colony busy with in 1933 besides the challenges brought by farm living? Its sons and daughters were schooled in three institutions a few kilometres apart from each other. At the Hirsch Central School, there was an "English Master" and a "Hebrew Master." The other two schools followed this arrangement. Hirsch had a Ladies Aid Society, a Zionist Society, and a Jewish Library. The library was no thrown-together affair, no dusty box of westerns, aged encyclopedias, and farmers' almanacs. In 1931, a de-accessioned library was sent from Montreal along with a carefully typed list of some eighty-eight titles, which included Dostoevsky's *The Idiot*, Eliot's *Adam Bede*, Darwin's *On the Origin of Species*, numerous titles by "B. Disraeli, Earl of Beaconsfield," Dante's *Inferno*, Dumas's *Le Comte de Monte-Cristo*, and Simon Dubnow's *History of the Jews in Russia and Poland*.

My grandfather's presence in Hirsch (not to mention Dysart) leaves remarkably little documentary evidence. At times, I feel as if I'm travelling back into the past to arrive at blank spaces, records of events where his presence should be noted but the documents do not include Yehuda Yoseph Eisenstein. Because the colony at Hirsch is well presented in its archival afterlife, we can imagine him there. It is in his own letters where his state of mind comes to the fore, his resolve to find a solution for his family. Still, major turns in the narrative are in store.

HOW TO BECOME A CHARACTER
IN A CANADIAN NOVEL

n the summer of 1934, my grandfather received, in response to a
letter to the Conservative premier of Saskatchewan, a short note.
The original is not in his file, but there is a typed copy, possibly
made by the JIAS.

The premier promised to take up the cause with the minister.
Like so many side rails in my grandfather's story, Anderson's role is
another loose end. His Conservative government, from the fall of 1929
to the summer of 1934, was an anomaly in the province, which had
been governed by Liberals since its inception in 1905. The Conservative

---

PREMIER'S OFFICE,
SASKATCHEWAN.

Regina, June 29th, 1934.

Reverend J. Eisenstein,
Hirsch, Sask.

Dear Sir:
    I beg to acknowledge receipt of your letter of June 26th and
in reply may say that I am taking this up with the Honorable W. A. Gordon.

                    Yours faithfully,

                            J. M. ANDERSON.

success in 1929 was thought to be accounted for largely by a nativist, anti-immigrant feeling stirred by the Ku Klux Klan. Was my grandfather aware that, a few years before his arrival in Saskatchewan, disgraced Klansmen from Indiana had decamped to Moose Jaw to start over, selling memberships to farmers and housewives? If he knew, he wouldn't necessarily have seen these events as a threat. Anti-Catholicism was the Klan's main line of rhetoric in 1920s Saskatchewan, along with an "anti-vice" campaign that targeted Chinese businesses, asserting that white women working in Chinese establishments were in moral danger.[1] In the late 1920s, Moose Jaw police busied themselves raiding chop suey houses on the lookout for gambling and opium. This must have seemed like a set of events on another planet to my grandfather. But I might overestimate his naïveté. The singularity of Jews and Chinese in little prairie places was part of a shared pattern of settlement. Louis Rosenberg, a JCA colony manager before he became a demographer, understood the shared experience of being a single representative of an ethnic group in a tiny prairie town. In an interview, he recalled that "there was a time . . . on the Canadian Pacific Railway Line going through Manitoba, Saskatchewan, Alberta. Every eight miles there's a whistle stop. The train stops. . . . So in every one of these places there's always one Chinese restaurant, one Chinaman, and one Jew, a storekeeper."[2]

The lead-up to the provincial election in 1929 might well have circulated in local lore upon my grandfather's arrival at Dysart in late 1931. Conservative political meetings included impressive Klan representation. The Liberal premier, James G. Gardiner, barnstormed the countryside accusing the Conservatives of being in league with the Klan and raising the spectre of American-style violence. A "Make Canada Great Again" credo flew from banners and from speakers on bandstands, with the implication that Continental European immigrants and French Catholic separate schools had diluted the country's Anglo-British identity. Crosses were burned all over the province, with special verve when the Klan's local "klaverns" honoured Empire Day.[3] In a weird social uprising, "klaverns sprang up in the towns and villages along the railway lines used by American immigrants, such as the CPR line running across southern Saskatchewan from Weyburn to Shaunavon."[4]

No evidence exists that Anderson—the first Conservative premier in a province full of Eastern and Central European new Canadians—was a Klan member. F.W. Turnbull—my grandfather's "Minister from Regina"—is known to have been a member.[5] But considering that he shows up early and late as a supporter of Reverend Eisenstein of Hirsch, it's clear that Klan membership in Saskatchewan was not necessarily connected with hatred of Jews. It might have represented a vote-getting strategy that proved, at least in the late 1920s, to be effective.

The Liberal premier, James Gardiner, the man whom J.T.M. Anderson ousted as premier in the fall of 1929, would have been a natural fellow traveller in my grandfather's efforts, an obvious source in the government of sympathy and support. That's a surprising story all its own. Gardiner was a long-time Liberal MLA for North Qu'Appelle—including Lipton and Dysart—before his rise to premiership in 1926. The farm that he bought during the First World War lay not far from Dysart and Fort Qu'Appelle, near Lemberg. That spot on the map—a whistle stop from Motherwell's Abernethy and a few from Dysart—was named for the major Polish city also known as Lvov. Gardiner was back in power in the summer of 1934, when my grandfather's efforts were mired in resistance by the federal immigration people. Like so many prairie men of his era, Gardiner came west from Ontario and rose to prominence in his new home province. He used his teacher training to gain his first position at the village of Hirsch. There he taught the children of the Jewish colonists farming near the village. And through this experience Gardiner became a kind of vanguard figure in the Canadian mainstream whose central Canadian background and culture, via his western experiences and educational training, came into meaningful contact with the Jewish newcomers on the Prairies.

In his letters, my grandfather often asked for advice from Jewish immigration representatives in an effort to gauge the usefulness of writing to opposition members and sitting members of both provincial and federal parliaments. Conservatives, in power in both governments for much of the first half of the 1930s, gained the bulk of his attention. But he sensed that a political shift might be in his favour in the summer of 1934. Writing to Louis Rosenberg, signing off as "Shoichet and Teacher Hirsch," he wondered whether Rosenberg was acquainted with the new Liberal premier.

Copy #672-34

Re:-Hirsch Central School-
Re:-J. Eisenstein, Hirsch-

Hirsch, Sask.,
Aug. 28, 1934.

Dear Mr. Rosenberg:

        As you are aware, I have been much occupied with
the difficult problem of bringing over my family. When I was in
your office last year, you told me that if the Premier of the Province
would give permission to bring my family in, then Ottawa would give
the permit. I would therefore ask you to do me a favor. As we now
have a Liberal Government, praised be the Lord and you are well
acquainted with Premier Gardner, I would ask you to see him and ask
him to give permission for the admission of my family for I am secured
of employment. Mr. Veiner and Mr. Gibbs always pointed out to me that
if Mr. Gardner becomes premier again, I will surely get the permit
with his help. I am enclosing the letter from the Hon. Mr. Gordon,
Minister of Immigration and Colonization, and a letter from Mr. Anderson
so that you may be acquainted with what has been done to date. Nothing
has transpired since then. My lawyer is Mr. Lynd of Estevan. I wish
to point out that Mr. M. A. Gray has already obtained a permit for a man
from Calgary in similar circumstances to myself.

        Let me remember you who helped to build my holy
synagogue. Please return the letters to me together with a favorable
reply for which I will always thank you.

        Wishing you a Happy New Year, I remain,

        Yours truly,

           J. Eisenstein,
             Shochet and Teacher Hirsch.

It's easiest to read his letter first and then to consider what it reveals about his efforts in the late summer of 1934.

Notable is its presentation in English, neatly typewritten, and signed in a rare variation of my grandfather's favoured professional moniker—in this case, "Teacher" was added to his usual assertion of his certification as a ritual slaughterer. It might be that in addressing Rosenberg, an administrator for the prairie colonies, my grandfather decided to assert both responsibilities for which he received his JCA salary. Nowhere in his Yiddish letters does he do this. The fact that the archive holds only a copy of the letter cannot be explained. Somewhere along the way the original was submitted but not returned to his file. But the manner designating it—"Copy #672-34"—reflects its movement through the JIAS, or the Lynd office, or some other bureaucratic system. The letter widened the circle of support that Rosenberg might consider in his efforts—M.A. Gray in Winnipeg, Lynd in Estevan, as well as long-time farmers Viner and Gibbs—if he were to alert the new premier to trouble in the colony where he himself had taught as a young man.

❋ ❋ ❋

When Gardiner arrived to take up his responsibilities at Hirsch in 1905, who should be there to meet him but the farmer-rabbi Berner. These two became true compatriots. Possibly, it was his British background that made Berner immediately sympathetic to a man like Gardiner. But there seems to have been more than accidental cultural affinity at work. Gardiner attended services led by Berner for his congregants. And when Berner needed an intermediary to draw up a document with a non-Jewish local, he called on Gardiner for help. In this way, Gardiner served as the rabbi's secretary when Berner contracted a mason to build the community's ritual bath.[6]

In this scenario, the numbers say it all. At the Hirsch village school, Gardiner taught forty-four pupils. Two were categorized as "Canadians" and two as Norwegians. Forty—let's say it twice—forty were Jewish children of Russian or Romanian background. Imagine the lessons learned by the teacher in his first assignment.[7] Rabbi Berner, though he wouldn't have known it at the time, nearly found his way into Canadian literature because of his time spent with Gardiner. It was in 1910, a few years after Lucy Maud Montgomery's Jewish peddler sold Anne some gruesome green hair dye, that Gardiner completed a novel manuscript titled *The Politician, or, The Treason of Democracy*. Gardiner gave his manuscript to the Methodist Book and Publishing House, which had on its list important early Canadian writers Robert Service and Catharine Parr Traill. The Methodists thought that Gardiner's work's fault was a tendency to moralize (one would have to check the Methodist list circa 1910 to see how well it steered clear of "moralizing").[8]

I encountered *The Politician* with some degree of astonishment. It offers one of the best portraits of life at Hirsch or any other Jewish prairie colony. No Jew has managed to write of Hirsch with the same novelistic detail; no Jewish or non-Jewish writer has managed, as Gardiner does, to place the Jewish prairie culture in its broader Canadian context. And he does this, for the most part, without pandering to the anti-Jewish stereotypes common in the years of his youthful prairie experience. We can travel back in time with young Jimmy Gardiner, in his fictional guise as Ronie McKinnon, to see the Jews of Hirsch, circa 1910.

Ronie is from central Canada. His training as a teacher is complete, and he has "secured a school in the new province where salaries were much better."[9] He is part of a decades-long effort by provincial leaders and social services—even the Masons got in on it—to make the Saskatchewan public school system an institution dedicated to the Canadianization of newcomers.

McKinnon gets off his CPR coach at dusk and gazes at a weird, haphazard array of Hirsch landmarks: "A boxcar for a station, . . . a loading platform, a water tank, an old tumbling-down building which had once been a store—a cow now stood in the doorway chewing her cud" (if Hirsch had a flag, maybe this could be on it: a lone cow in a doorway chewing its cud). McKinnon knows who he's come to teach, but he lets his reader experience a bit of dissonant surprise as he reports that "most of those who stood on the platform were talking a foreign language." Yiddish. The unnameable. If only the Methodists had said yes to *The Politician*, this would have been the first appearance of the language, however secretly presented, in Canadian literature. The Methodists might have taken the mighty high road as proto-multiculturalists. At this early point in his narrative, Gardiner panders to some low early-twentieth-century prairie caricature. McKinnon is approached by a "typical Hebrew of the Jewish Russian type."[10] We recognize the familiar confusion over how to categorize a Jew in Canada (not as a Jew but as the biblical archaism, a Hebrew, as ancient and unknowable as a Moabite or Phoenician), though in Gardiner's improved version the national background is added for narrative depth. It is out of the "peculiar odor . . . caused by the mingling of the breath of garlic-eaters with the purer atmosphere of the prairie" that the local Jew presents himself to McKinnon. This local knows who has stepped off the coach at dusk. "'The new teacher, is it?'" he asks.[11] And they are off. This is a picture in prose of the birth of the companionship that grew between Marcus Berner, the rabbi-farmer of Hirsch, and the young man who would become the premier of Saskatchewan.

The local who greets Ronie is said to speak a broken English, but he sounds savvy enough as he informs him that he "will be able to board with one of your own people who lives in the section house." Berner wrote and spoke the King's English with confidence. But

Gardiner—we wonder what instinctive urge led him to write Berner differently—portrays the farmer-rabbi as a kind of Jewish Black Peter, "thick-set . . . with a black beard, black hair, almost as black skin and the well-known Jewish nose."[12]

The Yiddish Black Peter, it turns out, is the secretary-treasurer of the school district. In the morning, he doles out keys to the school— not to the building, for its bolt is broken, but to the cupboards inside where the library books are kept, as well as a cupboard that McKinnon need not open, which contains the Torah used for Saturday services when the schoolroom doubles as a sanctuary.[13]

Ronie's initiation at Hirsch provides us with a portrait of the basics of Jewish observance. I set it down here at some length because it is among the few detailed ethnographic portraits of Jewish particularity in early Canadian writing:

> It was indeed a little Jerusalem. . . . The candlesticks still had their place in every home. The Rabbi had to draw his broad knife across the throat of the bound ox, or the chicken, or the sheep, before it could be partaken of by his people. Pork was an unclean thing from which the Hebrew shrank with horror. The lungs were blown up and examined carefully by the Rabbi after an ox was slain. The hindquarters were sold to the unbelieving Gentiles, while the front quarters were eaten by themselves. The Feast of Passover, of Tabernacles, and all the festivals and fasts of the old Jew in Palestine were sacred to the Jewish settler in Western Canada. Sunday was the busiest day of the week, while Saturday was kept sacred as the holy Sabbath. Would that we could induce such an adoration of the democratic institutions of our land. Our Canadian politicians do not give the Jew an inviting picture of the virtues of our institutions.[14]

Gardiner learned a few things. And Berner schooled him well. Ritual slaughter in McKinnon's Hirsch is an everyday encounter. When a Conservative bagman comes around with a vote-buying bribe, the rabbi is "engaged in dispatching a bullock for Charlie Zealoski."[15] Spooky and strange, isn't it, to stumble upon such a scene as we read, more than a century later, the bullock in the yard; its owner nearby; the ritual slaughterer at his work; the party bagman with his bottle in hand, the best that he can offer in exchange for the rabbi's all-important vote, for it is known that if the rabbi votes one way, most of his flock will follow him.

It gets better. It's one thing to know that, of Gardiner's schoolchildren at Hirsch, forty were Jewish. Gardiner offers us a portrait of the kids, lost as they otherwise are to Canadian history. He will not teach, he tells the "secretary-treasurer," until the schoolroom is cleaned and two broken windows are repaired. This is done. The children are ready to be taught. Outside the school, he finds "about fifteen rather dirty but intelligent-looking Russian Jewish boys lined up beside the school." And the girls? "On seeing the teacher about a dozen girls, more cleanly dressed than the boys, came out of one of the shacks and drew nearer the school." What we get is a little hint of *West Side Story* in the prairie schoolyard, with boys on one side, girls on the other, making their own way onto the stage. It is here that Gardiner offers some of what the Methodists might have dubbed moralizing: "Many little incidents gave" Ronie "insight into the true nature of the Jewish children. They were obedient, respectful children, who gave promise of being good Canadian citizens."[16] These comments are a fine response to the discussion, we might call it the clamour regarding "Continentals" in the country, and we can't but notice that the kids are rough and ready to learn. They're Jews, not mythical Hebrews. So it's history, not morals, that Gardiner's McKinnon is transmitting.

We don't hear anything more of those "little incidents" regarding the "true nature" of these children. Maybe Gardiner committed them to a diary. But he does delve more deeply into the life of the "secretary-treasurer," his fictional stand-in for Berner. Like Berner, he is a relatively recent widower. In the rabbi's house, Ronie encounters "rich eastern curtains and rugs, the oriental vases and candle-sticks," all with "traces of having once been placed in order by the hand of a woman who had been a careful housekeeper."[17]

In this the ingenious, hard-working Berner is cast, in his early private life at Hirsch, as a kind of Jewish Mr. Havisham. His home is a monument to the absent wife. In this, Gardiner's portrait of Hirsch comes full circle, having left behind the garlic-eaters in the pure prairie air in favour of real Jews in their public and private strivings. It's a great gift, this thing that the Methodists found outside the ken of their publishing list. It's early Hirsch, rough and true. Things would change, though, in the coming decades, before my grandfather held the knife to the bullock's neck.

THE IMMIGRATION PATH,
DARK AND TWISTED

Alongside the JIAS, including Paull and Gray, and Paull's office manager, Sam Kaplan, the local provincial MLAs, and federal members of Parliament came the lawyers. Before leaving Dysart, my grandfather corresponded with Sol Saper, "Barrister, Solicitor, etc.," as his Yorkton letterhead had it, in the fall of 1933. This was his first effort with a lawyer who claimed to be able to gain influence in immigration circles. The few letters from Saper in my grandfather's file reveal the contacts that my grandfather sought in order to gain access to the immigration department's permits. He approached Saper after his application was refused for the first time, and Saper acknowledged this failure when he wrote to Gray in Winnipeg asking for his "own views" on "this particular case." The same day Saper wrote to my grandfather assuring him that "I shall do all I can to secure the necessary Permit of Entry for your family from Poland." The method was straightforward, according to Saper: "seek the aid" of the local MP, the chosen target in this case being George Washington McPhee, who happened to be a fellow lawyer.[1] The going price to initiate such work was $100, with a retainer of twenty-five dollars up front. The impression given by Saper's approach to the file is that a reasonably well-connected lawyer working in a small city at the centre of Saskatchewan wheat country knew that access to elected representatives could result in immigration permits. For whatever reason, Saper falls out of the picture, and another lawyer appears.

The law office of W.W. "Wally" Lynd, KC, was on Estevan's main street. He played an important role in both local and national events, which ensured his influence and range of political contacts. Lynd, born in Ireland, was brought to southern Saskatchewan as a child. His parents farmed as early as 1906 outside Moosomin, which, coincidentally, was the site of the first Jewish farming colony in the province. He served in the Canadian Expeditionary Force during the First World War and was said to offer legal services to veterans at no charge.[2] Might my grandfather have intimated in some way that he too was a "veteran," in his case, of the Polish Army? These few biographical details help us to guess at Lynd's willingness to take on my grandfather as a client, but the actual background remains one of the unknowns of this story.

Lynd had already been appointed to the King's Counsel when labour troubles erupted in the Estevan area. His position of influence was key from the start. When the threat of a strike arose in the summer of 1931, Lynd represented the operators in discussions with the workers' representatives. It was widely known that he visited Regina to meet with government officials and that his offer of a "Conciliation Board" was refused by the workers' union. It was assumed that this was part of efforts by the operators and provincial government to undermine workers' claims.[3] Lynd was the go-between among J.A. Merkley, the provincial minister of railways, labour, and industries; his deputy minister, T.M. Molloy; and the mine owners. The federal government had its own western representative for the Department of Labour who took the measure of events for the Conservatives in Ottawa. And Molloy was often in Estevan to meet with operators as well as with Lynd.[4] Although Wesley Ashton Gordon, the minister of both immigration and mines, was at a remove from these discussions, he was in a sense atop the pyramid of influence to which Lynd reported.

An underlying concern for both provincial and federal governments during the Bienfait events was the effectiveness of union organizers and the perceived involvement of communist ideologues in the Depression-era economy. Lynd was a reliable aid in these efforts, and his role became the subject of public discussion. The November 1932 issue of the Toronto-based *Canadian Labor Defender* published the affidavit of

Roscoe Tuckner of Saskatoon, who sat on the jury trying the agitators of the Estevan strike. In cinematic terms, Tuckner described how he was approached on the street by Lynd, who wondered if he "ever took a drink." The men found their way to a "private bedroom" in Estevan's International Hotel, where a bottle was produced, and Lynd informed him that "we will have to get the whole bunch of red sons of bitches." The lawyers defending the agitators, Lynd assured Tuckner, could not win the case since they "did not know the jurymen." The *Labor Defender* editors underwrote the affidavit with a note that described Lynd as "influential in local politics."[5] My grandfather had found his man.

❀ ❀ ❀

I continue this narrative with some trepidation. What follows is in certain ways the most complicated part of the puzzle, yet in others the most telling, as it is the chapter that links Yehuda Yoseph Eisenstein's personal efforts to a broader national narrative. Since it deals with federal departments, Parliament, the Conservative prime minister, and people with access to him, it also highlights the contemporary role of immigration. This part of the story provides a lesson, by way of contrast, in how a country deals with newcomers and would-be newcomers.

My own relationship to this story growing up was not focused, however, on this broad national context. The little that I understood of the activities of my grandfather in the 1930s set him up as an exemplar of a person with a creative bent. The story that I heard was of how he'd changed his future and that of his family with a well-placed stroke of his pen. His literary flair had been his tool for better living.

A few of the letters in the immigration file—held back in my telling like high cards—have a special character all their own. They emanate from the upper reaches of Canadian political, bureaucratic, and social power. The most unsettling documents in the file are those that come directly from Department of Immigration commissioners to JIAS representatives, most often to its executive director. These bureaucratic officials rarely wrote directly to my grandfather, though in a few cases a Winnipeg representative of the Department of Immigration did respond to him, including C.E.S. Smith, the division commissioner of immigration in Winnipeg. Letters from the commissioner of immigration in Ottawa went to A.J. Paull in Montreal, never to Gray in Winnipeg. They are topped by the country's coat of arms and at times are signed illegibly. This renders the writer anonymous, possibly intentionally so. But by looking at unrelated immigration documents from the early twentieth century, especially those related to the aftermath of the *Komagata Maru* Incident in 1914 on the West Coast, it's clear that a key correspondent on my grandfather's file and hardliner at the Immigration Branch was Commissioner A.L. Jolliffe. One often finds his signature on documents from the 1910s regarding Sikh would-be immigrants. At that time, he oversaw the immigration office in Vancouver and was a key player in policies sent west from Ottawa by Superintendent of Immigration W.D. Scott. By the 1930s, Jolliffe had ascended to the position of commissioner for the Department of Immigration in Ottawa. He is the closest thing to a *bête noire* in my grandfather's story. If the much better-known doorkeeper, F.C. Blair, played any role in my grandfather's struggle, he left no trace in any of the documents beyond a shared penchant for the use of pompous and hectoring language that appears in letters in my grandfather's file.

❀ ❀ ❀

I aim to convey the voices of my grandfather's correspondents but have not tried, as I should, to convey his voice. As far as we are into his story, it should be in our heads. I heard it only once in my adult life in the strangest of circumstances. My grandfather had been dead for more than twenty years. I was visiting Vancouver and happened to go along with my mom to an unusual event, the fiftieth wedding anniversary of compatriots of her parents. Fifty years before, as it turned out, my grandfather had officiated at the couple's Vancouver wedding. Two artifacts of that event were on hand at the anniversary: one was a piece of wedding cake, which had turned the colour of wet cement. Then, without any preparation or announcement, a recording was played over the room's sound system, using a turntable set at 78 rpm. It presented a voice with a Yiddish Polish lilt blessing the now aged bride and groom. This was the voice that had, in *Dos Yiddishe Vort*, celebrated a *zaftig* Yiddish at a Dysart bar mitzvah brunch. Without any hesitation, my mother looked at me and said "That's my father singing." You couldn't have made it up.

But my grandfather's letters do convey his style—formal address, emotional tone, and willingness to return to repeated themes—and his state of mind. All of this is made somewhat remote in translation, leaving out the characteristic emotionalisms of Yiddish, but key aspects remain clear. They include his insistent questioning, an assertive style, an earnest or possibly slightly out-of-control willingness to reveal his own feelings as part of his effort to convince his correspondent of the rightness of his cause. Often he is businesslike but at times pleading. Occasionally, he strives to land on some ground of shared interest or understanding. This is the case in an early letter to M.A. Gray at the JIAS office in Winnipeg. My grandfather has read in Winnipeg's *Dos Yiddishe Vort* newspaper of Gray's involvement with the Labour Zionist Movement and his attendance at a Poale Zion convention on his way to Ottawa. "I ask of you," my grandfather writes to his *Chosheve freint*, "to please speak ... with Minister Gordon and plead with him to allow me to bring my family and you will with the help of God be successful" while acknowledging Gray's energetic Zionist commitments. The rhetoric that my grandfather was most likely to use is strange to our ears, overly emotional, unguarded, considering that often he was writing to people he did not know and whose range of influence was far above his own. But one finds an echo of his style and tone in letters written by Polish Jews of the period, directed at the head of the Polish government, Marshal Józef Piłsudski. Although Piłsudski's government was rightist in the early 1930s, it was not a Jew-baiting movement, and Jews wrote, often in Yiddish, pleading for aid in their daily struggles. The belief in the efficacy of a strongly argued missive, the offering up of what seems to our ears to be exaggerated platitudes, the willingness to plead intimately into the unknown, each had a certain moment among late-1920s small-town and urban-dwelling Jews.

As the correspondence in my grandfather's file developed, with a variety of letter writers in two languages, it's clear that my grandfather was not always sure of the best way to communicate with a particular correspondent. In one case, he sent a short English-language summary at the head of his Yiddish letter to Gray, as if, in late 1932, he was not confident that Yiddish, as a language of complaint, was effective enough. This letter was sent under the letterhead of "The Quality Corner Store H. Gibbs Prop. Dysart, Sask." The proprietor of the corner store must have been asked to write a few words in English, to be signed in English by my grandfather, before he embarked on a more detailed Yiddish missive. He signs off as "Yours Truly, Rev J. Eisenstein," and then in Yiddish, "Yehuda Yosef Kosher Slaughterer and Inspector Eisenstein," adding the abbreviation denoting his ritual role, just as a member of the military might append his rank to his name. All of this is followed by the bright but somewhat passive-aggressive finale: "Be so good as to send me a quick answer."[6] On the surface, the store owner's name, the breezily vernacular "Quality Corner Store," and the school-quality handwriting suggest that my grandfather's help might have been a non-Jewish neighbour. But it turns out that Gibbs was an early comer to the Saskatchewan prairie whose family was at Dysart as early as 1920. In that year, an S. Gibbs is listed among the representatives of Western Canada's Jewish Fund for the Relief of War Sufferers, which aimed to bring Ukrainian Jewish orphans to Canada.

The voice of official Canada increased in volume and unpleasantness as my grandfather, as well as his supporters at the JIAS, refused to take no for an answer. His efforts to bring in outside players to aid his cause at times riled up the bureaucrats as they sensed a challenge to their ability to keep files under control. In January 1933, Gray and Paull agreed that a "report" received from "the Member of Parliament of Regina" should "make it easier" for the JIAS to plead my grandfather's case.[7] This would have been Turnbull. But his "report" might only have riled up the immigration file minders. Not long after this, the division commissioner in Winnipeg sent what he must surely have believed to be his final word. It's worth revisiting the tone of Smith's rejection: "I beg to advise that inasmuch as the applicant effected entry to Canada by flagrant misrepresentation, the Department is not prepared to take any action with a view to facilitating the movement to this country of his alleged wife and children and you may advise him accordingly."[8]

This was the first official no from the Canadian government's immigration department. Whether he should or should not have been shocked that the government of Canada would behave this way, my grandfather appears to have been in his letters. Exactly who gave him the impression that there was hope, whether through his meetings with solicitous MPs or through the courteous and constructive efforts of Gray in Winnipeg, we can't know. Such hope certainly would have been raised by the letter that he received from the division commissioner's assistant, William Beatty, not long before Smith informed Gray that the rabbi and his "alleged" family were out of luck. Beatty's letter is dated December 21, 1932, and Beatty was a rare immigration department staffer who addressed my grandfather directly rather than through intermediaries, lawyers, immigration representatives, or elected officials. The letter, sent directly to my grandfather's postal box

IN YOUR REPLY REFER TO
No. 95365
KINDLY DO NOT WRITE ON MORE THAN
ONE SUBJECT IN ANY ONE LETTER

ADDRESS
DIVISION COMMISSIONER OF IMMIGRATION

CANADA

DEPARTMENT OF IMMIGRATION AND COLONIZATION

WINNIPEG, MAN., December 21st, 1932.

Sir:

I am in receipt of your application for the admission
to Canada of your alleged wife and her two children, and
note from correspondence on file that in all probability
you came forward as a single man, and now you are making
application for the admission of a wife and two children.
Please explain fully the circumstances with respect to the
reason why you described yourself as single at the time,
whether you described yourself as a rabbi, or as a farm
laborer, to what extent you supported your alleged wife and
her two children since your arrival in this country, your
financial resources with respect to cash on hand or on deposit in a bank, what housing accommodation is available,
and, definitely, such information as will satisfy me that
you are not only willing but financially capable of supporting your family after their arrival in this country, so that
they would not become public charges if admitted. I am also
desiring information as to whether transportation in favor
of your family has been fully paid for, or only in part.
If transportation is only partly paid for please advise what
cash payment you made, and what arrangements you have made
with the transportation company concerned for the payment of
the balance.

Kindly write very fully along lines hereinbefore indicated,
in order that we may give your application such consideration as
may be possible.

Your obedient servant,

W. M. Beatty.

Assistant Division Commissioner.

Rabbi I. J. Eisenstein,
Dysart, Sask.

address in Dysart, is a rare instance of the official voice of Canada's
Department of Immigration that allows a degree of human sympathy.
It reiterates the accusation of illegitimacy—"your alleged wife and
her two children"—but that is its single diminishing motif. The letter
has great artifactual character and is the first of a suite of letters that
provides a clear trail of the efforts of my grandfather and the voices of
those whom he and his helpmates corresponded with.

Beatty signs off with unusual courtesy, his signature perfectly leg-
ible. Why wouldn't my grandfather have viewed this as an opening, a

ADDRESS
DIVISION COMMISSIONER OF IMMIGRATION

CANADA

IN YOUR REFER TO

No.................................

KINDLY DO NOT WRITE ON MORE THAN
ONE SUBJECT IN ANY ONE LETTER

DEPARTMENT OF IMMIGRATION AND COLONIZATION

LJK/FF

January 16th, 1933,

WINNIPEG, MANITOBA,

Copy for; M. A. Gray, Esq., General Secretary, Jewish
Immigrant Aid Society of Canada.Your file 1917.

Sir: Your file 550775

Simply as further information for your
file as above, regarding an application from
Rabbi I. J. Eisenstein for the admission to
Canada of his wife and two children, I beg to
quote hereunder a letter from this party dated
29th ultimo and reading as follows:-

"In reply to yours of Dec. 21 inst. I am
obliged to reply to your inquiries. The
reason I described myself as single man is
at that time no married man was allowed to
enter Canada and from instructions and advice
from agents and transportation companys on the
other side,according to my permit I entered as
single, and described myself as private and
having the practice I became rabbi, and in-
structor to Jewish Missions, since here. I
supported my wife and children by sending them
$50.00 every three months,as to my financial
standing, I will have $300.00 left after I pay in cash
in full for the transportation of my family, and I
receive $100.00 per month from my Congregation. I
can provide for a decent home for my wife and children,
and assure they will not become a public charge in
this country. Your kind attention to my application
will oblige."

I advised the rabbi of Departmental decision on the
10th instant.

Your obedient servant,
C. E. S. SMITH
Division Commissioner.

Commissioner of Immigration,
Ottawa, Ontario.

first remarkable close call that signalled imminent success? The "here-inbefore" aside, Beatty writes plainly, asking realistic questions. He has gone back to the original text—my grandfather's application for permits and its particulars—and asked for clarification.

Beatty's lawyerly approach resulted in a carefully worded response from my grandfather that, with its smattering of legalese and formal English, was surely scripted for him by someone at one of the JIAS offices. Maybe it was Gray, the long-time alderman, who aided my grandfather in his use of the modulated tone.

The stilted tone assures the reader that this is *not* my grandfather's voice; rather, it is the official voice of the JIAS, struggling to arrive at an honest account of past decisions that might be said to have created the present state of affairs.

But at this point, it was a no go. Beatty, a mere assistant at the Winnipeg immigration office, was silenced in the correspondence by his boss, C.E.S. Smith, commissioner of immigration, whose letters entertain no sympathy or patience for the Eisenstein file. "Referring again to your application for the admission to Canada of your alleged wife and her two children," Smith writes to Gray, highlighting how "Juda Josef Ajzensztejn, described as a Hebrew, . . . stated he was *single* and a teacher by occupation. . . . He also claimed that his nearest relative in Poland was a sister." Smith composes a litany of the lies of Eisenstein: he was not single, he was not a teacher, and (though Smith does not make his point entirely clearly) his nearest relatives in Poland would be more properly stated as his wife and children. Smith, it is worth noting, "signs" his name with a full-caps rubber stamp—C. E. S. SMITH—as if he cannot bear to apply pen to document or can't be bothered and has had someone else in his office slam the ink stamp from pad to page. Another strong arm for Reverend Eisenstein and with a saucy tone this time—"no action can be taken with a view of facilitating the movement of your alleged wife and children at the present time."[9] The characteristic voice of the immigration department might not have rung in my grandfather's head as it reverberated in letters directed to the JIAS. Resistance to my grandfather's file in the immigration bureaucracy might have been driven partly by the kind of file it was. Not just Jewish, not just one that had a habit of returning like a boomerang, unexpected, but one of a group of particularly enervating files of men who had "secured admission by representation as a single man." At the same time that Smith was letting my grandfather know about the status of his "alleged" family, an immigration commissioner in Ottawa offered the opinion that deportation was the right response for such men in the country "illegally." They were not, the commissioner added, "entitled to any consideration."[10]

❊ ❊ ❊

The year 1933 was not as bad in Saskatchewan as it was turning out to be in other parts of the world; however, as far as my grandfather's efforts had gone to date, the year was off to a bad start. There was Smith with his rubber stamp. There was the haunting lie (or lies according to Smith) upon entering the country that operated as a Catch-22. One could say bye-bye to Beatty and his "obedience." It would be a good while before a federal agent wrote politely to my grandfather or a JIAS worker striving on his behalf. In Smith's letters, we find a commonly used government voice in its full-throated form. This included the indulgence of legalese, also loved by Jewish community workers, but from the pen or typewriter of the bureaucrat, the faux courtesy and legalistic lingo operated as part of the official hand of fate—the overly polite "I beg to advise that inasmuch" followed by the fist to the gut, the repeated punchline of the department's decision to do nothing at all for a "flagrant" self-misrepresenter and his "alleged" wife and children. The latter phrase is among the ugliest of the bureaucratic brush-offs since it besmears my grandfather with more than his own culpability—he acknowledged the central lie of his visa permit from the start—and offers the additional accusation of moral turpitude, pathological finagling, some kind of scam associated with a fake family back in Poland who *might not even be his own or exist at all.* When officialdom feels its oats, it indulges in this sort of casual character assassination. The Jewish functionaries—Gray in Winnipeg and Paull in Montreal, both of whom found their way periodically to Ottawa to call on ministers and their aides—knew far better than my grandfather what they were up against.

With Paull involved, my grandfather's efforts to have his case heard in Ottawa gained a new voice. Paull had access to Gordon, but he couldn't get him to change his mind on the Eisenstein file. The permits remained elusive. Based upon the materials that I have, 1933 was a washout, with little accomplished. Gray rounded out the year with a downhearted note: "Personally, I think that prospects of bringing wives to passengers who arrived as single are not good."[11]

Gray's comment reflects a substantial discussion in the immigration department about files like my grandfather's. In a memorandum prepared for Gordon by his deputy, Thomas Magladery, forwarded to him in mid-April 1934, the issue of men who have asked to bring wives after declaring themselves single is addressed. Magladery begins by targeting the previous Liberal government as the source of the problem, highlighting a period between 1926 and 1930 when admission to Canada of a resident's "unmarried son, daughter, brother and sister" took place without appropriate attention. There was, he writes, "considerable misrepresentation" in these files, the "chief offenders" being "the Hebrews." Although this is not a memo that directly addresses Jewish immigration, it does so. There were at least 100 such "aliens who have secured entry to Canada and who are pressing for the admission of their families." No specifics, names, or characterizations of files are supplied beyond this general description. What was to be done? The deputy minister offers four possible options. All of the families of these men could be admitted. This would result, Magladery opines, in the "admission of 1000 persons," read Hebrews. Special cases could be okayed, but this would trigger, he writes, "claims of discrimination." Applicants who lied about their married status could be deported, an option that would "no doubt arouse severe criticism." Or none of the family members could be allowed, letting the residents know that they could be reunited with their families "in some country other than Canada." That option was what my grandfather had heard from immigration officers and even, indirectly, from Gordon. This is as far as the deputy minister goes—though the archival record shows that Gordon sent the memo on to Arthur Meighen, a senator and past Conservative prime minister. Magladery signs off by asking Gordon for his "instructions" on these matters.[12]

In the spring of 1934, just around the time that Magladery composed his memo, a shift took place in relation to my grandfather's efforts. This was caused, it seems, by the lawyer Lynd of Estevan. Among the many figures of influence whom my grandfather enlisted, Lynd might have been the most decisive. In the 1920s, he ran three times, unsuccessfully, for the Conservatives in the Qu'Appelle constituency. In the 1930s, he wrote a pair of long letters to Bennett from his Estevan law office regarding the party's prospects in Saskatchewan. These letters gained the prime minister's promise to "advise" him upon "taking the matter up with my colleagues."[13] Later in his career, Lynd would be the president of the Law Society of Saskatchewan. To visit his office in Estevan, my grandfather needed to catch a horse and buggy ride with a Hirsch farmer headed into town or take the train a couple of station stops from Hirsch. Maybe he put himself up at the Singer boarding house by the railway line, with the "tramps" and their johns holed up in the neighbouring houses. Lynd's role is not accounted for in my

Copy #673-34

Re:-Hirsch Central School-
Re:-J. Eisenstein, Hirsch-

THE MINISTER OF IMMIGRATION AND COLONIZATION
OTTAWA, CANADA.

May 28, 1934.

Private and Confidential.

Dear Mr. Lynd:

I regret very much that when you were in Ottawa
you did not have an opportunity of interviewing me concerning
the admission to Canada of the wife and children of Rabbi Eisenstein.

Unfortunately, Rabbi Eisenstein is within the class
of those who have illegally gained admission to Canada and consequently
no action is being taken by the Department to condone the flagrant
disregard of this class for Canadian laws by allowing the admission of
their dependents. In view, however, of the strong representations you
have made, I am prepared to initiate an investigation concerning the
wife and family of the Rabbi, and if it is found that they are people
of good morals, good health, and in every way desirable citizens of
Canada, then the case will be again reviewed. This investigation will
take some little time, but it will be expedited to the greatest extent
possible.

Very kindest regards and best wishes for the future.

Yours faithfully,

W. A. GORDON.

W. Wallace Lynd, Esq., K.C.,
Barrister, etc.,
ESTEVAN, Sask.

grandfather's JIAS file by anything written by Lynd himself; rather,
there is a letter from—as the kids say, *wait for it*—Wesley Ashton Gordon, the minister of immigration and colonization himself. It is worthy
of full perusal in its original form (though my grandfather's file contains a copy, not a stately crested parliamentary original). At the JIAS
office in Montreal, someone in the typing pool copied it for the record.

What has happened? Gone is the nonsense, suggested to Turnbull, about returning to Poland to fetch the family left behind. We don't know what Lynd's "strong representations" were, or why they turned the minister's mind, considering that Gordon and Lynd managed to miss each other in Ottawa. And they were offered within a month of the Magladery memorandum, with its unforgiving options for men in the group of 100. What follows is *almost* an admittance, an investigation that the minister hopes will be "expedited to the greatest extent possible." Knowing the permit system at the time, which could turn on a minister's whim, and following private meetings among ministers, immigration commissioners, and activists from the JIAS, this was big news.

The second half of the minister's letter is rich and revealing. Its opening sentence rests on familiar official language and tone and on the department's habitual reliance on "rules" and the standing response received by most Jewish applicants. It refers to a special category of no, that received by those who have broken Canadian law by lying about their status on immigration papers. Here Gordon refers to the group of men who, like my grandfather, had come into the country claiming to be single and then struggled to bring their families after them. But in the second half of Gordon's paragraph, department boilerplate falls away. The minister will initiate a "review" of what has seemed, to date, to be a lost cause: the "allegedly" married man who entered the country by illegal means will be given consideration. Paull of the JIAS was in Ottawa regularly to promote a variety of immigration files, but nothing in the letters from Paull and Gray during these months suggests that they made headway. The background is lost, and we cannot gain a clear set of causes and outcomes. We do know that Gordon heard of the "rabbi" of Hirsch, formerly of Dysart. And the "rabbi" was among an unusual set of men for whom the immigration commissioners shared a special displeasure.

The Gordon-Lynd letter energized my grandfather anew. In the fall of 1934, he sent a copy of it to Louis Rosenberg at the JCA, his overseer as the colony teacher-rabbi at Hirsch. Rosenberg, the "MANAGER WESTERN OFFICE," forwarded it to his overseers, the Canadian Committee of the JCA based in Montreal, which included Member of Parliament S.W. Jacobs. The committee wrote to A.J. Paull to confirm that the prairie colony *shoichet* and teacher, quite rightly, should be reunited with his family. They would "appreciate anything" that he could "do in this connection."[14] My grandfather, with this support, was no longer an individual in dire straits, like so many others, a begging Jew who could be rendered "alleged," but an individual with a host of institutional backers, among them the settler infrastructure overseeing colonies in the West.

Gray in Winnipeg put his shoulder to the wheel anew. He wrote to F.W. Turnbull—Esq., MP—at Regina and enclosed an "original letter addressed to you by Mr. W. Wallace Lynd, Barrister, Estevan, Saskatchewan, in connection with the application of Rev. J. Eisenstein, of Dysart, and now at Hirsch, Saskatchewan, for the admission to Canada of his wife and two children, which was rejected by the Department of Immigration." In his letter, Gray acknowledges that the reverend "came forward under misrepresentation" but argues that "the applicant is now employed in Hirsch as a Rabbi" and "has steady employment at a monthly salary of $100.00 and housing accommodation. The application has been recommended by the Congregation and the settlement arrangements are satisfactory, there is no danger of the applicant or his family becoming a public charge. The Rabbi requested me to forward to you photographs of his wife and two children, which you will find enclosed." Oh, the enclosures! The letter notes them at the bottom: "Encls. 4." At least two were representations of the human drama at its best. The photo that my grandmother had sent of herself and the children was among them, taken in the studio in the old market square in Mława. The "alleged" wife and children became the prettily pictured, and so, it seems, the wheel of fortune began to turn in a new way. The immigration files from Gray's Winnipeg office reflect his ongoing efforts and my grandfather's in the direction of Turnbull, the Regina MP.[15]

Among the players in this narrative, Turnbull was long-lived—still alive in my youth, he died, at age eighty-nine, in 1971. He was another Ontario-born lawyer who headed west to practise law and then sought a Conservative parliamentary seat in Regina. Just as he heard anew about the rabbi of Hirsch, he was chairing a committee considering amendments to the British North America Act, which placed him among the MPs who promoted Bennett's "New Deal" program. Gray wrote to my grandfather in November 1934 that he had not heard back from Turnbull but added that "it may be advisable for you to try and get in touch with him yourself. After all, he is doing you a favor and is in no way obliged to reply to my letters should he not wish to do so. Probably, you could have your friend in Estevan write him again."[16] A great deal lurks between these lines. Gray betrays his own irritation with a bit of scolding and with a push for his client to take independent action. My grandfather's "friend in Estevan" was Lynd, and this advice signals, though we have no record of it, his attentive lawyerly work in contacting Turnbull himself. In early 1935, Gray wrote "please see Mr. Turnbull at your convenience in connection with your application for your family, as he will be leaving for Ottawa in the next few days." This note, woefully, leaves much out. The visit to Regina is assumed; Turnbull's interest, too, seems to be assumed; likewise assumed is the opportunity to motivate the MP to carry a message with him to his Ottawa counterparts. (The scenario of surmised encounter tempts speculation, which I resist throughout this narrative, but might Turnbull have come upon Gordon in some back hallway of Parliament and retired for a smoke and quiet discussion about one of "the hundred"?)

Through the fall of 1934 and early 1935, as events moved in a positive direction, my grandfather was enmeshed at the time in another set of circumstances—or was it an escapade of sorts?—that reflected his desperation. This is the only part of his narrative that touches on the United States. In October 1934, he found his way to the Worral Hospital, part of the Mayo Clinic, in Rochester, Minnesota. During a stay of two weeks, he was seen by a doctor who suggested that his ailments, which are not clear in his letters to Gray, were psychosomatic. Reuniting with his family, the doctor believed, would provide a cure, and the doctor prepared a letter arguing to this end. For good measure, the Mayo people removed from my grandfather his tonsils as well as "several teeth." While in Minnesota, he took a side trip to see a Radzanower, a relative in Chicago who was the first in his family to leave Poland. This was a man known as Mordecai *ganef*, Mordecai the Thief, who had taken part in a scheme to kill a czarist official in Warsaw and chose exile over prison. It was he who offered the first glimpse of the real America to the family back in the village square in Radzanów and other nearby towns, and it was his American sponsorship that allowed more members of the family to leave for America.

Upon his return to Hirsch, my grandfather took the doctor's letter to Lynd, who saw enough value in it to forward it to Turnbull in Regina. This is like something out of F. Scott Fitzgerald—let's say an unpublished story, since it lacks the pretty college ingénue at the heart

House of Commons
Canada

Ottawa, February 2nd, 1935.

M. A. Gray, Esq.,
General Secretary,
Jewish Immigrant Aid Society of Canada,
654 Main Street,
Winnipeg, Man.

Dear Mr. Gray:

Before and since the receipt of your letter of
November 30th, I have been trying to see what could
be done to obtain the entry into Canada of the family
of 'J. Eisenstein'. His trouble arises from the fact
that he himself is not legally in the country. At a
time when a married man was not admitted to Canada, he
obtained entry by representing himself to the authorities
as being single. There is the further situation I believe,
of which you probably know, that there are quite a number
of others in the same position and to admit one would be
to admit all. However, I am also in receipt of another
letter from the Rabbi himself which I am passing on to
the Department to see if they know of any way in which
the Rabbi's request can be granted.

Yours truly,

F. W. Turnbull

FEB 4 1935

FWT/LM

---

of the narrative, but there is train travel on the plains in autumn along
with deep longing and misspent energy. What could Turnbull have
made of the Mayo Clinic letter? Somehow Lynd thought it worth
sending. It's beginning to seem that almost anything was worth a try.
And it was getting late in the year. The Depression on the Prairies was
deepening. Fewer Jews were managing to enter Canada under any circumstances. What would finally move my grandfather's goals forward?
A letter from Turnbull under House of Commons letterhead.

Turnbull's letter proves a number of things without saying them outright. Gray was by no means a side player once Paull was leading the way on files in Ottawa. It was the western link here, the Regina MP's response to a Winnipeg alderman, about a constituent, that resonates. Turnbull was not above rehearsing the "trouble" associated with this file—misrepresentation was the first problem, and the "situation" associated with a "number of others" in my grandfather's limbo was the second problem. The letter's opening astonishes us: "Before and since the receipt of your letter of November 30th, I have been trying to see what could be done. . . ." Turnbull was knowledgeable and, we might say, motivated. He heard about this file from different angles, including Lynd, a true insider. And now the studio photo of wife and children sat on his desk (or on that of an assistant) to enliven the reality of the story. Somehow, anew, my grandfather wrote himself into the midst of Turnbull's considerations for action. This late-coming effort would be aimed at the cold hearts at the Department of Immigration. The "Rabbi's request," as Turnbull put it, was circulating on Parliament Hill.

ENTER THE
GREAT LADY

By early 1935, A.J. Paull was hopeful, writing less guardedly than usual to my grandfather: "I am doing all possible to bring the matter to a close. I have communicated with the Department of Immigration again and hope to get results shortly."[1] But he did not signal the source of his hope, for he was entirely allergic to the kind of interpretive chatter that my grandfather sometimes received in long typed Yiddish missives from Paull's assistant, Sam Kaplan. This might have been a protocol issue—the boss had to remain mum, whereas his helpers could offer succour. None of my grandfather's letters was addressed to Kaplan, but he often answered them at length and clearly was managing the file.

It was at this point of apparent momentum—with all of my grandfather's letter writing, JIAS efforts, Lynd's doings, and signals from Gordon and Turnbull—that everything was brought to a halt by the redoubtable A.L. Jolliffe, the commissioner of immigration in Ottawa, whose experience with difficult files reached all the way back to the send-off of the *Komagata Maru*. Some degree of bureaucratic heft would have to be brought to bear, considering the variety of interest in the "rabbi" from Hirsch. Required was a bigger and badder version of the rubber stamper, C.E.S. Smith, back in Winnipeg. Jolliffe was a lifer in the immigration department. Born in 1885 in Southampton, England, he became an immigration officer in Vancouver in 1913 just in time to stand behind the government's rejection of 376 immigrants aboard the *Komagata Maru*. He must have felt relieved, his job accomplished, when the Canadian Navy towed the ship out of the harbour and sent it on its way back to India. This event presaged the outcome of the *St. Louis*, a ship that departed from Hamburg carrying roughly 900 Jews and was denied landing permission by the Canadian government, leading it to return to Europe in June 1939. In the 1930s, Jolliffe was a counterpart of the more notorious F.C. Blair, overseeing the immigration staff in Ottawa, answering to and advising Minister Gordon. In the postwar years, Jolliffe was appointed director of the Immigration Branch. He appears as a minor player in the "none is too many" narrative, with his most telling portrait offered in relation to wartime events when he was Blair's deputy. "Blair and Jolliffe," Abella and Troper write, "did not get along. Jolliffe, a thirty-year veteran of immigration work when appointed to replace Blair, was, by all accounts, a more flexible, accessible and agreeable individual with whom to deal. One observer was later to recall of Jolliffe that he consistently endeavoured 'to interpret Canada's immigration regulation in a generous and liberal sense.'"[2]

Not so in our case. Two letters—one epic in its argumentative approach, for a bureaucratic document, the other terse—reflect Jolliffe's intention to bring to a halt the doings regarding my grandfather's file. First the longer one.

In this letter, Jolliffe's tone is one of barely contained emotion—frustration, fury?—but the letter remains a lawyerly covering of ground, as well as a slamming on of the brakes, regardless of what Paull or others might have viewed as sympathetic "representations" (in fact, the department had signalled the possibility of "favourable consideration" through the correspondence between its head, Gordon, and Lynd). There must be an end, Jolliffe writes, to this Eisenstein business. This letter in many ways is the centrepiece of my grandfather's immigration file for appreciating the point of view of the Department of Immigration at the time. It is the most effusively argued, under the country's coat of arms with its lion crowned, above the slashing signature of the immigration commissioner. The backhanded compliment regarding "the Rabbi's standing" is surely not a good example of Jolliffe's potential, as Abella and Troper have it, for fair-handedness in contrast to Blair.[3] And there is something heightened in the delivery of its report,

ADDRESS
COMMISSIONER OF IMMIGRATION

CANADA

IN YOUR REPLY REFER TO
No. 530775

KINDLY DO NOT WRITE ON MORE THAN
ONE SUBJECT IN ANY ONE LETTER

DEPARTMENT OF IMMIGRATION AND COLONIZATION

OTTAWA, January 29th, 1935.

JAN 30 1935

62057

Dear Sir,-

      I am in receipt of your letter of January 23rd, your file No.17808, regarding the application of Rabbi Eisenstein of Hirsch, Saskatchewan, for the admission to Canada of his wife and children.

      There would appear to be some misunderstanding in the information which has been furnished you in respect to the above application. The Department has not at any time indicated that we would be prepared to give the matter favourable consideration. On the contrary, it has been pointed out to all concerned upon a number of occasions that the case is not one in which favourable consideration would be warranted. Rabbi Eisenstein was admitted to Canada in November 1930, destined to a brother in Vancouver, B.C. At that time he was described as a teacher and single and his entry was arranged under the regulations which permitted the admission of single brother and sisters but not of married brothers and sisters. The applicant in Canada described Rabbi Eisenstein as single and the latter declared the same thing before our Examining Officer at Danzig and upon arrival at the Port of Quebec. Rabbi Eisenstein is one of many persons who effected entry to Canada by this misrepresentation of their status. In some cases the excuse has been set up that the immigrant did not know any better but this can scarcely be advanced in the case of a person of the Rabbi's standing.

      The Department has been obliged to take a firm stand in these cases, as we cannot condone deliberate misrepresentation and evasion of the law. The situation in which these applicants now find themselves is one of their own making, and, while the Department has refrained from instituting deportation proceedings, we are not prepared to extend facilities in respect to the admission of their dependents. If they desire to be reunited with their families they have open to them the course of returning to their native country.

Yours truly,

A. J. Paull, Esq.,
Executive Director,
Jewish Immigrant Aid Society,
4226 St. Lawrence Blvd.,
MONTREAL, P. Q.

Commissioner.

as if the writer has *had it up to here* with this file—too many representations, follow-ups, and reviews. The letter sums up Jolliffe's view that a "firm stand" is required in response to "evasion of the law." And then a threat: "While the Department has refrained from instituting deportation proceedings, we are not prepared to extend facilities in respect to the admission of the dependents. If they desire to be reunited with their families they have open to them the course of returning to their native country."

A glance at other materials in the immigration file from January 1935 offers evidence of what might have riled up Jolliffe. At this time,

Paull informed my grandfather that he was "doing all possible to bring the matter to a close" and hoped "to get results shortly."[4] At the same time, Paull had his office manager, Sam Kaplan, send a letter to Jolliffe, reasserting Gordon's letter to Lynd, as if its contents would provide the key to unlock the barred door. This reply from the Montreal JIAS office reflected its workers' boundless and outwardly upbeat efforts against all odds, even in the face of the most *shreklich* (here the Yiddish word for scary sets the tone) dressing down by government bureaucrats. In response to Jolliffe, Kaplan—in Yiddish correspondence, he calls himself a "field organizer"—did not respond directly to the commissioner's letter's contents. Rather, he sent a copy of a "letter addressed by the Hon. W.A. Gordon Minister of Immigration and Colonization, to Mr. W. Wallace Lynd, K.C., of Estevan, Sask.," which contained Gordon's unusual allowance that a "review" of the file would be "expedited to the greatest extent possible." "The above letter," Kaplan added, "raised the hopes of Rabbi Eisenstein to a considerable extent and should be taken into consideration by the Department when dealing with this case at the present time."[5] The Gordon letter was the JIAS trump card, played in spite of Jolliffe's obstruction.

What temerity the field organizer applies in his missive to the commissioner. Still, there is a kind of mellow thoughtfulness, too, almost like a game, in the response offered to Jolliffe's lecture in the letter of January 29. Kaplan raises him one ministerial missive to Lynd. This behaviour was a direct outcome of the reigning "permit" system. Although the status quo was a grim one, the routine "no" to any particular file might come back as a "no" many times until some powerful higher up on the ministerial ladder drove things in a new and surprising direction. No became yes.

Kaplan wrote again to Jolliffe without waiting for a response to his previous letter: "Rabbi Eisenstein writes us that your Department has been conducting an investigation concerning his family and that if it were found that they are people of good moral and good health, and in every way desirable citizens for Canada, the Department would be prepared to give the matter of his application for the admission of his family favorable consideration."[6] Kaplan's tone would seem to be oblivious if not for further evidence in the file that more was going on behind the scenes.

In the same week that Jolliffe sent his second refusal, ordering Eisenstein to cease and desist, Paull wrote to my grandfather. This

Dear Rev~~. Eisen~~stein:

    I spent two days in Ottawa last week and again discussed your case with the Department.

    As your application needs an Order in Council it was referred to the Minister who will render his decision shortly. I expect favorable action.

        Yours very truly,
    JEWISH IMMIGRANT AID SOCIETY OF CANADA

        Executive Director.

Rev. J. Eisenstein,
Hirsch,
Sask.

letter suggests a new order of activity. If the permit game in Canada's immigration department was an ongoing drama of forays and parries, efforts rebuffed and redeployed, then the order-in-council was the high card that beat all. S.W. Jacobs, in his eloquent early-1920s presentation to Parliament, decried the use of an order-in-council as a method of passing laws without parliamentary debate. An order-in-council—brought for consideration by a group of cabinet members—could contain many items: those of national or local scope, those affecting Canadian society or just a few individuals. Ministers with various goals signed off jointly on each other's projects of the moment. The minister whose contribution to an order-in-council might include permits for my grandfather was Gordon. And, regardless of Jolliffe's hot air, Paull expected favourable action.

Just six days later came another hopeful letter from Paull.

This letter suggests an even wider range of discussion at this late date—Lynd, Gordon, and, though it's difficult to imagine, Bennett. Can it be true that my grandfather's having opened a correspondence with the prime minister, by way of the mail train at Hirsch, required continuation? This seems to be otherworldly. Yet there's more to come.

Jolliffe's first letter was designed to be the death knell of my grandfather's efforts. Its tone is brutal, in this case offering the sinister advice to a Jew in 1935 that he has the opportunity to return to European

Dear Rabbi Eisenstein,

            With further reference to your case
I would advise that you again communicate with
Mr. W. Wallace Lynd, K.C., who was instrumental
in advancing your case with the Minister.

            Since you have written to the Prime
Minister with regard to your family it will also
be necessary for you to further communicate with
the Prime Minister, because you must realise that
no action can be taken until such time as the
Prime Minister has indicated his intentions in
the matter.

                    Yours very truly,
            JEWISH IMMIGRANT AID SOCIETY OF CANADA

                    Executive Director.

Rev. J. Eisenstein,
Hirsch,
Sask.

Hitlerism at a time when refugees were heading west from Poland and Germany en masse. The letter uses, as well, the niggling, self-satisfied logic of the many letters and pronouncements of Blair quoted in Abella and Troper's *None Is Too Many*. It infers and accuses. And it holds Canadian citizenship up as a rare prize that certain kinds of people do not deserve. The letter was Jolliffe's most concrete foray into my grandfather's file, but it wouldn't be, as Jolliffe likely thought it would, his last.

Two weeks later Jolliffe wrote again to Paull, more concisely this time. He did not rehearse my grandfather's sins. He left more to the imagination, as if he had decided that it would be safer not to rehearse the narrative at hand. He reveals in the letter that my grandfather's file has raised its share of talk on Parliament Hill, including the consideration of the prime minister.

We can't know which "representations" to Prime Minister Bennett Jolliffe is referring. The possibilities include, in descending order of influence, Gordon, Turnbull, and Lynd. Exactly what could "careful review" have been at this point, or was this mere bureaucratic boilerplate? Still, Jolliffe arrived once more at the bureaucrats' favoured insistence that the department was "unable to vary its former decision"

ADDRESS
COMMISSIONER OF IMMIGRATION

CANADA

DEPARTMENT OF IMMIGRATION AND COLONIZATION

OTTAWA, February 14th, 1935.

Dear Mr. Paull:-

      I duly received your letter of January
31st, with reference to the case of Rabbi Eisenstein of Hirsch,
Saskatchewan, dealt with on your file 17808.

      In this connection I have to advise you
that recently upon representations received through the office
of the Right Honourable the Prime Minister the case has again
been made the subject of a thorough and careful review. The
Department, however, has reached the conclusion that it is unable
to vary its former decision and in consequence it cannot facilitate
the entry to Canada of Mrs. Eisenstein and her two children.

        Yours very truly,

Commissioner

A.J. Paull, Esq.,
Executive Director,
Jewish Immigrant Aid Society of Canada,
4226 St. Lawrence Blvd.,
Montreal, P.Q.

and could not "facilitate the entry to Canada of Mrs. Eisenstein and her two children." They had so many ways of saying the same thing, topped with a "yours very truly."

Not enough for my grandfather was the cast of players in his drama to date. To add to it, he undertook what might have been his *coup de grâce*, his masterpiece of inadvertent genius. The best trace is a note card dated January 21, 1935, under the letterhead 149 Somerset Street, Ottawa, signed with overdue courtesy.

149 SOMERSET STREET,
OTTAWA.

January 21-1935-

Dear Rabbi Eisenstein —
        I received your letter
some time ago — but as
I was ill for several weeks
was unable to do anything
about your case. However
— I have now taken steps
to have it taken up at
the Department of Immigration
and I hope they will
be able to do something

The date of writing, in what must not have been a coincidence, was a week ahead of Jolliffe's nasty letter, which aimed to end things once and for all. And the note card is signed, in contrast to Canadian government correspondence, with simple courtesy.

Sincerely yours –

Mrs. A.J. Freiman

Who, most anyone would ask, was Mrs. A.J. Freiman of 149 Somerset Street, Ottawa? Canadians should know her, but they don't. This is the sort of thing schoolteachers say that puts their students to sleep. But in this case it's the truth. Canadians, Jews and non-Jews alike, should know about Lillian Freiman. Alongside the other players in my grandfather's narrative, she can be said to be the most surprising and unique. Certainly, she is central to its outcome, though pinpointing her exact role is not an easy task.

This part of my story has its roots not in documentation found in archives but in family lore, much rehearsed. It was, in fact, the only facet of my grandfather's story that I knew growing up, and it stood for us as the explanation of how my grandfather was able to confront the brutal Canadian immigration regulations of the early 1930s. I connect this version of his narrative with the photograph of him holding me. He looks happy to be holding his third-born New World grandchild in the room in his Vancouver house, circa 1965, which I knew as the "den." It was a sunroom with a view of the backyard, a low, white, old-style Vancouver picket fence and wonderful fruit trees—pear, apple, and cherry. In 1965, they bore too much fruit for one family to handle, but by the time that I knew the sunroom as an adult the cherry tree had given up.

Family lore went as follows: my grandfather had spent all of his energy fruitlessly on lawyers and Jewish immigration representatives and was on the verge of returning to Poland (it's notable that this motive never arises in the archive that documents his efforts; maybe it existed in our folkloric version as a trace of Gordon's initial insult: *Tell the Rabbi of Hirsch that he can go back to Poland and bring his family with him to this country from there*). My grandfather had talked to so many professionals and to so many compatriots about his efforts to bring his family over, with each offering sometimes semi-sensible, sometimes crackpot, advice. One day at Hirsch he was in a farmer's home and noticed a photograph of a woman on the wall. In the version of this story that I remember, the photo was high up, near the ceiling. Was this how they hung portraits in the houses of Hirsch? My grandfather asked if the woman in the photo was the Queen of England. The farmer laughed and said no, not the Queen. Even better, this was a Jewish woman who lived in Ottawa named Lillian Freiman. She'd saved Ukrainian Jewish orphans after the First World War, bringing them back to be adopted by Canadian Jewish families. And the King of England, George V, had given her a medal for her various charity-related efforts. The farmer was about to offer a longer list of Freiman's accomplishments when he drew himself up, gazed at my grandfather, and pointed at the photograph on the wall. "You should write to her," he advised. "She might be able to help you bring your family here."

And so, faithful and unstinting to the end, my grandfather sat down that evening and wrote a letter to Freiman. How he determined her address—whether on Somerset in downtown Ottawa or via the main office of the Hadassah women's Zionist organization that she headed—I can't say. Nor can I confirm whether he sent a letter in Yiddish, which Freiman hardly spoke, or had what he wrote translated in the careful and businesslike way of other JIAS-translated letters in his file. It's certain that with the letter he included the photograph picturing his wife, Chaya Dina, the boy, Berek, serious faced, and the girl, Henna. Family lore had it that my grandfather had a knack for writing a good letter—which the letters in his immigration file prove without a doubt, so this aspect of the lore is reliable—and that this skill was complemented by impressive penmanship. So letter and photo went winging off to Ottawa. And Freiman wrote back on a note card to confirm that she "had taken steps."

THE TRAIN I RIDE

My grandfather's story—apart from its Polish starting point, a side trip to Rochester for medical help, and to Chicago to see Mordecai *ganef*—is a prairie tale until the power centres of Canadian life in the 1930s take the lead. Montreal is in play, at one address, the JIAS office on St. Lawrence Boulevard. But the focus moves to Ottawa unavoidably, because this is where the answer to his troubles lies. My grandfather would never see the city, but he became a sustained subject of discussion there. How about that? He knew the Polish countryside, where he'd traded with grain growers and millers; he knew the Warsaw streets, where he had done the bidding of a Polish officer; he even came to know the Atlantic Ocean aboard the *Ascania* and much of Canada via the CNR train line west. But these routes and byways did not hem him in. He went where the power and influence lay, by way of his letter writing, which today would be called "networking," his cajoling, begging, and soliciting. And he understood that what he sought—a permit for his family to enter Canada—was manufactured in backrooms in Ottawa. As he repeatedly told Paull and Gray, "please see to it, with all your powers and influence, that I shall now receive a permit."

I took the train myself to Ottawa to follow the final lines of the story, in the hope of finding yet unseen documents, parliamentary or private, that might confirm how my grandfather's efforts brought the influence of MPs, of ministers, along with immigration workers, Mrs. Freiman, even the once-Calgarian in the Prime Minister's Office, to lay their shoulders to the wheel of his grand undertaking: permits for three from Poland to the land that held itself aloof from Europe's oncoming catastrophe.

❀ ❀ ❀

It was appropriate that I rode the train to Ottawa since, in so many ways, this is a train story of a time when great journeys, especially in Canada, took place by rail. It was a CNR train that I rode—I had not considered when I planned the trip that VIA is owned by the company that itself was so intently involved with bringing settlers and newcomers west. It was the line, more or less, that my grandfather took inland as he departed from the port at Quebec City. This part of his travels was likely booked along with his steamship ticket since immigration agents were anxious to arrange these things all at once as a kind of immigrant's package deal. The CPR in particular built long-standing and close relationships with the settlement agents and representatives of organizations like the JCA's Louis Rosenberg. These men facilitated settlers' travels west and often rode with them, or went from hamlet to hamlet, investigating their progress. In the late 1920s, the CPR sent Rosenberg a pass for travel throughout the year "covering stations West of Fort William," which had been a gateway between the eastern and western parts of the country since the days of the fur trade. It was only in 1933 that the CPR dropped this custom, informing Simon Belkin, Rosenberg's boss at the JCA, that the days were over when the railway would pay for the "transportation to those not carried on payrolls" of the railway.[1] Why, one wonders. Why this new cost-cutting measure? Was it just one more shutting down of the now roughly fifty-year process of settling newcomers in the West, now in so many ways "settled"?

I set out from Montreal. The city is under an early layer of snow. Just a sprinkling, really, in late November. I follow the route that my grandfather took in the very month that he travelled it. The sky is grey, with a wash of brightening cloud in the southwest and a hint of pale blue winter light where the cloud cover has thinned. The city's backside: from the train, I see a section of the city invisible day to day. The train route reveals hidden aspects of the city; new neighbourhoods and old can be seen over gullies and rail barriers that separate them. Freight cars along the rails are coloured gloriously by graffiti tagging in yellows, greens, and pinks. Old streets at the bottom of the downtown dead-end at the tracks. On the north side of the track is Saint-Henri. In the 1920s and early 1930s, it was a factory community of smoke-stacks and working-class Irish and French Canadians. I pass a building with faded stencilled block letters—manufacturing graffiti—intact. They read "FACTORY #1." The Lachine Canal is a diminished old dowager, given over entirely to its new identity as a route for pleasure craft and a source of pleasant condo views. The streets of Saint-Henri, even in 1930, were like nothing that my grandfather would have seen in Poland. Working-class Warsaw, on the far bank of the Vistula River, was grand in comparison.

"Will you take coffee with your breakfast?" So it goes in business class.

No one had an offer like this for my grandfather as his train rolled west. What did he eat as he crossed the country, with the conundrum of a kosher diet underlying the basic need for sustenance? Hard-boiled eggs and fruit? Maybe he'd already faced this challenge in the Polish Army and had decided that Polish borscht was Jewish borscht, Jewish challah was Polish *chałka*. I eat my eggs but leave the bacon in the corner of the tray. The train whistle sounds over fallow fields. It is something that hasn't changed much, though the whistle was steam-driven eighty years ago like the locomotive that pulled the passenger cars.

What had my grandfather seen of his native country before leaving it for good? He had family members in the villages that lay sixteen or thirty-two kilometres from his hometown. In Szreńsk. In Drobin, where his father was born. Sierpc was near Radzanów. It was a large place with a few thousand Jews before the war. My grandfather travelled to Mława for his short-lived stint at the Gerrer *shtibel* and then later to visit his wife's family. He went to Warsaw for his battle-free term in the Polish Army, attending to an officer's whims. And then, in the process of leaving, he might have gone to Warsaw for a medical examination given there by the Canadian immigration services and his ship's doctor. Then to Gdańsk, and the port of Gdynia, his final Polish place.

Everything along my route speaks of the past and of other places. The train threads its way over this bit of the globe on a link that might take us, by connected rails, any which way. Even backward into the past.

❀ ❀ ❀

Like a lot of streets at the perimeter of Ottawa's downtown, Somerset Street is a mixture of 1960s high-rise apartment blocks, recent condo developments, and a few red and sand-coloured brick buildings that have hung on from the old days. The house at 149 Somerset maintains some of its Victorian stateliness, as it's been retooled over the years to serve a variety of organizations as a kind of glorified clubhouse. Currently, it serves as the Canadian Army Officers' Mess. The lawns have been paved to provide parking, but the winter garden is still there, with a view of the asphalt.

I simply walk in. The front rooms are quiet, so I sit down at a table with armchairs that offer a good look around. The dark wood wain-scoting and coffered ceilings might be original, all the way back to the first owner, C.B. Pattee, a late-nineteenth-century American lumber baron who came north. After him, the house was owned by Carlings— beer magnates—and then by A.J. and Lillian Freiman, who moved their family there in 1913 and stayed for three decades.

On the walls of 149 Somerset hang portraits in oil of Prince Philip and Queen Elizabeth when they were young royals; General Arthur Currie, who led the Canadian Corps in the First World War; Brig-adier A. Hamilton Gault, who funded his own infantry regiment in the First World War; Lieutenant General G.G. Simonds, a tactician of the Normandy Invasion in the next war; and two portraits of Col-onel Elizabeth Lawrie Smellie, who oversaw nurses in France and England during the First World War and was appointed to the King's Commander of the British Empire order. In one portrait, she wears a Mona Lisa smile, a smartly buckled belt at her waist, a cape over her shoulders, and leather gloves in hand that seem to say "At your service."

Where was Lillian?

You must walk toward the back of the house, by the stairs, at the end of the hallway that gives onto the bar and the dining hall, to find a poster-sized set of photos of A.J. and Lillian. Each is seen sitting at a desk. The photo of Lillian is from the mid-1930s. She is at her big wooden desk, surrounded by knick-knacks. It might be the desk where she wrote to communicate her willingness to help Reverend Eisenstein of Hirsch. And she did a thing or two there for the Canadian Army, its veterans of both wars, and their families. As with Smellie, the King found Freiman worthy of his Order of the British Empire.

I've found Lillian, and that's when someone finds me and asks what I am doing there. I am interested, I say, in the history of the house associated with Lillian Freiman. This gets me a certain distance, but the place, I am told, is private. How about that. When Lillian ran the house, she brought home refugees spared from deportation and broken-down vets and let them sleep in the front room. She organized the ladies who made the first Canadian poppies from cardboard in the living room and brought in sewing machines and a corps of volunteers to make clothing for the forces abroad. But now that the army's got the run of the place it's private? I'll say it again: how about that.

I am surprised, I say, because the website makes the Army Officers' Mess out to be a public place connected with our military. I could have told my questioner, the mess staff guy, *You know, my dad was a veteran—two harsh years on Canadian Navy corvettes in the Atlantic, and up to Murmansk and Archangel, like a spaceman in the Pacific winter, escorting Allied merchant ships full of munitions. Once he watched a guy swabbing the deck get swept overboard. Just his shoes left behind. Like a bad joke. How's that for private?* I could have told him, too, that Lillian's OBE trumped Colonel Smellie's CBE, though Smellie did have a swell pair of gloves, and it was time for an *oil portrait of Lillian in the front room of her house.* Tell the army boys, I might have said. Framed. Over the dining table. But my dad never once referred to himself as a veteran, and I didn't come to 149 Somerset to get sassy with the house manager. He offers to take my name and have the real head guy who knows the history of the house—all about the Freimans—give me a call and a tour. But you know what? That call never did come.

※ ※ ※

Jews make their debut in Canadian literary history in a curious, slap-dash way. It's the early twentieth century on Prince Edward Island, and who comes around, gypsy style, selling odds and sods to well-meaning Canadian girls? Well, Italians. But Jews too. It's a "German Jew" who shows up on the doorstep to be greeted by Anne of Green Gables. The Jew has a story, and it is familiar to us: he is "working hard to make enough money to bring his wife and children out from Germany" (lucky for him that, at the turn of the century, "enough money" might be all that it takes to pull that off).[2]

Anne—good Prince Edward Islander that she is—"wanted to buy something from him to help him in such a worthy object." And what does he have of interest to her in his "big box full of interesting things"? A bottle of hair dye. For fifty cents, the peddler promises that this dye will turn Anne's red hair a "beautiful raven black."[3] But the treatment hawked by the German Jew turns Anne into a kind of witch, her hair a "queer, dull, bronzy green with streaks here and there of the original red to heighten the ghastly effect."[4] And off he goes, singing his song to one unwitting householder after the next.

What's to be done? The hair must be cut.

Peddlers. Most of us are too young to have met one. When I was a teenager in Calgary in the 1970s, Jewish men did well as scrap dealers—they had scrapyards, an early version of the conservationist ethic of putting cast-off things to a second or third use, with car bumpers, copper pipe, radiator coils, and whatever else might be torn from old houses. The rag collector with his horse and cart is an iconic presence in early Yiddish Canadian stories. He came down the alleyways in the Jewish quarters of Montreal, Toronto, and Winnipeg singing his song: "Rags, bottles, rags, bottles, top dollar! *Alte zachen!* Old things!"

When Lillian Freiman's father started out in Canada, he was a peddler of watches. That's a few steps up from hair dye. He parlayed this work into success as a jeweller on the way to greater business success in Ottawa. When he wasn't focused on business, he put his shoulder to the wheel of an array of Jewish communal organizations, and the family home operated as a de facto communal shelter where the Bilskys welcomed newcomers from Europe. Lillian's mother could be found laundering and mending their clothing in an effort to send them out ready for their new Canadian lives. As an adolescent, Lillian was included in these activities, and they made an impression that led her to emulate her parents' projects. As a teenager, she established a pattern that would guide the rest of her life; she committed herself to the Ottawa Ladies' Hebrew Benevolent Society and the more ecumenical Children's Aid Society. Whether it was by following the family example or the outcome of living in a small Jewish community, this willingness to involve herself in both Jewish and general causes characterized her for the rest of her life.

Too little attention has been paid in recent decades to Lillian Freiman, though she was designated a "Person of National Historic Significance" by the Canadian government in 2018. She has an entry in the *Dictionary of Canadian Biography* (as does her father), and she is highlighted by websites devoted to influential Canadian and Jewish women of the twentieth century. A biography appeared in 1961, but it doesn't do her justice—the book is divided in two, with the front half dedicated to her and the back half to her husband, A.J. It has a grandiose tone and fails to place her in any real context beyond the lengthy lists of her accomplishments. It reads like a compilation of announcements and news clippings. Privately released, it did not reach much of an audience.

So who do we meet at this juncture, having busied ourselves up to this point with Polish émigrés, Jewish homesteaders, "half-breeds" (as the explorers in 1858 called their workmates on their Qu'Appelle Valley travels), cabinet ministers, small-town lawyers, and Jewish immigration workers? We meet someone unlike any of them. And though each of us in many ways is unlike anyone else, it would seem, from a consideration of her life, that Lillian was *more unlike* the rest of us than anyone else.

Her family story is of the kind peculiar to central Canada and to the place of Jews in the country's early years. Her father, Moses Bilsky, was Lithuanian born, and her mother was born in Berlin. Moses fit the form of the early Jewish Canadian merchant to a T. He fought for the Union forces in the American Civil War and began a family with Pauline Reich in New York City. His rise to social and economic success began with a gold strike in the Cariboo Mountains of British Columbia. He moved first to Mattawa, a riverside Hudson's Bay Company fur trading post, but took his family to Ottawa in the 1870s, where he opened a pawnshop and a variety of other businesses. Lillian Bilsky, born in 1885, grew up first in Mattawa, and then in her parents' house on Nicholas Street, where the first Jewish religious services in Ottawa were held. There it was, too, that newly arrived immigrants stayed before they were helped on their way to a new start in the city. When Bilsky died, his funeral was reported on the front page of the *Ottawa Citizen*. As would be the case at his daughter's funeral, it was attended by the city's mayor and MPs.[5]

Married in 1913 to A.J. Freiman, who became an influential merchant in a more modern vein, Lillian enjoyed a private life of wealth and remarkable access to the leaders of early-twentieth-century Canada. As a newly married woman with a young family, on her morning walks she often crossed paths with the top-hatted ex-prime minister, Wilfrid Laurier, pearl pin in his cravat, who lived around the corner from her home on Somerset Street.

The Figler biography of Lillian and Archie Freiman reads like a Jesuit's argument for sainthood. It's true, though, that the list of her accomplishments lends itself to this kind of argument. Lillian was an activist in aid of displaced Polish and Russian Jews at the end of the First World War; her support for convalescing veterans led her to found the Great War Veterans' Association in 1918, which would become the Royal Canadian Legion; she managed Ottawa's response to the flu epidemic in 1918 almost single-handedly; she initiated the Canadian poppy campaign for veterans in her living room in 1921; the list—evidence of actual hands-on goodness—goes on and on. A notable aspect of it all is the fact that, even though her family had financial resources, which played a role not only in what she accomplished but also in her access to elite circles in Ottawa, it was her organizational skills and far-reaching practical commitments that characterized her efforts. The list of accomplishments is never a catalogue of philanthropic gifts but a resumé of hard work.

For a Jewish woman of Freiman's time, her access to government authorities was singular. Lillian was thirty years old in 1915 when she was in discussions with the Conservative federal labour minister, Thomas Wilson Crothers, about her efforts to aid displaced Eastern European Jews.[6] This success in bringing federal bureaucrats over to her side continued in the early 1920s when Lillian undertook two unlikely schemes to aid Jews caught in the European calamities of the time. The first of these schemes was in 1920 in response to the number of Jewish orphans in eastern Poland and Ukraine following the upheavals of war and national revolutions. F.C. Blair—the toughest nut to crack when approached with tales of Jewish heartbreak—agreed to her request that she bring 200 of these orphans to Canada. They discussed the terms of the plan in his office, and he followed up with a letter, which spelled her name as "Freeeman."[7] In this case, it could have been her involvement with veterans, and her inclusion of the prime minister's wife, Isabelle Meighen, on her committee's charitable work, that rendered her an unstoppable force.

Freiman travelled across the country to raise funds for these efforts as well as to secure homes for the orphans as adoptees. Only 150 such homes were on offer. In this way, her fellow Jewish Canadians failed her. She travelled to Antwerp, where the 150 would-be travellers were gathered by two colleagues who chose them from among the thousands they saw in Poland and Ukraine. In photos on board the *Scandinavian*, her ship home, Freiman wears pointy high-heeled shoes of light leather. She stands with a group of eight children in one photo and alongside Feige Azarowa, who became Fay Green in Ottawa, in another.[8] At Quebec City, Freiman oversaw the children's dispersal to new Canadian homes. In true saint's narrative fashion, the children wept and threw their arms around her as they were parcelled off to their new families. She adopted one herself—a daughter, Gladys, who grew up on Somerset Street.

In a more convoluted case in 1921, Freiman stepped into the midst of the kind of immigration scenario that would become *de rigueur* in the 1920s and early 1930s under both Liberal and Conservative governments. This set of events began with an order-in-council of July 1921, which put new limitations on access to the country by "Non-Preferred Europeans." Hundreds of Jewish immigrants already okayed for travel and aboard or ready to board steamships for Canadian ports were not alerted to these changes. As many as 500 were interned upon arrival at Halifax, where the threat of deportation hung over them like a death writ. Freiman visited the internees at the port, greeting them in her limited Yiddish. Contacts with the immigration and justice departments of the time under Conservatives James A. Calder and Charles Doherty led to the government's reluctant acceptance of some of the hundreds into the country, while the remainder were sent off to Cuba, from where a further number managed to return to Canada.[9]

This sort of outcome with regard to deportation orders wasn't taking place in 1920s Canada. Increasingly, deportation had become a tool of choice of the federal government. By the late 1920s, it was a kind of national project, regularly and cruelly applied. Most of those deported had emigrated to the country a few years before. Finding themselves out of work, and in some cases leaving a failing farm for an urban centre, they were branded as "public charges." This did not mean that they cost the government a cent; rather, it simply meant that they were unemployed mouths that might seek to be fed. The *Toronto Star* followed the outcomes of these policies to the port at Halifax, where it found ships leaving for Poland, Germany, and Sweden, each with its complement of ex-new Canadians heading back to where they'd come from without any say in the process itself. "The deportees arrive in special railway cars," the *Star* reported, "drawn from all parts of Canada. Some, according to immigration officials, have been detained for weeks awaiting a sailing of the steamship line which brought them to Canada."[10] This part of their ordeal was explained by the Canadian government's ability to tell steamship lines that they were owed return travel costs for having brought "failed" immigrants.

In Parliament, the leader of the Cooperative Commonwealth Federation, James S. Woodsworth, argued against these policies. In the early 1930s, when W.A. Gordon had the immigration portfolio, he pushed back. One wonders what he had at stake in supporting such an embarrassing government project. Was it perceived public opinion about "Continentals"? Or panic about "malingerers" of the kind who'd brought out the RCMP shooters at Estevan? Was it word from higher up—from Bennett, concerned about relief costs that he did not want the federal government to carry?—that insisted deportations were a necessary ill in response to rising unemployment? Gordon offered the argument, likely true in certain cases, that his government was doing the bidding of municipal politicians. But he relied on the rhetoric of an increasingly anti-immigrant era, suggesting that he had encountered "many cases of 'pure malingering'" among those being sent back to Europe. Using a canard that remains familiar in the present era, he suggested that, among those being shipped home, "many people had been deported at their own request."[11] To counter this claim, there was Louis Baum with his six children, "moving continuously on his feet," murmuring "Not Poland. No, not Poland." There were the Mylkas— three brothers and three sisters, "tall, gaunt, silent."[12]

In the midst of all this—the parliamentary arguments, the special railway cars, the families waiting for the one kind of free ship's passage that they did not want—there was a familiar Canadian Jewish response: begging. In a telegram to Gordon from Winnipeg in October 1930, the city's Jewish community promised that a boy named Freedman would not become a public charge. The community promised to "pay all hospital charges" and insisted that "there are extra ordinary reasons why boy cannot be returned to Poland please do everything in your power to stop deportation."[13] We don't know the response from the minister, but he and his commissioners must have recognized their superhuman powers to offer life or scratch the Freedman boy from the list. The telegram landed on the minister's desk as real and true as lunch or a glass of ice water. What to do? Chat with Jolliffe (chatting with Blair was like wrestling with a boa constrictor or debating with the proverbial devil). Make an exception and buck the system? You choose.

When one reads the stories above—orphans and snookered internees at Halifax—and considers Freiman's capabilities, they themselves seem to have some kind of superhuman power. Freiman was up against the same self-satisfied upper crust of Christian-born Anglo-Saxons who stalled and denied the efforts of the Jewish MPs Heaps and Jacobs. Was it the force of her personality that got agreements out of these men? Was it her early activism in support of the welfare of veterans, of flu victims, of "incurables" at the Perley Hospital in Ottawa that made her somehow undeniable even when she came calling regarding Jews? Was it her unusual wedding of mainstream and Jewish causes? Access to ministers—for both Lillian and her husband—led to good relations, even companionship, letters of friendship, and condolences from both Liberal Prime Minister King and Conservative Prime Minister Bennett. When Freiman led a campaign for the United Palestine Appeal in 1934, she brought Bennett on board for a radio speech that inaugurated the fundraising program. "All Canada is interested" in this appeal, he told his listeners. This opportunity to communicate directly with Canada's Jews might have led to other efforts—both in English and in *idishe iberzetsung* (Yiddish translation); how many other prime ministers have been so *ibergezetst*?—that Bennett sent to a Winnipeg Yiddish newspaper in 1934 at the Jewish New Year. One wonders who wrote his New Year's message to "all Canadians of Jewish ancestry," with its acknowledgement of their "patriotism" and their contribution to the "learning, the arts and the literature of mankind." Bennett's message ran in direct opposition to the denigrating myths that circulated among government representatives regarding Jews, asserting instead that Jews arrived in the Dominion early, "as throughout the British Empire," and that they "have engaged in all professions and pursuits" (not just peddling fraudulent pharmaceuticals alongside Italians). Yet the prime minister acknowledged that "the daily press continues to remind us we are still living in a troubled world," that world, of course, being one in which *flichtlingen* found little chance of safe haven in Bennett's Canada.[14]

Blair—the *bête noire* of any story of 1930s and 1940s Jewish immigration to Canada—gave Freiman no effective backtalk. In a letter from the later 1930s, when Blair had taken up the role of director of the Immigration Branch within the Department of Mines and Resources, we find him responding by letter to a morning telephone call to Mrs. Freiman. Her call was regarding a Jewish couple seeking entry to Canada from Italy (this, unlike my grandfather's story, was deep inside the "none is too many" period). Blair expressed agreement with a guarantee of $25,000 to be brought by the couple; if "they are in good health," he would "recommend" their admission. Abella and Troper's book, *None Is Too Many*, is full of narratives in which Jewish families guaranteeing the transfer of larger sums of money are blown off summarily. Blair noted that the Immigration Branch had "no previous approach from any person concerning this couple," as if to suggest that he was happy that the present deal could be made directly between him and Freiman via a private backroom handshake. Then he went one step further, telling her to have the couple get in touch with the commissioner of migration in London, who "will authorize immediate sailing under non-immigrant status," with the plan to "secure the authority later for permanent admission." What more could he have done? He signed off with "yours very truly," and either he or his typist had learned to spell Freiman's name correctly.[15]

The unique aspect of Freiman's undertakings was its ecumenical character—what we would recognize today as a cross-cultural impetus. Accomplishments in this regard included being president of the Dominion's Hadassah organization; president of the Ottawa Girl Guides Foundation; vice-president of the Ottawa Branch of the Canadian National Institute for the Blind; president of the Ladies Auxiliary of the Perley Home for Incurables in Ottawa; founder of the Canadian Legion; and originator of the British poppy movement in Canada in support of veterans, which led to the first commemorative poppies. These accomplishments have a ladylike ring, being the duties that a good-hearted socialite might choose. But many of her undertakings were more rough and ready. When the flu epidemic of 1918 needed a coordinator in Ottawa to respond to the crisis, Freiman camped out at a city office where she managed the job. Upon awarding her in 1934 the Order of the British Empire—the medal from George V that the farmer near Hirsch had heard about—the King commended her for her work "on behalf of ex-servicemen as well as his Jewish subjects throughout Canada."[16]

Freiman's activities were so well known in her day that her home on Ottawa's downtown Somerset Street was deluged by way of mail and telegram with mountains of begging letters. Freiman shared this experience with Prime Minister Bennett. His begging letters came from all over Canada, with a heavy accent on the Prairies, whereas Freiman was best known to those who sought help in central Canada.

The prime minister had two secretaries opening his mail. Freiman had one. "Dear Sir," wrote Charles Grierson of Winnipeg to Bennett in January 1934, "I have been unemployed for nearly four years."[17] In the early 1930s, this was often the undercurrent of Bennett's correspondence with Canadians. On February 22, 1932, a Vancouver Islander wrote the following:

Dear Sir

before we are much older there is going to be trouble in Nanaimo & Cumberland owing to the foreigners having jobs while the men & boys who are borne British subject & who rightfully belong to these jobs have to go without jobs....[18]

In October 1933 from Saskatchewan:

Dear Sir, — I am a girl thirteen years old and I have to go to school every day its very cold now already and I haven't got a coat to put on. My parents can't afford to buy me anything for this winter....

My name is

Edwina Abbott

In reply, Bennett sent five dollars.[19] At times, when he sent money, the recipient wrote back with thanks, as did Dorothy Franklin in 1935:

> I got each boy a suit of clothes and a hat for the money you sent and if you could have seen the expression of mingled pleasure and pride which overcame their faces when they got ready for Sunday School yesterday you would have been glad it was in your power to give such joy to a couple of boys.[20]

Like Bennett—a rich man sitting in the most powerful office in the country—Freiman, often called the first lady of Canadian Jews, stood out as a figure of access and hope. The letters that she received, at least those that have been gathered in files at the Ottawa Jewish Archives, are both handwritten and typed. They are at times businesslike and at other times desperate. They are a kind of archive of human woe and hope in a period when Canadian and international events seemed to bring calamity upon calamity and authorities were of little help. In January 1934, from Montreal's early Jewish quarter on Papineau Avenue, a lengthy letter, finely handwritten, described a family's inability to send money home to destitute relatives in Romania. "For twenty-five years," the writer explains, "our family has been in the habit of sending 'home' regular sums of money in aid of our relatives there (aged uncle, motherless children—all the usual relatives one aids)." But the family itself on Papineau was now "in dire circumstances" because of unemployment. "Would you not, Mrs. Freiman," the writer asks, "send direct to 'Meir Lofar, Burdujiani, Roumania,' $25.00, considering this a loan to me, repayable as soon as possible?" In May 1934, Rabbi S. Levin of Hamilton (Harav Shmuel Halevi Levin on his Yiddish letterhead) asked for Freiman's help in preventing the deportation of Rabbi Solomon Kaplan. This, he writes, was his second letter on this matter to Freiman. "As his time for remaining in Canada is getting short," the rabbi adds, "please reply with what information you can get on the said matter, as soon as possible." The rabbi's letter is dated May 15, 1934. Two days later Freiman sent a note much like the one that she sent to my grandfather, short and to the point:

My Dear Rabbi:
    I have your letter
of the 15th instant relative to
Rabbi Solomon Kaplan and in this
connection I wish to inform you
that I am looking after the case
and will do all that I can.[21]

Letters in this vein appeared with regularity. In September 1934, from Markham Street near Toronto's Kensington Market, Sarah Lasowsky wrote at length, acknowledging her understanding that "immigration has been abolished" but wondered whether Freiman could help to "secure a permit" for her brother back in the old country. The writer signed off with thanks for "all your past favors," adding that Freiman was her "only hope." For many of these letters, we lack responses, and without great effort (a book for each like this one) it's impossible to know each letter's outcome. Once in a while a result, or at least the sign of a likely one, shows itself. This is reflected in a letter with the signature of A.L. Jolliffe, dated January 18, 1935, the very week that he sent Paull his epic rejection regarding my grandfather. Freiman phoned Jolliffe about the application of "Mr. Max Steinkopf of Winnipeg, for the admission to Canada of his brother-in-law, Mr. Ernest Mayer, wife and two children." Jolliffe wrote back, and here a pattern emerges, for a phone call from Freiman led to a letter to her from the department. Jolliffe asks whether the family possesses a "valid passport" and "what financial resources Mr. Mayer possesses, exactly how much money, if any, he would be bringing to Canada," as well as his intended occupation. "With this information," Jolliffe would be "glad to give the case further consideration and to let you know without delay the final decision."[22] The tone and absence of the usual runaround echoed Blair's in the case of the couple from Italy.

How did it go after this? Well, we can guess. These things went on throughout this period. Jews did enter the country even though overall the immigration policies and regulations were designed to keep them out. How strange. A kind of quiet traffic in Jews, with Freiman directing a portion of it from her desk at 149 Somerset Street, beneath a big oil portrait, a chunky sculpture beside her, by the light of a lamp hung with a Victorian-era fringe. In the years before her early death in 1940, the combination of ill health and overwork led her husband to write to S.W. Jacobs to ask that he "discontinue sending Mrs. Freiman any more immigration cases. As it stands, life isn't worth living—my office and my home have been turned into immigration offices," a state of affairs that he thought was "practically killing Mrs. Freiman."[23]

Outside their home, Somerset was a perfectly preserved Victorian streetscape. Modern urban change had yet to come to its big lawns shadowed by mature trees, their branches above the roadway. Amid this staid setting of Canadian wealth and status, Lillian Freiman directed traffic.

GOING TO
THE ARCHIVES

A lot of the work teasing out my grandfather's story is done, alas, while sitting on my ass. But sometimes I have to get out in the world too. I nose my way into the Officers' Mess even though it is dubbed private, or hunt about in archives for traces, spoor, the past's imprint, which lays there, so ready at hand that I often feel tempted to steal a piece of the past and take it home with me. My hoped-for discoveries in the capital focused on a number of things that I'd not yet seen: a third immigration department file associated with my grandfather, a part of the overall departmental materials kept on microfilm at Library and Archives Canada; a substantial Freiman Family Fonds, as they call archival collections, there; and the Ottawa Jewish Archives with its own collection dedicated to Lillian Freiman. That's where the trove of begging letters is filed, neatly set aside by her secretary. As I moved through the folder full of them, arranged by date from early to late, I approached the early months of 1935, where I assumed that my grandfather's written plea would sit. But no such luck. For whatever trivial reason, his letter was not preserved. Perhaps it would offer nothing that we don't know already from other letters that my grandfather sent. But the absence sent me back to my long-standing impression that his doings had somehow been lost, erased, mysteriously made unfindable in the archives and other accounts of the period of his activity.

Writing directly to Freiman fit within the frame of my grandfather's try-anything approach but with the sensible notion—after having written to all available players locally and farther afield—that she was a Canadian Jew with real access to power and with her own powers of influence. How much of this relevant background my grandfather understood is an open question. One can view his letter to her as an act of desperation at a point well into his efforts when not much seemed to be working. At the house on Somerset Street, in late winter, I imagine her opening his letter. She might have sat to read it in the winter garden on the house's hip. Or it might have been on a seat by the bay window where I found myself years later. Along with my grandfather's letter, she would have been presented with a photo of the three faces from Mława. Here was the rabbi of Hirsch writing to the great lady of the capital, whose many undertakings and deteriorating health easily could have kept her from responding to his plea.

It was late in 1934 that he wrote to his two heavy hitters, Bennett and Freiman. It was around this time, in early February 1935, that Turnbull wrote to Gray on his parliamentary letterhead: "Before and since the receipt of your letter of November 30th, I have been trying to see what could be done to obtain the entry into Canada of the family of 'J. Eisenstein.'" At the same time, Turnbull noted that he was "*in receipt of another letter from the Rabbi himself which I am passing on to the Department to see if they know of any way in which the Rabbi's request can be granted.*"[1] I italicize these lines because they deserve to stand out. They set the scene that my grandfather was setting: turn from your desk where one letter lay and another one came winging into view.

On it went. No matter how many barriers he met, no matter what form of bureaucratic insult and denial he put up with, no matter how far-flung his existence down by the American border in southeastern Saskatchewan, he pursued further channels. And lo and behold, these efforts paid off. Well-meaning elected representatives and professionals followed through and made their own efforts to bypass the naysayers, the rubber stamp wielders. The lesson to be learned from my grandfather's approach is do not cease in your efforts if you wish to arrive at the goal that you have set.

In a letter to Paull in Montreal in February 1935, my grandfather followed up on these events. He wrote that "two months ago" he "made a great appeal to Prime Minister Bennett. Yesterday, I received a reply from his office, saying that he was taking my letter into consideration and that my letter had been forwarded to his colleague, Mr. Gordon for consideration." It was around this time, too, that he informed Paull that "Mrs. Freiman promised me that she would work for me and my case," adding, correctly, as if Paull did not know, that she "has great influence in government circles." A few weeks later he reiterated that Freiman "promised me two months ago that she would help me with my case. Since that time I have not received a reply from her to my correspondence. So, I plead with you to please see Mrs. Freiman in Ottawa." The lone piece of documentary proof regarding the lost correspondence with Freiman is the note from Somerset Street, dated January 21, 1935. The original is in the immigration file for my grandfather, as if at some point he forwarded it to Paull in Montreal as a motivator, as proof of the worth of their ongoing efforts. There it was in plain language from the great lady: "Dear Rabbi Eisenstein—. . . I have now taken steps . . . at the Department of Immigration and I hope they will be able to do something for you."[2] How many times must my grandfather have read and reread these words? Maybe, in the style of a climactic Broadway scene, he roared them out the doorway of his Hirsch home at the empty prairie sky, at the Canadian wilds, and at all of the forces of the country's bureaucratic and ideological apparatus that had been aimed at him like a military onslaught bearing the message of the times: No. The Great Canadian No of the early 1930s. Not for him, though, the Reverend Eisenstein of Hirsch. He was not capable of hearing it.

The vehement no offered by Jolliffe in his letters, short and long, was the bureaucratic last gasp, an effort on the bureaucratic side to head off doings on the ministerial side. "There would appear to be some misunderstanding," Jolliffe told Paull, regarding the "application of Rabbi Eisenstein of Hirsch, Saskatchewan, for the admission to Canada of his wife and children."[3] Jolliffe rehearsed the lying behaviour of the rabbi and his brother, bringing the "Examining Officer at Danzig" into the picture, *for he, too, was lied to! That good man, who must slave away in the Polish emigrants' encampment, guarding the gates against the "Continental" European immigrant wave.* A "firm stand" was what the Department of Immigration applied in such cases. But a bureaucrat is only as powerful as his last letter, and even with regard to little people like my grandfather the wheels of government can turn unpredictably.

The letters tell the tale. Sometime between the end of January and the middle of February 1935 someone walked into the office of Jolliffe and told him what to do. That led to a succinct letter to Paull just two weeks after the rejection seemingly had been finalized. The JIAS people had been writing and visiting, and Jolliffe had to "advise" Paull that "recently upon representations received through the office of the Right Honourable the Prime Minister the case has again been made the subject of a thorough and careful review."[4] This, however sketchily presented, brings all of the players into one room, a kind of game show scenario that we might call "Who Gets the Last Word?" The Office of the Right Honourable Prime Minister; as my grandfather said, he'd written to Bennett and been told that his case was being considered. Turnbull suggested as much. Lynd, as we know, was active in his lawyerly network. And though Freiman had a few other fish to fry in these darkening times, most often she was as good as her word when she told a correspondent that she has "now taken steps . . . at the Department of Immigration." What she did most often was mop the floor with whoever was on the other end of the phone line or across the desk. I can feel it in my gut as I write; can you? A change was afoot.

Still, the bureaucratic dam held, and Jolliffe, having raised the reconsideration, threw down one of the great bureaucratic words— *however*—and reconfirmed in a letter on February 14, 1935, that the department was "unable to vary its former decision and in consequence it cannot facilitate the entry to Canada of Mrs. Eisenstein and her two children."[5] At least the wife of the rabbi was no longer dismissed as "alleged."

Strange and compelling. The ins and outs are lost to us. At different stages, consideration was offered by the prime minister, the minister of immigration and colonization, Freiman in Ottawa, Paull in Montreal and on visits to Ottawa, Gray in Winnipeg, Turnbull and even Anderson in Saskatchewan. Against all of this was Jolliffe with his two hands up against the door, dropping a final "however" from the corner of his thin lips. We sent that ship full of Asiatics back to India, he might have thought, watched it fade in the harbour light, but the "Rabbi of Hirsch" we cannot stop?

The letters in my grandfather's immigration file are a puzzle with key pieces missing. Everything there starts to shift in early 1935, and the view varies depending on who is writing. "I spent two days in Ottawa last week," Paull wrote to my grandfather in mid-February, without revealing the full picture, "and again discussed your case with the department. As your application needs an Order in Council it was referred to the Minister who will render his decision shortly. I expect favourable action." But it was a dance of contradictory possibilities. On the 14th, Jolliffe, writing to Paull, dismissed all hope, regardless of recent representations "received through the office of the Right Honourable the Prime Minister." My grandfather's own letters, having nothing to hide, reveal a more complex backstory. On February 8, he said to Paull that he had received in reply to his letter to the prime minister a guarantee that it had been forwarded for "Mr. Gordon's consideration." It's worth wondering who composed my grandfather's letter to Bennett. Lynd? A farmer with a literary touch? We don't know since these things are not in the JIAS files and not found in the immigration files at Library and Archives Canada. In a letter to Paull in March, my grandfather sets out his own timeline for the shifting status of his reception in Ottawa. On March 20, he says, he received a telegram from Freiman informing him that she "had obtained the permit" for his family. She had, he reports, "personal interviews with Minister Gordon and Prime Minister Bennett regarding my case," during which the family photo had gained him sympathy.[6] The 20th was a notable date for her to send a telegram, being one day after an order-in-council was signed in Ottawa authorizing the permit that my grandfather had sought for so long.

❁ ❁ ❁

Library and Archives Canada in Ottawa is way down Wellington Street, past the Parliament buildings, past the Bank of Canada, past the Supreme Court on its oddly featureless lawn. The archives are housed in a big white boxy building built in the 1960s. Its entrance hall is all white marble and gold accents—modern luxe. The reference room and document-viewing rooms one floor up have an unimpeded view of the Ottawa River. Across the water is Hull, Quebec. As one works, the view is of the country's greatest divide. Having ordered everything that I wanted to see in advance via the LAC website, boxes arrive, ready to be opened, on a grey rolling truck of the kind that a children's librarian might use to reshelve DVDs. And there you are. Answers or not-answers. Discoveries or the great drudgery of sifting through irrelevant stuff. The day that I visit there are nine researchers in a room the size of

a gymnasium, with the ceiling high enough to put on a circus performance. They sit at some remove from each other, hold their weathered
sheets, and gaze into storage boxes.

I have ordered both paper files and microfilm. The Freiman materials are made up of actual artifacts. The Department of Immigration
files are all on microfilm. And the orders-in-council from the first
months of 1935 are gathered in manila files in slim banker boxes. At
this point, we should return to a crucial question: what is an order-in-
council? In our family lore, it operated as a kind of holy grail, though
I don't believe that any one of us could have said what it actually was.
It was something that ordered lives to be saved. There was the mystery, of course, of human events, wilful effort, luck, and happenstance
that allowed it to happen. In the 1930s, a lot of governing in Canada
was done by way of orders-in-council. Once each order was passed,
it was formalized as a "Report of a Committee of the Privy Council
ON MATTERS OF STATE." And then it was the law of the land.

I begin with the box marked "Orders-in-Council 12 March 1935—
29 March 1935" because I know from letters by my grandfather that it
would include the week in which he received news that his permits
were assured.[7] But he never would have understood the order-in-council himself unless Lynd took the time to instruct him on its character.
And it remained a much-mentioned mystery in our family until I set
out to discover its life-saving power.

Each order itself—at least as it appeared in the middle 1930s—is a
work of artful presentation, typewritten on a paper of foolscap length,
heavy enough to be vellum; decorated with the country's coat of arms
in red; a blue ribbon tied in a bow binding it at the top left-hand corner. This must be a leftover of the old customs associated with candle
wax, tassels, and thread that decorated official documents of ancient
regimes. Each order-in-council is covered by a letter titled "GOVER-
NOR GENERAL AND COMMANDER IN CHIEF OF THE DOMINION
OF CANADA" because, even though the men who came together to
decide the day's accounting and business were cabinet members of the
national government, the governor general, the king's representative,
was given final signing responsibility. On the order-in-council from
March 18, 1935, just preceding the one that refers to my grandfather,
this is the case. The governor general at the time was a posh Brit
named Vere Ponsonby, 9th Earl of Bessborough. His oversight of the
Privy Council on March 18 was assured by his mark: "Bessborough."

For whatever reason, on the order-in-council enacted March 19, the one that we are most interested in, it is the deputy governor general's upward-slanting signature that stands for the king's pleasure at the doings of the Privy Council that day. The deputy's signature is stupendously illegible. Duff? Ouff? O'duoff?

The idea of an order-in-council as a kind of holy grail is given an added flourish by the archaic way that the governor general is designated at the head of the document: "Captain the Right Honourable the Earl of Bessborough, a Member of His Majesty's Most Honourable Privy Council, Knight Grand Cross of the Most Distinguished Order of Saint Michael and Saint George . . . may it please Your Excellency." The committee that gathered to discuss the orders-in-council brought forward was made up of the governing cabinet, MPs under the chairmanship of one of their peers.

In March 1935, the Privy Council issued orders—each one a detailed and thus dense document with a variety of concerns—acknowledged by the governor general and his deputy on March 12, 14, 15, 18, 19, 21, 22, 25, 26, and 29. That was a lot of orders. What were they up to when they weren't okaying the entry of Jews? Some of it was trivial. In one case, it was the sale of chicks in Nova Scotia. Agricultural policy. The RCMP in Saskatchewan—Ituna, Yorkton, Kamsack, and North Battleford—were okayed for new "motor transport," mostly Ford V8s, with the odd Chev thrown in for variety. One order delved into the Canadian government's rental of machines for postal cancellation from the United States. More vehicles for the RCMP in Winnipeg. What was up with all this vehicle buying? Had the RCMP been walking and horseriding prior to 1935? V8s. Big tough cars.

But there were also weighty things to discuss. In the order for March 12, the relief necessary for unemployed ex-servicemen was on the council table, with the men in need divided into categories including the "Disabled non-pensioner" and the "old and Totally Disabled." The Privy Council, apparently, was also the final arbiter of death penalty sentences. On March 26, the council members, one hopes, came prepared to discuss the transcript of the trial of the accused, Joseph Alisero, "28 years of age, unmarried and . . . living with his parents, reputed to be respectable people." A Quebec court had sentenced him to death by hanging for the murder of "Graziella Viens, 28 years of age, . . . a divorcee and a woman of rather loose morals." She was found "in the rumble seat of a coupe belonging to the accused . . . covered with blood." No interference in the sentence of death was the council's decision. In the Internet age, one need only type the name Alisero into Google to confirm that he was indeed hanged at the Bordeaux jail on May 3, 1935, after his resourceful lawyer went above the heads of the Privy Council and tried an appeal to George V.[8] Then there were matters presented without enough background detail for us to understand how a decision was made. Why, we might wonder, did the Chiefs of the Bella Bella Band of Vancouver Island "surrender" the "merchantable timber on the Echo Reserve No. 6" in return for "50% of the sale" value of the trees? Some deeper history of the trading away of reserve resources must be told, but it would take another researcher to tease this out.

Permits for would-be immigrants were on the table, too, in orders that preceded my grandfather's. On March 18, twenty-four waivees were added to a list to be brought before the Privy Council. Among them were Jews. Reading the list for that day's order-in-council, one would have to admit that "none is too many," even at mid-decade when it had become particularly difficult for Jews to enter Canada, does not properly describe the state of affairs. It's true, counting by ones and twos, even by fives and tens, considering each case's drawn-out backstory on its way to success, does not create an upbeat picture, but, still, here are the facts. On the list, dated March 9, is Annie Devorah Shteren, who would "come forward" to be a Hebrew teacher in Canada. She was a "citizen of Poland, aged 25 years, presently residing at Vilno." Symcha Binem Lipshitz was "a citizen of Poland," twenty-one years old, and would work as a "Hebrew teacher and assistant Rabbi." Some declared the "intended occupation" of "merchant," which could not have been further from the government's desired agricultural and domestic work-ers. One can always discern non-Jewish Poles from Polish Jews since the latter are referred to as citizens "of Poland of Hebrew race." In the case of Shteren, it was A.J. Paull at the JIAS who pursued the permit application. The 350 pupils at the Montreal Peretz School would have a new Kindergarten teacher. Paull argued that "there are no qualified Hebrew teachers available in Canada or the United States." This surely was not the case, but Shteren would fill the gap and save herself from the oncoming European disaster. Paull apparently "submitted" another on the day's list, Julia Obler Sauberman, a sixty-seven-year-old widow who would join her daughter and her husband in Montreal. To assure the department that this proposed immigrant "will not be permitted to become a public charge in Canada," a cash deposit of $300 was "placed with the Department." (It's worth noting that these were not people related to the 100; rather, they were a group with different kinds of immigration stories.)

Applicants' supporters offered receipts to prove that they regularly forwarded funds to their families in Europe; they stated their annual earnings; they made claims regarding cash on hand and bank deposits. In one case, a "cash deposit" of $300 was placed with the department as a guarantee that a proposed immigrant wouldn't become a "public charge." This concern hovered over application after application. Members of Parliament often put their names on applications, highlighting the importance in the early 1930s of gaining the ear of one's M P. An Italian-born coal miner, Innocente Basso, who wanted to bring over his daughter, was supported in his claim by the "Hon. H.H. Stevens, M.P."

To get the full sense of the complement of twenty-four approved on March 18, 1935, one should not assume that they were all refugees caught up in the oncoming global disaster. Among them was Jean Bosser, a "beauty specialist" from France, expected to be an employee of the T. Eaton Company. In a previous order-in-council, Eaton's need for hairdressing skills had led to the admission of Jean Semard. But that Jean was now unable to come to Canada. In support of Bosser as Semard's replacement, Eaton's supplied its business plan, a new "Style Shop" in its Toronto store, which required "specially trained men" of a kind "absolutely impossible to procure . . . in Canada." No recommender of this plan was cited—no lawyer, MP, or immigration organization representative. It was as if Eaton's business plan simply recommended itself.

As is the case elsewhere in this narrative, one must look carefully to sense the hand of Wesley Ashton Gordon, at the time acting minister of immigration and colonization, in these undertakings. But covering the list of those "coming forward" is a telling prefatory paragraph, which, in the case of the order approved the day before my grandfather's, reveals that one of the key reasons for meeting was the recommendation of Gordon.

This order-in-council asserted its right to "waive" the determinations of an earlier order in which strict immigration regulations were brought into effect. This reflected an ability—understood to exist by those in the know—of the minister to "issue a permit in writing to authorize a person to enter Canada without being subject to the

The Committee of the Privy Council, on the
recommendation of the Acting Minister of Immigration
and Colonization, advise that the provisions of
Order in Council P.C. 695 dated the 21st day of
March, 1931, prohibiting the landing in Canada of
immigrants of all classes and occupations, with
certain exceptions, be waived in the cases of the
immigrants (twenty-four in number) named on the
attached list dated March 9th, 1935.

provisions" of the Immigration Act, without interfering with the status of those provisions. Georges Pelletier, editor of the Montreal-based *Le Devoir*, criticized this very activity in an editorial in late 1929, promoting the popular notion in French-speaking Quebec that this capability would contribute to large-scale Jewish immigration to the province.[9]

❀ ❀ ❀

To arrive at the order-in-council addressing my grandfather's case, I run through the full month of March 1935 until I hit one that includes

my grandmother, "Chaje Dine Eisenstein" (a new effort at transliteration, more or less correct), and the children, "Berek and Hene," ages
five and six. They appear as part of another list of twenty-four coming
forward, as if this has been decided on as a group of manageable or
presentable size. The Privy Council had to deal with chicks and Ford
V8s, and then the "recommendation of the Acting Minister of Immigration and Colonization," Gordon, who advised—and, based upon
the previous order list prepared for March 9, we know that Gordon
was "advising" in this way on a somewhat regular basis—that the Privy
Council waive "the provisions of Order in Council P.C. 695 dated the
21st day of March, 1931, prohibiting the landing in Canada of immigrants of all classes and occupations, with certain exceptions."

A great deal is revealed by this repeated "waiving," to use the Privy
Council's term. Order-in-Council PC 695 of four years earlier was
the work of the Bennett government, overseen by Minister Gordon,
which implemented "the tightest immigration admissions policy in
Canadian history."[10] It capped the trend that had begun under the
Liberals in the 1920s limiting newcomers to subjects with means from
the United Kingdom and United States, agriculturalists with means,
and wives and children of Canadian residents. It was this immigration
order-in-council—routinely waived in the council chamber, as we've
seen—that would allow the Liberal government under King to deny
entry to the refugee passengers of the *St. Louis* in 1939. But behind this
"closed door" policy lay the demonstrably strange but working system
by which a wide variety of immigrants continued to attain permits.

These orders-in-council of the troubled mid-1930s addressed everyday business—the chicks and the Fords; even the doomed murderer,
for in what way, really, was he the business of the Privy Council?—and
then in inadvertent ways they responded to and reflected much more
serious national undertakings. With respect to waiving immigration
regulations, they signalled a covert way of contravening the government's stated brutal entrance regime, whose de facto outcome was the
continued refusal to undertake any open responsibility for the plight of
Jews fleeing the refugee crisis touched off by German anti-Jewish policies. Jews from Poland, Czechoslovakia, Austria, and Romania were
unlikely to enter Canada without the special attention of the Privy
Council, which alone had the power to "waive" regulations. And that is
what the Privy Council gathered to do in March 1935.

❁ ❁ ❁

The list of twenty-four up for approval on March 19—the day that my grandmother and her two children were waived—is a smorgasbord of cultures and characters, of old and young, of male and female. There are Dutch, Czechoslovaks, Jugo-Slavs, Romanians, Maltese, Italians, and Poles. Some are coming forward to join children, siblings, and grandparents. There are toddlers such as twenty-month-old John Neusatz with his nineteen-year-old mother, who will join her husband in Canada. The intended occupations of the men coming forward include draughtsman and carpenter, whereas the women will be housewives or domestic helpers. Those given permits are accounted for in the order on two separate lists, each describing the proposed immigrants' cases. The first list is a summary of each case and fits on two pages. It is followed by a more detailed narrative for each person or family coming forward. These parts of the order-in-council have their own artifactual character: they are no less fascinating to hold, to study in the light, than a shard of pottery dug out from a midden or an outmoded tool washed out of a badlands hillside by spring rains. Their handmade character is in the heavy paper, the typist's underlining, the absence of typos, as if there is something grave about these lists, in which no errors can be seen to creep.

This is the short entry for the three Eisensteins, oversigned by the council's chair of the day.

```
11.     Chaje Dine Eisenstein, aged 30 years, and two children —
        Berek and Hene Eisenstein, aged 6 and 5 years,
        respectively, citizens of Poland, presently residing
        at Radzanow, nad Wksz, Starosto Mlawa Z. Warszawska,
        Poland; coming forward to join husband and father,
        respectively.
```

It is in the more substantive description later in the order that, in cases including my grandfather's, a novelistic narrative takes shape. One learns, among the other details, which recommender made an argument forceful enough for the minister to add names to the list of the saved. Just under the name of my grandmother, we find Josiel Lejzerowicz of

Poland, thirty-one years old, a carpenter by trade. His permit application was supplied by "Miss Pearl Berman, of Montreal," who would marry him and "assist him in becoming properly established in this country." She agreed to place a "bond" with the department "as a guarantee that she will marry the proposed immigrant within thirty days after his arrival," and, in a proposition often seen in these documents, she promised that "immediately on her marriage she will discontinue" her "outside employment" as an "operator on cloaks." Merit befell the married woman who defaulted to housework. Ottawa barrister Samuel Lepofsky promoted this permit recommendation (his name appeared in other cases, suggesting a busy immigration legal office).

The account of my grandfather's application is told in much greater detail than those of companion cases. Let's say that it is the most novelistic and that its main author, Rabbi Eisenstein of Hirsch, and his many collaborators and networks and correspondents, assert the most substantial storyline. Maybe I see it this way because I have studied it so carefully, but I think that's not the reason. Of the stories brought forward on March 19 to the big boys of the Privy Council, chaired by the Right Honourable Sir George Perley, MP for Argenteuil, Quebec, it's the weightiest, the most *zaftig*, to use a word that my grandfather liked. Fulsome.

Here it is.

11.   Chaje Dine Eisenstein, aged 30 years, and two children - Berek and Hene Eisenstein, aged 6 and 5 years, respectively - These proposed immigrants are citizens and residents of Poland of Hebrew race who are desirous of coming forward to join husband and father, Rabbi J. Eisenstein, of Hirsch, Sask. The last named, who is 33 years of age, was admitted to Canada from Poland in November, 1930, as a single man destined to a brother in Vancouver; he was, however, married at the time and thus his entry was obtained by misrepresentation. He has for some time been endeavouring to arrange to have his wife and children join him in Canada but, in view of the circumstances under which he secured admission, these members of his family are not admissible under the regulations. It is stated that Mr. Eisenstein has been engaged as a Rabbi since his arrival in Canada, now being stationed at Hirsch, and that he is in a position to receive and provide for his family to whom he has been forwarding funds for maintenance since coming to this country. Representations have been submitted in support of his application for the entry of his wife and children on various occasions through a number of sources, including the Hon. W.R.Motherwell, who took the case up in July, 1932, and again in 1933; the Hon. J.T.M.Anderson of Saskatchewan; Mr. Robert McKenzie,M.P., and the Jewish Immigrant Aid Society of Canada, Montreal; Mr. F.W. Turnbull, M.P., is also interested in the case and has recently submitted additional representations in support of the same.

It would be interesting to know who composed this version of my grandfather's odyssey in striving for the acceptance of his Polish family by the Canadian government. Immigration documents don't reveal the mid-level strivers, the names in the typing pool, the roundabout way that this documentation was set down for the Privy Council. All of the sass and high-hat attitude has been ironed out of the final account. The angry and defiant commissioners are forgotten. The "Rabbi" of Hirsch "has for some time been endeavouring. . . ." Well, yes, you could say that and then some. His misrepresentation of himself is reiterated. Why hide it? If the order-in-council can "waive" government regulations made by two governments over the previous decade, then the rabbi's acknowledged flouting of the system is not going to provide a roadblock. Flouting regulations is one of the purposes of the order-in-council. But one wonders, too, if this isn't a kind of coded presentation, like a bid in bridge that signals to a partner what's in the hand that can't be shown; by allowing that "Rabbi J. Eisenstein" is one of the 100, there might be a sign to those in the know that some kind of shift is taking place on that front.

My grandfather's good work and status as a small-town salaried functionary on the prairie with money sent back to his family in Poland spoke in his favour. But then witness the slew—you'd have to call it a slew—of supporters and recommenders. Alongside the unflinching JIAS people were politicians along the political spectrum: W.R. Motherwell, with his farming theories; J.T.M. Anderson, who taught at Hirsch as a young man (and now the premier of his province); Robert McKenzie, another transplanted Ontarian, a Liberal, elected in my grandfather's Assiniboia riding. To top things off, the Regina Conservative member of Parliament F.W. Turnbull was "interested" and "recently submitted additional representation." It was a lively group of Liberals, Conservatives, provincial and federal representatives, and immigration officials, with background efforts by a well-connected Estevan lawyer and Conservative bagman. Among the unmentioned but likely important aspects of all this was the influence of Lillian Freiman. Her background activity wasn't suitable, of course, to gain mention in an order-in-council. And this might account for why Freiman is less recognized today than she should be. Her efforts ran under or around traditional lines of influence, though the immigration people did leave a record of her influence in their correspondence regarding actions that they would take once "having spoken with Mrs. Freiman."

The impressive number of my grandfather's Saskatchewan-based supporters is also worth noting. In his letters, my grandfather mentions visits to Regina to see these people, though we don't get proper descriptions of the visits. In an earlier and less hectic political era, perhaps these men were accessible in ways that politicians no longer are, and they might well have viewed my grandfather's story with some personal sympathy. His commitment to small-town prairie life might have impressed them. Perhaps they viewed him as the minder of a flock, however small, of Jewish voters. His perfectly respectable Depression-era salary of $100 a month might have impressed them too. The fact that he misrepresented himself to the federal government to enter Canada might not have surprised them, and the increasing bias against "such people" in Ottawa might not have gained the traction that it did in the federal government among Westerners who knew that their constituencies were made up of large groups of ethnic Europeans. The Ottawa ideal of an Anglo-Saxon mainstream already might have seemed like a pipe dream to men like Motherwell as he managed his own farm near the Qu'Appelle Valley. Saskatchewan was a patchwork of Central and Eastern European settlement, some of it in blocks and some of it scattered more precariously over the prairie. Rabbi Eisenstein of Hirsch was at home there.

The order-in-council's longer account of my grandfather's efforts, sealing their outcome, is revealing but naturally partial. It is accurate on certain fronts, obfuscating on others. Although it's true that my grandfather performed the duties of a rabbi, first at Dysart and then at the Hirsch colony, he was not one and had no official rabbinical certification. Calling him rabbi acknowledged him at a time when the government had decided that he deserved to be one. He had been sending money back to Poland, and the details of his status upon entering Canada were crushingly true. They proved to be central to his difficulties in bringing his family after him. But whoever scripted the summary paragraph stepped back from the language of illegality used by immigration commissioners such as Jolliffe and Smith in their letters to the JIAS. The arguments in favour of the three prospective new Canadians were offered with sympathy, at a point at which they were de facto successful.

❀ ❀ ❀

What does the order-in-council allow us to see of my family's counterparts—the other waivees—that day? In each case, the description of prospective immigrants includes their "current residence," the one detail in addition to name and age that gives their existence solid shape. The specificity of this information differs from case to case. In certain cases, it's just a country, Poland; in others, it's a city or town, Figlini, Vegliatruo, Italy. As with other aspects of my grandfather's file's description in the order, there's more than might truly be necessary: "Chaje Dine Eisenstein, aged 30 years, and two children—Berek and Hene Eisenstein, aged 6 and 5 years, respectively, citizens of Poland, presently residing at Radzanow, nad Wksz, Starosto Mlawa Z. Warszawska, Poland; coming forward to join husband and father, respectively." It wasn't the case, at least not in early 1935, that the Eisensteins interested in "coming forward" resided "at Radzanow, nad Wksz." This is the village where both my grandfather and his wife were born, where three of their four parents were born, and where their children were born. It was their original Polish home. The phrase "nad Wksz," properly spelled Wkra, designates the Radzanów on the Wkra River, in the district of Mława, northwest of Warsaw, which differentiates it from the other Radzanóws in Poland on different riverways. In fact, my grandfather's wife and children received news of visas to Canada in Mława, the much larger place down the country road an hour or so, where more than 6,000 Jews lived before the war in relative cosmopolitan calm. My grandmother and the children had gone there to live with her half-sister, known in the family by the Polish moniker Ciocia Mariam (Aunt Miriam). Her photo from 1936, when placed alongside the commonly used photos of Jews in the press and railway promotion, is notable for her Polishness.

The market basket, the shawl, her uncovered hair, and even the delicate shoes on what appears to be a rural pathway mark her identity by way of her locale and its influence. Anyone looking at the photo to caption it with the word *Jew* would falter. *Who have we got here?* the railway official would wonder. My grandmother's family in particular experienced the final years of their Polish century in middle-class comfort. Ciocia Mariam, with her successful Mława store, was representative. It was to her home that my grandmother and her children went to live during the last period of separation from her husband

far away in Canada. So the studio photo, said to have gone up the Canadian line of power to the prime minister, whether it was Gordon who came down the hall with it or Freiman, presents a family of good middle-class standing. European, yes, but not in any definable way Jewish. It would be impossible to know this about the three coming forward upon looking at the photograph: they look like nicely turned-out Europeans. But here the idea of determining what a Jew "looks like" at any given time or place reveals itself to be a hare-brained idea. I've never written that word before, but it applies here. If you think you know, reliably, what a Jew looks like then you're hare-brained.

❊ ❊ ❊

It's revealing to look at the others among the twenty-four approved by the order-in-council on March 19, 1935. Before I tell you about them, I must say that they put me in mind of Leona Helmsley. Remember her? Hers was the only palace where "The Queen Always Stands Guard." This is what the magazine ads trumpeted in support of the Manhattan Helmsley Hotels, part of her husband Harry's real estate realm in the big city. When it was discovered that "the Queen" did not like to pay taxes, and in fact hadn't paid any, she brushed this issue off with the ripe witticism that taxes were for "the little people."[11] Well, those twenty-four souls okayed for entry to Canada by the Privy Council were the true little people of 1935. Swept quietly, supra-legally, into Canada with the stroke of a pen and some neat typing, in the cosiness of the Privy Council chamber, with the willingness of sixteen MPs who agreed to follow the guidance of Wesley Ashton Gordon, the acting minister of immigration and colonization. This was happening with some regularity in the early 1930s, under R.B. Bennett's Conservatives, when Canadian immigration had clamped down fiercely on Europeans looking for an exit visa from their troubles. These were the ones who, like my grandfather, defied the idea of none. For them, none became one, two, three, sometimes more.

Not all among them, of course, were Jews, but they were from countries that Canada's immigration officers were steadfastly aiming to deny visa permits. A good number of those coming forward planned to live with family members who had been residents of the country for some time. Ksenia Wowk, eighteen years old, would "join sister and engage in domestic work." One wonders about the parents back in Poland—were they gone or simply unwilling to start over in a new country? Elizabet Smaga, of Roumania, was thirteen years old, and her aunt and uncle were "desirous of adopting her." An eleven-year-old, Maftej Paryniuk of Bukowina, Romania, would come "forward to reside with" his grandfather on his Manitoba farm. There were young women, travelling alone, whose "intended occupation" was "housewife." And one unusual family group: "Clement Polycarpe Calleya, aged 52 years; wife, Cornelia Calleya, and four children—Ada Clementina Calleya, Tris Antoinette Calleya, Yolanda Rosa Calleya and Anaclet William Calleya, aged 21, 19, 16 and 13 years, British subjects of Maltese race, presently residing in Smyrna Turkey; intended occupation of first named—draughtsman." Along with a Dutchman, Johan Oosterink, the Calleyas were the lucky holders of citizenship from a "Preferred" country, as singled out in early orders-in-council. Of the fourteen discrete groups of immigrants, some in pairs or larger family units, there were few Jews. It's true. There were the three Eisensteins and lucky Josiel Lejzerowicz, for whom "Miss Pearl Berman" agreed to stop making cloaks and to contribute $1,500 as a bond, guaranteeing her ability to undertake her "duties of housewife." The lawyer Lepofsky arranged for that fund to "remain in effect for a period of five years" to ensure that the Berman-Lejzerowicz household would remain intact. This was different from anything in play in my grandfather's case. These Jews agreed to invest $1,500 in Canada. If they missed the mark as an immigrant couple, then the national budget would be that much richer.

The portion of the orders-in-council overseen by Gordon is a story of little people. Almost all whom we encounter, apart from representatives of established Canadian authority and organizations, were among the vulnerable and the lucky. Emigrating from Europe to Canada in the 1920s and 1930s often meant that one travelled alone, disembarked alone, and took the train cross-country alone—if one wasn't about to stay put where the ports led into the big cities—till one met some familiar face, embraced, and began at that moment to construct a new life. There's a story to be found in these first tentative steps on Canadian ground that I haven't told in this book.

What of the first days out west spent by my grandfather? When he arrived in Vancouver, it flashed its Edwardian-era building boom. There were new bridges and an art deco office tower or two. The expectation was that the port would become increasingly important. But parades of out-of-work men would soon overtake the streets. Did his brother take him down to English Bay or to the view at Brockton Point in Stanley Park, when the First Narrows, between the park and West Vancouver, had not yet been linked by Lions Gate Bridge? Immigration was ever in the air, a subject of upset and disagreement. Shortly before my grandfather's arrival in late 1930, Immigration Commissioner A.E. Skinner made it into the papers by decreeing that the American "King of Jazz," Paul Whiteman, could bring his orchestra to town to play at a concert but not at dance parties. Taking an all-or-nothing approach, the orchestra left for Seattle without playing a note. The players were almost all white, though Whiteman sometimes included black musicians. It's not clear why Skinner, defying reason, fancied his port duties to include the realm of jazz performance, but he insisted that playing the foxtrot for dance parties was not properly "entertaining."[12] He succeeded A.L. Jolliffe as Vancouver's lone local commissioner of immigration, the latter having moved on to Ottawa, where he would eventually hear of Reverend Eisenstein. In my grandfather's first summer in Vancouver, there was a substantial fiasco under Skinner's watch as the RCMP investigated a long-standing underground market in permits, false birth certificates, and naturalization papers, organized by the Japanese interpreter at the Vancouver Immigration Branch office. That summer the RCMP busied themselves seeking the status of recently arrived Japanese Vancouverites.[13] Immigrants found to have entered Canada illegally were deported.

My grandfather's brother would have provided access to the Jewish community in Vancouver, and he helped my grandfather to undertake the ritual slaughterer's training, which enabled him to apply for the job on the Prairies. I don't know when a daily life led in Yiddish gave way to a more Canadian mix of English and Yiddish. My grandfather's project of a new life took shape over years that included his sojourn at Dysart, the move to Hirsch, all the while pursuing a future with his family left behind in Poland.

But even as his story is resolutely one of little people, I can't tell it without what I've been calling the big boys. Through them, we see Canada more broadly, from its top authority down. Anderson. Turnbull. Motherwell. McKenzie. Even Lynd. All players in 1930s Saskatchewan. Gordon in Ottawa. And the one lady among the gents, Freiman. They all vouched for the little guy—Rabbi J. Eisenstein, as they knew him—to the big boys of the Privy Council. How much could each of them have understood the full story that pointed back to Radzanów nad Wkra? Let's say that Freiman knew a newcomer from that part of Poland in an intimate way. She'd argued for and brought in people like my grandfather using her powers of management and sympathy. The rest had at least read at some point a letter or two or heard the case described to them in their offices by Paull on one of his permit-fishing visits to Ottawa.

The final circle, the prime minister's Privy Council, which okayed the arrival of my grandfather's family and their twenty-one compatriots, likely knew nothing of and possibly cared little for the would-be new Canadians on that March-morning agenda. The councillors sat in their high-backed leather armchairs, around a circular board table, beneath a gauchely elaborate electric bulb chandelier, and under photographic portraits of past grandees who stared down from the wallpapered walls, to sign off on the day's business. Who were they, these big boys of 1935 who acted like joint landlords willing to open the gate of their property just a crack? The chair of the Privy Council that day was Sir George Halsey Perley. An American come north, he'd been the director of the Bank of Ottawa. By coincidence, his family had been in business with the Pattees, who had built the house that the Freimans had bought on Somerset Street. Hugh Guthrie. He'd led Canada's delegation to the League of Nations. In 1935, he was the Conservative minister of justice. R.J. Manion was Bennett's minister of railways and canals. Arthur Sauvé was Bennett's postmaster. Charles H. Cahan was a journalist and lawyer, and once in politics he used his legal background to criticize the very thing that the Privy Council did: that is, apply its own legal prerogatives to diminish and evade parliamentary oversight and government acts as they were legislated. In 1935, Cahan was the secretary of state in Bennett's cabinet. D.M. Sutherland was the minister of national defence. Alfred Duranleau oversaw the Department of Fisheries. Maurice Dupré was Canada's solicitor general. Of course, there was W.A. Gordon, now made the acting minister of immigration and colonization. Many of these men would lose their seats when the Bennett government was defeated later in the year. But in the spring of 1935, they were the big boys, among others, in Bennett's Depression-era cabinet who sent word to His Excellency Vere Ponsonby, 9th Earl of Bessborough, that, on the advice of Acting Minister of Immigration and Colonization Gordon, Rabbi J. Eisenstein's application to bring Chaje Dine, Berek, and Hene

1139

TO HIS EXCELLENCY

Captain the Right Honourable the Earl of Bessborough, a
Member of His Majesty's Most Honourable Privy Council, Knight
Grand Cross of the Most Distinguished Order of Saint Michael and
Saint George,

GOVERNOR GENERAL AND COMMANDER IN CHIEF
OF THE DOMINION OF CANADA

Report, of a Committee of the Privy Council ON MATTERS
OF STATE.

PRESENT:

The   RIGHT HONOURABLE

SIR GEORGE H. PERLEY

THE HONOURABLE

HUGH GUTHRIE

E. N. RHODES

R. J. MANION

J. A. MACDONALD

ARTHUR SAUVE

H. A. STEWART

C. H. CAHAN

D. M. SUTHERLAND

A. DURANLEAU

T. G. MURPHY

M. DUPRE

W. A. GORDON

R. WEIR

R. C. MATTHEWS

R. B. HANSON

G. STIRLING

May it please Your Excellency

APPROVED
19 MARCH 1935

208

over from that mysterious place Radzanów nad Wkra had their assent. In the government's reckoning, the Privy Council members are listed as on the previous page.

The order-in-council triggered a letter to Paull from Jolliffe, indirectly conveying the news to my grandfather. This letter acknowledges that the immigration biases of mid-1930s Canada have been overruled by the prime minister's cabinet at the advice of the minister of

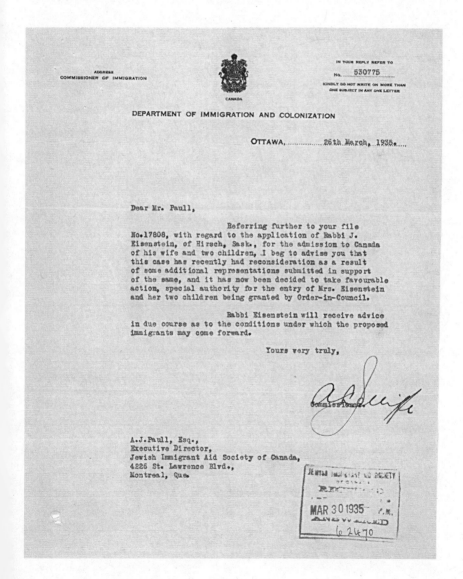

immigration. The likes of Jolliffe (with Blair in the wings) have been brushed aside, their excuses and diversions and feigned outrage at Jewish manipulation of the system diminished to nothing. If not for the years of care by archivists, whether in the Jewish community or in the government, all of this would have been lost. Not simply forgotten. Gone.

YOU COME FROM FAR AWAY:
THE DANZIG STORY

S ometimes, though it's rare, you think that you are reading something that might change your life or, even more, *change the order of things*. Something in the writer's voice, the contents, or the focus of a passage opens a door, clarifies, provides a new focus. To take such an experience out of context and set it down here might be bound to fail; describing the experience is never the same, of course, as having it. The timing of such reading and recognition might be key: why, in the middle of 2020, when Montreal was "locked down," did Norman Mailer's account of Lee Harvey Oswald's meandering months in Minsk seem to reveal *the heart of the matter*? And, more so, the great catalogue of Alice Munro stories buried in the archive of *The New Yorker* magazine. Each one—well, nearly every one—caused me to wonder how does the author manage to open this world, one that I have never encountered in time or place, in such minute and resonant detail? Are the transcendent scenes fully imagined? Did some aspect of what Munro describes happen so that she could tinker and shade and deepen the effect to convey whatever it is the reader recognizes as clarity, as the world clicking into focus?

I will risk here an example from Munro's work. The story, from a *New Yorker* in 1986, is called "The Moon in the Orange Street Skating

Rink." It is, like this book, a piece of deep and heartfelt recovery, in Munro's case a late-middle-age vantage point on youth, which for her characters was scruffy and failed, even grotesque. In the story is a trio—a girl with a penchant for dressing like a boy and two boys who are both drawn to and take advantage of the girl. The story's end returns to an earlier scene, already a scene of recognition among the three. For one character, their "moment of happiness remained in his mind, but he never knew what to make of it. Do such moments really mean that we have a life of happiness with which we only occasionally intersect?"[1]

My grandmother's "life of happiness" was lived entirely in Poland. The rich, loving, varied life among family, the parents who did not want to give her away, the devoted half-sister and her husband, the children thriving in their middle-class nest. And it was a nest. Often contemporary Jews, whose ancestry is Eastern European, wipe the slate clean by referring to all Jews who came to Canada in the early twentieth century as pauperized *flichtling*, to use my grandfather's carefully chosen word for German Jewish refugees from Nazi Germany. Not one of these Jews my grandmother. Her home, in Mława, up to her departure in the summer of 1935 for the ship to Canada, remained its cosmopolitan, suave self.

There is a remarkable archival visual record of Mława at this moment: the great darkness and depth of violence as yet unseen. The city was well served by photo studios, like the one that my grandparents went to for an engagement photo. Photo albums must have been carried in great numbers by departing Mlawers. So many photos—now in archives at Yad Vashem in Jerusalem and the Ghetto Fighters House north of Haifa—could not all have circulated by mail, though this is how some of the photos included in this book made their way to safety in the years before the war. Via these images, Mława comes to life before the patient researcher's eyes, in all its variety and uncanny modernity. It was the modernizing, Polonizing side of Mława Jewish society that went in for having their pictures taken. Clearly, there was a belief that, if one were in an organization—religious, social, labour-oriented, political—or a graduating-year class at school, then a photographic record was necessary. These photos portray the range of political affiliation in the city: Poale Zion and Ha-shomer Ha-tsa'ir on the left; He-Halutz and the Bund, with their differing views on emigration; and, on the far right, Betar with young members in military-style uniforms. One sees in many photos the characteristic Polish fashions of the times, particularly for young women. Some of the dresses are formal, with collars and frills, but more often they evoke American flappers, even bohemians, with the ever-present high-heeled shoes with one thin strap over the ankle. One finds engagement photo after engagement photo, taken in the same pose as that of my grandparents, using the same backdrop scrim with its image of a large windowsill and box of wildflowers.

It was not a trouble-free time. The Endek—the nationalist anti-Semitic party—met public events with leftist politicians with vandalism and violence in the style of right-wing chaos being fomented in Nazi Germany and Austria. Jewish stores were targeted. Signs—some hand-painted, a kind of homegrown graffiti art—pictured a Chassid being booted in the rear, with a slogan insisting that Poles buy from Poles (*nic od zydow!*). The booted Chassid looks nothing like any of the Jews in Mława in thousands of photos from the 1930s. He is a fantasy figure, a particular European mania of the time.

The reality of leaving arrived abruptly, with news of the permits arriving in March and my grandmother's passport being issued in June. The ship was booked from abroad for July. But there was a pattern underlying emigrant travel, even if each family had its own story. The train station in Mława before the war was impressive, red brick, with gables and dormer windows. The trip to the Baltic port at Gdynia was not overly long. Gdynia was a product of Poland's new national urges. In 1935, it was a modern, white, art nouveau set of buildings housing immigration infrastructure a few kilometres from the port of Gdańsk.

Here the point of leaving overlapped with history that my grandmother would not necessarily have thought was part of her own experience: the aftermath of the First World War in Europe; new Polish national projects; the departure of emigrants, waning but still strong in the middle 1930s. Poles were on the go, and most who left found their way out of Continental Europe at Gdynia, becoming by leaving, according to the Canadian government, "Continental Europeans." So Gdynia, a place unknown to Canadians, was at the heart of the matter. My grandmother's first encounter with anything Canadian took place there. By the time that my grandmother arrived there with her two children, to join the other émigrés, Canadians had had a little more than a decade of experience managing the outflow from the Baltic port.

Gdańsk, or Danzig, as it was known before the Second World War, was the source of rising tensions between the defeated Germans and the ascendant Poles, who, after the First World War, for the first time in many decades, were masters in their own nation-state. As a port city, Danzig had the status of a "free city" as guaranteed by the League of Nations. In 1924, the league gave the Poles control of the Danzig harbour. At the same time, the city's political representative body, a mini parliament, was weighted heavily toward the city-state's majority German population. A restive German citizenry, stoked by rising Nazi influence, watched unhappily as Polish projects went forward that integrated Danzig into Polish economic and political life.

Canadian Department of Immigration documents from the early 1920s reflect efforts to position Canadian immigration inspection activities in the new Polish state, with Danzig at the centre of discussions. This was in part because of the practicality of gathering prospective immigrants near the port, but the Poles themselves promoted this idea, seeing it as part of their goal of autonomy on the Baltic coast. In a letter to the "Canadian Quarantine Inspector" at Danzig in 1923, an emigration attaché of the Polish government highlighted what his government was putting in place. An "unclean camp" would have beds for 400 and a "clean camp" room for 800. Surgeons would attend to issues of "disinfection," and migrants would be transferred from the camp to the port "in special sanitary trains." The question of where to "examine" those headed to ships had been in the air for a year.[2]

Some of the players in these discussions are familiar. F.C. Blair was the point man in Canada as the scenario at Gdynia was decided. He was the kingpin, the head manager of the commissioners and inspectors and medical examiners who acted abroad on Canada's immigration goals. Blair's management of this part of Canada's immigration bureaucracy reflected little of his later focus on keeping unwanted refugees and immigrants from entering the country. In the early 1920s, in correspondence with colleagues in Antwerp, and on the poetically named Auswandererlager Avenue in Danzig, he behaved like a property manager as he oversaw lease agreements and the pros and cons of setting up a Canadian immigration office in Warsaw or Danzig. This latter question runs through letters in 1922 and 1923, though the reasons for proposing Warsaw—far from any coastal point of departure—are never made clear. Perhaps to some the free city looked precarious politically. But most Canadians on the ground favoured Danzig. This was where Canada's immigration office was established in two rooms, with requisite furnishings, supplied at no charge by the Poles.

Blair, a central figure in the "none is too many" narrative, absent from any documentary track record in my grandfather's story, was responsible for setting up the infrastructure by which Polish Jews and other Eastern Europeans abandoned their homes for the New World in the prewar years. He was the overseer of my grandfather's place of exit in late 1930 and then that of his family in the summer of 1935. Danzig, before it was destroyed in the Second World War, was an ancient settlement with a medieval centre and port machinery. It was the last of Europe for emigrants and their first encounter with Canadian officials. At Danzig and nearby Gdynia, the Old World and New World met and danced at a distance from one another. For the lucky traveller, Gdynia was the place where old was exchanged for new. It was also the place where a Canadian-bound emigrant would be supplied with a visa or rejected.

The status of immigrants from Eastern Europe in the minds of Canadian bureaucrats is not always clear in their correspondence. Inspector John A. Jepps wrote to his colleague T.B. Williams, in Antwerp, of the risks inherent in moving the Canadian immigration office to Warsaw. On this, he agreed with Blair, for "large numbers of persons more or less undesirable" would find it much easier to knock on their office door. Jepps vouched for the supply of what he called "undesirables" in the Polish capital, whose population was one-third Jewish. He noted that he had just visited what he dubbed the "slums and ghettoes of Warsaw" to witness "the filth and squalor there . . . beyond description." Danzig represented, in his mind, "the neck of a funnel through which come streams of emigrants from Warsaw, Lemberg, Posen, Galicia, Upper and Lower Silicia, and other parts of Poland. Roumanian emigrants sometimes come through here, as also do Lithuanians, Czecho-Slovaks, Yugo-Slavs and Russians."[3] Most likely the "slums and ghettoes of Warsaw," as Jepps deemed them, were found along the great Jewish streets of the prewar city—Krochmalna, Nalewki, Grzybowska, Twarda, Chłodna—presented in their prewar state in Isaac Bashevis Singer's masterly memoir, *In My Father's Court*, as well as in his postwar novel *The Family Moskat*. On every page of these books, down to the sound of a horse carriage on cobblestones, the Jewish streets are rendered with force and honesty. One must go there to encounter an alternative to the judgment of men like Jepps. Blair put things plainly in a letter to the Antwerp Canadian immigration office: "Since we are not seeking immigration from these countries it is not essential that we have any display window nor yet is it necessary that we have an office on a busy and expensive street."[4]

Well, the Canadians got what they paid for (or didn't). Two rooms with the address on the letterhead: Auswandererlager 27/28. One room was for the inspector himself. The other housed two stenographers, Misses Niedwiedzki and Voss. The former, Blair was told, was indispensable, since "being a Pole herself and having lived in that country and traveled over practically all parts of it" she was "in a position to at once advise Inspector Mitchell during the examination of an immigrant whether he comes from an agricultural or manufacturing district."[5] Leave it to Miss Niedwiedzki, head stenographer, to sniff out the "Bona Fide Farmers with Capital over $1000" so dear to the Canadian immigration policy makers of the time. Maybe she had her nose out for a few other things too. We can't know. The two rooms where the inspector met all comers did not convey diplomatic politesse. T.B. Williams of the Canadian Antwerp office was tasked with a visit to Danzig to produce a report on the department's Polish setup: "The location of our office in such a building, owing to the number of people occupying the premises and the various kinds of cooking going on, makes it anything but pleasant to work under such conditions."[6] One expects that the cooking smells of the Auswandererlager were not so different from those in the "slum" avenues of Warsaw.

Blair, back in Ottawa, might not have been "seeking" immigrants from the Polish lands and the surrounding Eastern European countries, but a great number were coming forward, both non-Jewish and Jewish. These numbers threatened to overwhelm the trio in the Canadian inspection office. As many as 600 a month visited the office in the 1920s. Along with a visit to Inspector Mitchell, every prospective immigrant underwent a medical examination by a Canadian doctor. It followed an examination by a Polish doctor employed by the steamship companies. In this way, immigrants okayed by a Polish physician could still be rejected by the Canadian examining doctor in the "emigration camp." The late 1920s saw the firming up of Canada's network of immigration inspectors, including medical examiners, abroad. This was the final accomplishment in a decade-long bureaucratic push to regularize and control the processes by which Europeans came to Canada. In 1928, Canada's chief of the Immigration Medical Division of the Department of Health confirmed that the country had placed medical officers at suitable European sites to examine "*all* prospective immigrants prior to leaving their home." Canadian medical inspectors were placed in Liverpool, Bristol, Birmingham, Aberdeen, Glasgow, Belfast, Riga, Hamburg, Paris, Antwerp, as well as Danzig.[7] At the last site, Dr. Arpin stood guard. Thorough exams in these cities abroad were necessary considering that receiving Canadian examiners at Halifax, Saint John, and Quebec City could see as many as 300 prospective immigrants per hour and could hardly provide reliable results.

Immigration examiners had a full complement of concerns. The categories included "epileptics, insane persons," "mentally or physically defective" persons, including the "dumb" and blind, and two categories that one would think were difficult calls in the context of a single meeting: "constitutional psychopathic inferiority" and "chronic alcoholism."[8] Could the first mean shyness? And the second raises the question of how many prospective immigrants showed up for their medical exams drunk. For those stupid enough to do so, how would the examiner confirm that the drunkenness was chronic? Oh, to be a fly on the wall during these examinations, with their language challenges as an added twist. One wonders if regulations and categories of refusal were not touted to please the taskmasters back home, such as Blair. No one would be able to say that immigration offices abroad were playing free and easy with the large numbers pressing to emigrate from "Non-Preferred" countries.

In 1929, the year before my grandfather's departure, the outcome of a negative medical report was laid out in correspondence from the Danzig immigration office to Ottawa. In a group of thirty-nine families okayed for travel by steamship doctors, two were rejected by Arpin, the Canadian physician. In later groups destined for Danzig from Warsaw, eight families out of ninety were not allowed to proceed to the port. A few weeks later thirteen families out of a group of seventy-five were blocked from travel. Arpin, who headed Canadian medical examinations in the early 1930s, was expected to examine hundreds of people in a day. When he could not complete a full complement because of travel, their ship did not sail.[9]

With these challenges considered, the late 1920s and early 1930s remained a time of great leaving from Poland. I have found no record of my grandfather at Danzig in 1930 or of my grandmother and her children in 1935. They might have presented themselves to Mitchell, their passports up to date. My grandfather must have been seen by Arpin, but how attentively could the doctor have engaged with him?

(If Miss Niedwiedzki remained on guard, then her ability to translate would have been useful, for my grandfather had no fluency in English, French, or any other European language besides Polish and a smattering of Russian). His hometown, Radzanów, was neither an important agricultural centre nor known for its manufacturing, but his experience minding grain merchant networks might have suggested agricultural skills to his interviewer. The waterways of the Wkra and neighbouring rivers, with their rich fishing stocks, might have been known to Niedwiedzki. Then my grandfather would have gone to the "emigration camp" near Danzig, at Wejherowo. There the Canadians maintained their "clean camp" and "unclean camp." Immigration correspondence routinely records the processes of and care taken with "disinfecting and delousing" ship-bound travellers.[10] An emigrant could spend four or five days at the "emigration camp" before departure. One wonders if this sort of undertaking was characteristic of emigrant treatment at the time in other parts of Europe, or were aspects of this treatment specifically concocted for Poles and their even less preferred compatriots of the "Hebrew race"?

As the orders-in-council from the mid-1930s show, Jewish Poles continued to make their way through these rigorous emigration routines. The Canadian immigration office at Danzig prepared detailed monthly reports of those it admitted and those it rejected. An exemplary month was August 1925: 140 Poles and 60 Hebrew Poles admitted; 9 Poles and 4 Hebrew Poles rejected. In the 1920s, Danzig bookkeepers counted "Polish Hebrews" and "Poles" as two distinct national groups. The "Summary of Admissions and Rejections" added a note when an order-in-council supported a traveller's progress. The total number of persons travelling to Canada from Danzig in August 1925 was 302.[11] At times, these summaries highlighted when a Jewish immigration aid organization was responsible for groups of travellers. In this way, Jews always stood out among the Poles, Germans, Czechoslovaks, and Danzigers travelling alongside them. Their immigration, in some cases, was organized (though not for my grandfather) by immigration aid workers in Canada, men like Paull and Gray, who busied themselves with hundreds of files. The efforts to process this case load are found, too, in the Department of Immigration files directed to Winnipeg MP A.A. Heaps in the hope that he might gain access to department officials. Everyone was scrambling. On the Polish side. On the Canadian side. Among the families striving to bring people over. At the immigrant aid societies. At Danzig, the number seeking exit threatened to overwhelm the small Canadian staff on Auswandererlager. All the while the ships awaited their passengers.

It was the SS *Pulaski* that awaited my grandmother at Gdynia, as the Poles and the Canadian Government Return form had it. It was midsummer, July 18, when she and the two children set out for Halifax, without the trouble of a mid-trip handover at Southampton in England. The ship arrived on July 28. Chaja, as the form has it, was thirty; her son, Berek, was six, and her daughter, Chana, was four. Their "Race or People" was "Hebrew." Chaja's father was properly named— Mendel Margules—as her closest relative back home. The passports were new, issued in Mława. Chaja would continue in the "Trade or Occupation" of "Housewife" upon her arrival in Hirsch, Saskatchewan. She would travel by prepaid CNR ticket.

On the *Pulaski* with them were Poles, whose "Race or Peoplehood" was Ruthenian, Polish, or Ukrainian. But there were other "Hebrews" travelling with them, all of whose files would have been handled, like my grandfather's, at the endpoint of Bennett's Conservative government. Among them was the Low family, a mother with her daughter and son, sponsored by the husband in Canada. The Lows listed their "Language" as Polish. Ita Kleindorf, sponsored by a fiancé, travelled alone. She was from western Poland—Miedzyrzecz—and her given language was "Jewish." Rachel Gurman from Bransk, Poland, was with her son. Two Kierbels were sponsored by an uncle. Among these emigrants, the most interesting for our purposes are the Lows. Why? It is possible that their presence on the *Pulaski* was facilitated in part by my grandfather's efforts to bring his family from Poland.

The predicament of Meyer Low—one of the notorious 100, so now we know two such men—tagged along with my grandfather in the course of his efforts, making cameo appearances here and there in the immigration and JIAS letters. His efforts to right himself after having lied to enter the country ran aground. Like my grandfather, Low had no marriage certificate and lacked his children's birth certificates. In Winnipeg, he drove a bread truck for Buckwolds' Bakery, earning twenty-five dollars a week. His application to bring his family from Poland was rejected, appealed, and rejected again. Immigration files at Library and Archives Canada in Ottawa refer to his file, but in scattered form, interspersed with other departmental business—a letter here, an affidavit there. In 1933, C.E.S. Smith (his name stamp not handy, he signed by hand) dubbed himself Low's "obedient servant" as he informed Low that "the Department is not prepared to favourably consider the admission of your wife and children." As late as March 1935, Gray in the Winnipeg JIAS office was soliciting MP Heaps to do "everything possible. Although I have many similar cases," Gray added, "I have never referred one as yet to you."[12] What must have been "similar" about Low and others was their membership among the much discussed 100.

An affidavit that Low drew up in Winnipeg offers a *mea culpa* not so different from that appearing in my grandfather's JIAS file. Low "Solemnly and Sincerely Declares" that "conditions in Poland were very hard and there was no means of making a livelihood for my wife and two children and as I could not come forward to Canada being married, I decided to proceed as single as my intention was to save my family from starvation. . . . I have been legally married to my wife, Regina Low, and that Chaja and Abraham Low are my lawful children."[13]

It was early in 1933 when the two files—my grandfather's and Low's—first overlapped. Paull wrote in February to Gray about both men. Eisenstein, Gray responded, should be left "in abeyance as I understand that a member of Parliament of the Rabbi's constituency is interceding on his behalf." But he would "appreciate if a special effort be made" on behalf of Low's family. This file, for reasons that we can't guess, attracted Gray's energies.[14] In another letter, Gray described how "greatly interested" he was

> in having this case developed and would appreciate if you would do everything possible to obtain a permit. May I suggest that you proceed personally to Ottawa. The appli-cant is prepared to pay all the necessary expenses in con-nection with this case which I, personally, guarantee. There are many factors in this particular case which require our utmost endeavors. . . . You may rest assured that I would not urge so strongly if the case were not so important.[15]

Nowhere in my grandfather's correspondence with Gray does he assert himself this way: his boss, Paull, "must do everything possible," including proceeding "personally to Ottawa." At times in his letters, my grandfather makes what seem like unseemly offers to pay JIAS workers for their efforts, but these offers were never taken up or even acknowledged. Here the offer is taken one step further—Low's offer to pay for expenses will be guaranteed "personally" by Gray. One could argue that every case that the JIAS offices dealt with was treated as if it were important, but Low's wife and children were promoted overtly as such.

Low's documentation record is a good deal slimmer than my grandfather's. It includes the affidavit, which might not have proved to be very helpful: a typo in its "solemn" declaration renders Low "unable to receive, maintain and support my wife and children upon their arrival."[16] Someone with a sharp eye in the JIAS office caught this and circled it with a pencil. In Low's file, there is a letter of support from V. Buckwold of Buckwold's Bakery, attesting that his "services are very satisfactory."[17] The file does mirror my grandfather's in its focus on the family left behind: Regina, age thirty-five; Chaja, age seven; and Abraham, age three. But the paperwork trails off in the spring of 1933. Gray's enthusiasm notwithstanding, nothing was placed in the file for two years, until the week of March 25, 1935, when a letter marked "Confidential" shows up from Paull to Gray. What's in the immigration file is a copy, but it provides a startling read.

Unusually, Paull's letter to Gray deals not with a single file but with a large group, "the wives and children of men who came in as single." Paull advises against "publicity" but suggests that Gray "secure the applications of these men and send them to me." Paull would then submit them to Gordon at the Department of Immigration. March 25 was within a week from the day that the department concluded its work on my grandfather's file, the order-in-council having been approved on the 19th. Jolliffe, without much pleasure, alerted Paull that the Eisenstein permit was being reconsidered, and on March 26 Jolliffe wrote to Paull—dubbing him "Esq." and signing himself "Commissioner"—to advise him that "additional representations" led to "favourable action, special authority for the entry of Mrs. Eisenstein and her two children being granted by Order-in-Council."[18]

The timing seems to be beyond uncanny; it cannot have been a coincidence. The somewhat hushed tone of confidentiality, along with Paull's tone of controlled panic ("secure the applications . . . and send them to me"), signalled that something bigger was afoot than a single file's correspondence. And then, lo and behold, there they were on

AJP/AK
Confidential
March 25, 1935

18084
18146

Dear Mr. Gray,

Dear Mr. Gray, this will acknowledge the receipt of your

letter dated There may be a possibility to secure
the admission to Canada of the wives and children
of men who came in as single. Without giving this
any publicity in your paper secure the applications
of these men and send them to me.

I will submit them to the Minister and
most probably an investigation into the settlement
arrangements will be instituted by the Department
of Immigration.

On the results of this investigation
will depend the final outcome of our applications.

For your information I am listing below
the following applications in which you are interested:

Your File #1908 - Meyer Low - wife & 2 children
            1849 - Leib Frank of Canora, Sask.-wife & child

Yours very sincerely,
JEWISH IMMIGRANT AID SOCIETY OF CANADA

Executive Director.
Ald. M. A. Gray, General Secretary,
Jewish Immigratn Aid Society,
a Main St., Winnipeg, Man.

654

the *Pulaski*, the three Lows headed for Magnus Avenue in Winnipeg.
Their passports were even fresher than those of my grandfather's family, as if they had been made in a rush so that the mother and children
could make it on board the ship.[19] Turnbull, in his last letter to my

grandfather, reiterates that he is not alone in his predicament and that if something is to be done for him—a married man who entered Canada saying that he was single—there are others for whom something, too, should be done. Without thought of my grandfather's family's shipmates, one might read this as an evasion, a retreat by the MP from Regina into the bureaucratic rule-mongering beloved of immigration commissioners. But it seems to be reasonable to suggest that Rabbi Eisenstein's permits in March, followed by his family's sailing alongside Regina, Chaja, and Abraham Low, was not a coincidence but a final saving grace, a flourish at the late stage of my grandfather's story. Lying Eisenstein. Lying Low. The Liars. Let's let 'em in.

I have not followed the trail of any of the other lying 100. They surely could be the subject of a country ballad. Let's call it "The Lyin' Marrieds." It would be a song about loners who threw themselves over the barriers of early 1930s Canadian immigration restrictions and then found themselves in the greatest struggle of their lives to bring their families after them. It seems to be likely—and here I indulge in guesswork by way of detection—that by never taking no for an answer my grandfather nullified, without ever knowing it, the no meted out to another mother and her two children.

LAST THOUGHTS
UPON LEAVING

have not seen it asked of Jewish emigrants to Canada what it felt like in the days before leaving their homes in Poland. This, among the many things that I cannot recover associated with this story, is one of the gaps, the unknowables, that haunts me. In my case, there is the anecdote associated with the departure of my grandfather that, as he left Radzanów, he "tore himself from a house of wailing women." This says it all or at least goes a long way toward doing so. But in my grandmother's case, of her departure from Mława by train with her two young children in the midsummer of 1935, I have no anecdote or document or record. Perhaps my grandmother told me of this leaving more than once, but I have forgotten if she did. The setting for the telling would have been the house that she lived in as a widow for many years in what had been Vancouver's postwar Jewish neighbourhood of choice for those able to put a few thousand dollars down on a house. There she would have told me who saw her off, how the family reacted, whether they feared for her travel alone with two young children, or, more stereotypically, if they felt sad that they were being left behind. I do not know how my grandmother prepared, what she took with her, if the objects from Poland that she had in Vancouver—leather-bound volumes of the Talmud printed in Lvov in the late nineteenth century, a silver candelabrum and kiddush cup, an unusual art nouveau glass decanter—had travelled with her on the *Pulaski* or if these things were sent afterward. Either way, no trunk travelled with her, as one hears in some family stories, to bring large amounts of property. Her leaving was not a flight. Hers is not a refugee narrative. Her extended family was staying put, the bulk of them in the fairly comfortable bourgeois Jewish context of the small city of Mława, northwest of Warsaw.

One might think that the train to the port at Gdynia, not far from Gdańsk on the Baltic coast, would pass through the capital, but this was not the case. From the Mława train station—a fairly modest but handsome red brick outpost of the burgeoning rail network in interwar Poland—my grandmother travelled west and then north. Polish train timetables for this period are available online, so the routes available to her are easily found. There would have been whistle stops, but the major through-points included Malbork, a 600-year-old settlement with its ruined Teutonic castle. There one saw a fanciful Gothic rail station, which still stands, like the one that would present itself later upon arrival at Gdańsk. After Malbork, Gniew, another ancient place, and after it Tczew, magestically positioned on the bank of the Vistula River. In a few years, the Second World War effectively would break out at Tczew, where Polish sappers struggled to blow up a bridge before German bombers blew them up as part of the brutal invasion in early September 1939. There was much for the children to see. Maybe this offering appealed more to the boy. He was not much older than his sister but still officially her minder. The backsides of train stations often don't present the nicest views. At Tczew, it would have been the river that drew the eye. Then the big-city activity of Gdańsk Glowny, the station at Danzig, as it was known to the rest of the world by the name preferred by its German ethnic population. Then Gdynia, the exit point, the point of leaving for so many Poles, both Jews and non-Jews, in the early decades of the twentieth century. When my grandmother saw Gdynia in 1935, the number of Jews passing through the Canadian immigration network there had dwindled to a few hundred a year. Although my grandfather's story, beginning as it does in 1930, can be said to take place largely outside "none is too many" territory, my grandmother's travel in the summer of 1935 was well within it. My grandmother was making the dream passage, countering "none" with a well-presented three. Mława fell behind her as the train rattled past

פאמיליע פון רבי י. י. אייזנשטיין דא פון פוילן

עכטס, העגעלע אייזנשטיין, 5 יאר, לינקס, בערעיע, 6 יאר, אינמיטן,
מרם. אייזנשטיין

Teutonic castles and Dickensian train depots and the wide, slow Wisła, as the Poles know their river.

The Canadians at Gdynia were trying to keep things under strict control, whether at the Polish port or farther on at Southampton and then ultimately at Halifax. But elements of the process remained haphazard and, one would have to say, mysterious. At Gdynia, where a medical examination was *de rigueur*, the medical officers were issued a booklet that included the "vocabularies of foreign languages for use in questioning aliens," with a list of prospective questions in Greek, Yiddish, German, French, Italian, Swedish.[1] But having asked, via transliteration, "Zite ihr krank?" what of the answer in Yiddish, beyond a head shake, would have been understood? And of course, as was likely the case for my grandmother, it was known that it was best to say as little as possible in these circumstances. In fact, she travelled with the knowledge that she had early symptoms of tuberculosis, a deal-killer for any emigrant, and had made up her mind to spend the ten days of travel in her cabin to avoid further questions or revelations on this front. Young Berel was tasked with bringing her food, not understanding until years later why his usually grounded and sensible mother seemed to be so anxious.

This was departure. The passage through ancient Polish settlements. The newfangled emigration port. The Canadians on their guard but somehow clowning at the same time. My grandmother must not have been very sick, because her medical inspection at Halifax went without any cause for worry. She lacked the key to open the can of sardines given to her before embarking on the long train trip to the wheat lands of Saskatchewan.

The Winnipeg Yiddish daily *Dos Yiddishe Vort* announced her arrival, alongside a picture of "Henele Eisenstein, 5 years, left, Berele, 6 years." The photo and the accompanying text provide the endpoint, provocative punctuation, to my grandfather's half-decade effort to find them a way into Canada. It's a Polish photograph, supplied to the paper by my grandfather. So in it my grandmother and her children gaze out of the past into their New World lives.

For Avrum Eisenstein,
translator and expert reader,
and for his sister, Hannah, and brother, Bernie

ACKNOWLEDGEMENTS

This book provides its own extended acknowledgement of key informants in my understanding of Canadian and Polish life and history. Only through its reading can these players be properly revealed. My uncle, Avrum Eisenstein, a Yorkton-born Brooklynite, proved to be a true collaborator through my years of work on this project. His translations of handwritten Yiddish letters opened those documents in unexpected ways. To each translation he appended a commentary on historical and personal themes worthy of a professional historian and genealogist. His work made this book possible.

Archivists Janice Rosen, Andrew Morrison, Rebecca Murray, and Saara Mortensen helped me find key resources.

David Ravvin, Shelley Butler, and Howard Dancyger provided support for and interest in the book's direction.

Robert Lecker, David McLennan, Kelly Laycock, and Dallas Harrison helped it reach a happy conclusion.

NOTES

ANOTHER SHIP, ANOTHER TIME

1   Mawani, *Across Oceans of Law*, 36.
2   "The Ships List."
3   Mawani, *Across Oceans of Law*, 92.

LEAVING

1   Duncan, *The Story of the Canadian People*, 261–72, 267.
2   England, *The Central European Immigrant*, vii.
3   England, 17.
4   England, vii.
5   England, 8.
6   England, xiii.
7   England, 218–19.
8   Quoted in "Quality," *Globe*, October 25, 1928.
9   "Advise," *Globe*, June 5, 1928.
10 "Trafficking," *Toronto Daily Star*, May 15, 1928.
11 Anderson, *The Education of the New-Canadian*, 24.
12 Anderson, 49.
13 Anderson, 87–88.

14 Jamieson and Sandiford, "The Mental Capacity of Southern Ontario Indians," 540.

15 Anderson, *The Education of the New-Canadian*, 86.

16 Pagé, "Medical Aspects of Immigration," 368.

17 Pagé, 370.

18 Jeffs, "Overseas Immigration Medical Service," 283.

19 "Juda J. Ajzensztejn."

20 Lepore, "But Who's Counting?," 14.

21 Quoted in Lepore, 14.

22 Lewando, *The Vilna Vegetarian Cookbook*, xxvi.

23 Weiss, "Availability of Kosher Food."

24 "RMS *Queen Mary* Kosher Dinner Menu."

25 "Cunard Tourist Third Cabin Accommodation."

26 Quoted in Beaud and Prevost, "Immigration, Eugenics and Statistics."

27 Quoted in Beaud and Prevost.

28 Greenway and Keyfitz, "Robert Coats," 314–18.

29 Greenway and Keyfitz, 321.

30 Coats, "The Growth of Population," 2, 5.

31 Coats, *Origin, Birthplace, Nationality*, 3.

32 Coats, 12–13.

33 Coats, 11.

34 Coats, 44; see also Rosenberg, "The Jewish Population," 33.

35 Coats, *Origin, Birthplace, Nationality*, 24, 164.

36 Coats, 25.

37 Coats, 25.

38 Coats, 23.

39 Beaud and Prevost, "Immigration, Eugenics and Statistics."

40 Quoted in Beaud and Prevost.

41 Weinfeld, "Introduction," xii.

42 Weinfeld, xvii.

43 Coats, *Origin, Birthplace, Nationality*, 114.

44 Rosenberg, *Canada's Jews*, 259.

45 Rosenberg, 90.

46 Rosenberg, 128.

47 Abella and Troper, *None Is Too Many*, xii–xiii.

48 Rosenberg, *Canada's Jews*, 128.

"PURE RUSSIAN, JEW, GERMAN"

1   "John Murray Gibbon."

2   *The New Canadian Folksong and Handicraft Festival*, 3–4.

3   Gibbon, *Canadian Mosaic*, ix.

4   Coyne, "Foreword," 5.

5   Foster, *Our Canadian Mosaic*, 78.

6   Foster, 18.

7   Foster, 7.

8   Foster, 46–47.

9   *The New Canadian Folksong and Handicraft Festival*, 32.

10   *The Great West*, 22.

11   *The Great West*, 28–29.

12   *The Great West*, 4.

13   *Canadian Folk Song*, 24.

14   England, *The Colonization of Western Canada*, 273–74.

15   *The Great West*, 5, 14.

16   *Canadian Folk Song*, 22.

17   Bissell, *The Imperial Canadian*, 105.

18   Rosenberg, "The Jewish Population," 43.

19   Osborne, "Constructing the State," 176.

20   Osborne, 171.

21   Library and Archives Canada [hereafter LAC], Canadian National Railways, RG30, vol. 5893.

22   Osborne, "Constructing the State," 183–84.

23   Osborne, 185–86.

24   Osborne, 180.

25   "Some Types," 13.

OH, OTTAWA

1   Belkin, *Through Narrow Gates*, 149.

2   Belkin, 149–50.

3   King, *The Mackenzie King Diaries* , January 2, 1932; January 5, 1932.

4   Belkin, *Through Narrow Gates*, 152.

5   Belkin, 150–51.

6   *"Dos schwindlerishe arbet."*

7   Belkin, *Through Narrow Gates*, 155.

8   Belkin, 126.

9   Belkin, 155.

GO WEST, SLOWLY WEST, KNOWING NOTHING AT ALL

1   Hall, "Clifford Sifton," 69–70.

2   Arnold, "Sir Wilfrid Laurier."

3   "America."

4   JIAS-CA-71-17808.

5   Clarke, *Souris Valley Plains*, 22–23.

6   Clarke, 27.

7   Stegner, *Wolf Willow*, 41.

8   LaDow, *The Medicine Line*, 91.

9   Clarke, *Souris Valley Plains*, 23.

10   Stegner, *Wolf Willow*, 116.

11   LaDow, *The Medicine Line*, 29.

12   Clarke, *Souris Valley Plains*, 39.

13   LaDow, *The Medicine Line*, 62.

14   Huyda, *Camera in the Interior*, 3.

15   Huyda, 5.

16   Hind, *Reports of Progress*, 46.

17   Huyda, *Camera in the Interior*, 13.

18   Huyda, 16.

19   Huyda, 19–20.

20   Hind, *Reports of Progress*, 3–4.

21   Hind, 57.

22   Hind, 53.

23   Hind, 50–53.

24   Bryce, "The Immigrant Settler," 40.

25   Culliton, *Assisted Emigration*, 26.

26   "Immigration Act, 1906."

27   Chan, "Chinese Head Tax in Canada."

28   Trant, "Jew and Chinaman," 251.

29   Trant, 254.

30   Hedges, *Building the Canadian West*, 360.

31   Moir, "Canada West," 13.

32   Belkin, *Through Narrow Gates*, 125.

33   Hedges, *Building the Canadian West*, 361.

34   England, *The Colonization of Western Canada*, 92–94.

35   "Immigration Project."

36   "Advise Government."

37   *British Family Settlement*, 18.

38   *British Family Settlement*, 6.

39   *British Family Settlement*, 16.

40   *British Family Settlement*, 36.

41   *British Family Settlement*, 29.

42   *Winning Through*, 19–20.

43   Hedges, *Building the Canadian West*, 360.

44   "Order-in-Council PC 1931-695."

45   Rosenberg, *Canada's Jews*, 136.

COMING FORWARD FORM RADZANÓW

1   LAC, S.W. Jacobs Fonds, MG27 III C3.

2   Bohi and Kozma, "Interwar Rail Construction," 47.

3   Boulet, *Vistas*, 84.

4   Rosenberg, *Canada's Jews*, 20–27.

5   Rosenberg, 312–13.

6   LaDow, *The Medicine Line*, 213.

7   Stegner, *Wolf Willow*, 112.

8   Rosenberg, *Canada's Jews*, 314.

9   Stegner, *Wolf Willow*, 261.

10   Stegner, 248.

DYSART, SASKATCHEWAN, CAPITAL OF THE FORGOTTEN WEST

1   Osborne and Wurtele, "The Other Railway," 122.

2   McManus, *Happyland*, 114–15, 120–22, 136, 175.

3   "The Qu'Appelle Valley."

4   Carter, *Lost Harvests*, 25–29.

5   Carter, 54–57.

6   "File Hills Indian Residential School."

7   "File Hills Colony."

8   "Dysart."

9   "Dysart, Sask.," December 5, 1932.

10   "Dysart, Sask.," October 27, 1933.

11   "Dysart, Sask.," May 12, 1933.

12   White, *In Search of Geraldine Moodie*, 16, 26, 28.

13   Mandelbaum, *The Plains Cree*, 183.

14   Mandelbaum, 186, 234.

15   Brown, *First Nations*, 117.

16   Cadzow, "The Vanishing American Indian Medicine-Man," 418.

17 Friedgut, "Jewish Pioneers," 399–400.

18 JCA, KC, Lipton Colony Reports.

19 JCA, KC, Lipton Colony Reports.

THE BENNETT YEARS

1 Abella and Troper, *None Is Too Many*, xxiii.

2 Waite, *The Loner*, 29.

3 Fortney, "Bennett Revisited."

4 *Calgary City Directory 1934.*

5 *Land of Promise*, 257.

6 "Mrs. I. Kesnick."

7 *Land of Promise*, 257.

8 Marr, "House of Jacob."

9 "Bennett Richard Bedford Department of Immigration."

10 Kelley and Trebilcock, *The Making of the Mosaic*, 216.

11 Kelley and Trebilcock, 222.

12 Kelley and Trebilcock, 227.

13 O'Leary, "Cabinet Portraits," 33.

14 "Gordon, W.A.," LiPaD, April 8, 1926.

15 "Gordon, W.A."

16 "Influx of Migrants."

17 "Hon. Wesley Gordon."

18 "Deportation."

19 "Frederick Blair."

20 Jolliffe, "Report of the Commissioner of Immigration," 76.

21 Jolliffe, 76.

22 "Order-in-Council PC 1931-695."

23 Rosenberg, *Canada's Jews*, 136.

THE IMMIGRATION FILES: THE HEART OF THE MATTER

1 JIAS-CA-71-17808.

2 JIAS-CA-71-17808.

3 "Motherwell, W.R."

4 *House of Commons Debates*, June 5, 1922, 2514–15.

5 *House of Commons Debates*, June 5, 1922, 2517.

6 *House of Commons Debates*, June 5, 1922, 2518.

7 JHC 148, file 18, JIAS, "Rev. J. Eisenstein."

8 JHC 148, file 18, JIAS, "Rev. J. Eisenstein."

9   JIAS-CA-71-17808.

10 JIAS-CA-71-17808.

11 JIAS-CA-72-18084.

12 JIAS-CA-71-17808.

13 JIAS-CA-71-17808.

AT HIRSCH ON THE SOUTHEASTERN BORDERLANDS

1   JCA MAI DB 14.

2   Goodman, *Gezamelte Shriften*, 221.

3   Belkin, *Through Narrow Gates*, 70.

4   Belkin, 72.

5   Belkin, 213.

6· Rosenberg, *Canada's Jews*, 219–20.

7   "Bienfait."

8   Endicott, *Bienfait*, 65.

9   Endicott, 87, 132.

10 Hanson, "The Estevan Strike and Riot," 99.

11 LAC, MG26-K.

12 Endicott, *Bienfait*, 36.

13 "Historical Tours."

14 JCA MAI DB 14.

15 Grossman, *The Soil's Calling*, 47–48.

16 "Hirsch."

17 JCA MAI DC 7.

18 JCA MAI DC 7.

19 JCA MAI DB 14.

HOW TO BECOME A CHARACTER IN A CANADIAN NOVEL

1   Pitsula, *Keeping Canada British*, 26, 35.

2   Anna Feldman Fonds, box 814, f. 28, "Louis Rosenberg."

3   Pitsula, *Keeping Canada British*, 99.

4   Pitsula, 106.

5   Brown, "Protecting the Individual," 267.

6   Benson, *None of It Came Easy*, 66–68.

7   Benson, 88.

8   Ward, "Editor's Foreword," x.

9   Gardiner, *The Politician*, 113.

10 Gardiner, 113.

11 Gardiner, 114.

12 Gardiner, 114.

13 Gardiner, 116.

14 Gardiner, 115.

15 Gardiner, 119.

16 Gardiner, 117.

17 Gardiner, 116.

THE IMMIGRATION PATH, DARK AND TWISTED

1 JHC 148, file 18, JIAS, "Rev. J. Eisenstein."

2 Park, "Deep Lessons Learned."

3 Hanson, "The Estevan Strike and Riot," 99.

4 Hanson, 99, 168.

5 "How They Framed Sam Scarlett."

6 JHC 148, file 18, JIAS, "Rev. J. Eisenstein."

7 JHC 148, file 18, JIAS, "Rev. J. Eisenstein."

8 JHC 148, file 18, JIAS, "Rev. J. Eisenstein."

9 JHC 148, file 18, JIAS, "Rev. J. Eisenstein."

10 Rome, *Clouds in the Thirties*, 207.

11 JHC 148, file 18, JIAS, "Rev. J. Eisenstein."

12 LAC, Meighen Papers, MG26 I.159.

13 LAC, MG26-K.

14 JIAS-CA-71-17808.

15 JIAS-CA-71-17808.

16 JHC 148, file 18, JIAS, "Rev. J. Eisenstein."

ENTER THE GREAT LADY

1 JIAS-CA-71-17808.

2 Abella and Troper, *None Is Too Many*, 156.

3 JIAS-CA-71-17808.

4 JIAS-CA-71-17808.

5 JIAS-CA-71-17808.

6 JIAS-CA-71-17808.

THE TRAIN I RIDE

1 JCA, Canada Collection, L100, box 57.

2 Montgomery, *Anne of Green Gables*, 300–01.

3 Montgomery, 301.

4   Montgomery, 299.
5   Speisman, "Bilsky, Moses."
6   Berman, "BILSKY, LILLIAN (Freiman)."
7   Jewish People's Relief Committee, "Correspondence."
8   "Mrs. A.J. Freiman."
9   Rome, *Clouds in the Thirties*, 227–28.
10   "Back to Native Land," 1.
11   "Opposing Move."
12   "Back to Native Land," 2.
13   LAC, Immigration Branch Fonds, RG76, vol. 245.
14   "Message of the Prime Minister."
15   Blair, "Dear Mrs. Freiman."
16   Berman, "BILSKY, LILLIAN (Freiman)."
17   Grayson and Bliss, *The Wretched of Canada*, 68.
18   Grayson and Bliss, 18.
19   Grayson and Bliss, 56.
20   Grayson and Bliss, 120.
21   OJA, Freiman Family Fonds.
22   OJA, Freiman Family Fonds.
23   Rome, *Clouds in the Thirties*, 217.

GOING TO THE ARCHIVES

1   JHC 148, file 18, JIAS, "Rev. J. Eisenstein."
2   JIAS-CA-71-17808.
3   JIAS-CA-71-17808.
4   JIAS-CA-71-17808.
5   JIAS-CA-71-17808.
6   JIAS-CA-71-17808.
7   This resource and related order-in-council files from March 1935 are listed in Archival Materials.
8   "Hangings in Montreal."
9   Anctil, *A Reluctant Welcome*, 96.
10   "Order-in-Council PC 1931-695."
11   Rampell, "The Little People Pay Taxes."
12   "The History of Metropolitan Vancouver."
13   Cameron, "Canada's Struggle with Illegal Entry," 51–52, 55.

YOU COME FROM FAR AWAY: THE DANZIG STORY

1   Munro, "The Moon in the Orange Street Skating Rink," 44.

2   LAC, Immigration Branch Fonds, RG76, vol. 245.

3   LAC, Immigration Branch Fonds, RG76, vol. 189.

4   LAC, Immigration Branch Fonds, RG76, vol. 189.

5   LAC, Immigration Branch Fonds, RG76, vol. 245.

6   LAC, Immigration Branch Fonds, RG76, vol. 189.

7   Pagé, "Medical Aspects of Immigration," 368, 370–71.

8   Pagé, 366.

9   LAC, Immigration Branch Fonds, RG76, vol. 245.

10 LAC, Immigration Branch Fonds, RG76, vol. 245.

11 LAC, Immigration Branch Fonds, RG76, vol. 245.

12 LAC, Immigration Branch Fonds, RG76, vol. 245.

13 LAC, Immigration Branch Fonds, RG76, vol. 245.

14 JHC 148, file 18, JIAS, "Rev. J. Eisenstein."

15 JIAS-CA-72-18084.

16 JIAS-CA-72-178-18084.

17 LAC, Immigration Branch Fonds, RG76, vol. 245.

18 JIAS-CA-71-17808.

19 "Ryfka Low."

LAST THOUGHTS UNPON LEAVING

1   LAC, Immigration Branch Fonds, RG76, vol. 349.

SOURCES CITED AND CONSULTED

ARTICLES, BOOKS, DIARIES, DOCUMENTS, PAMPHLETS, THESES

"1911—First Synagogue Cornerstone Ceremony Attracts Donors, Dignitaries." *Journal of the Jewish Historical Society of Southern Alberta* 14, no. 2 (2004): 1–2.

Abella, Irving, and Harold Troper. *None Is Too Many: Canada and the Jews of Europe 1933–1948.* 1983; reprinted, Toronto: Key Porter, 2000.

"Advise Government to Secure Settlers from Great Britain." *Globe* [Toronto], June 5, 1928, 12.

Aleksiun, Natalia. "Regards from My *Shtetl*: Polish Jews Write to Piłsudski, 1933–1935." *Polish Review* 56, nos. 1–2 (2011): 57–71.

"America." In *The YIVO Encyclopedia of Jews in Eastern Europe.* https://yivoencyclopedia.org/article.aspx/America.

Anctil, Pierre. *A Reluctant Welcome for Jewish People: Voices in* Le Devoir's *Editorials 1910–1947.* Translated by Tonu Onu. Ottawa: University of Ottawa Press, 2019.

Anderson, J.T.M. *The Education of the New-Canadian: A Treatise on Canada's Greatest Educational Problem.* Toronto: J.M. Dent, 1918.

Arnold, Abe. "Sir Wilfrid Laurier and Canada's Jews." Canada's History. https://www.canadashistory.ca/explore/prime-ministers/sir-wilfrid-laurier-and-canada-s-jews.

Backhouse, Constance. *Colour-Coded: A Legal History of Racism in Canada, 1900–1950.* Toronto: University of Toronto Press, 2001.

"Back to Native Land." *Toronto Star*, December 12, 1932, 1–2.

Baltzan, Jacob A. *Memoirs of a Pioneer Farmer in Western Canada at the Dawn of the Twentieth Century.* Toronto: privately printed, 1994.

Beaud, Jean-Pierre, and Jean-Guy Prevost. "Immigration, Eugenics and Statistics: Measuring Racial Origins in Canada (1921–1941)." *Canadian Ethnic Studies* 28, no. 2 (1996). https://search-pro-quest-com.lib-ezproxy.concordia.ca/central/docview/215640280/fulltext/67EB5E0D5EC04FA1PQ/1?accountid=10246.

Belkin, Simon. *Through Narrow Gates: A Review of Jewish Immigration and Immigrant Aid Work in Canada (1840–1940).* Montreal: Eagle Publishing, 1966.

Benson, Nathaniel A. *None of It Came Easy: The Story of James Garfield Gardiner.* Toronto: Burns and MacEachern, 1955.

Berman, Shirley. "BILSKY, LILLIAN (Freiman)." In *Dictionary of Canadian Biography*, vol. 16. Toronto: University of Toronto; Laval: Université Laval, 2003. http://www.biographi.ca/en/bio/bilsky_lillian_16E.html.

"Bienfait: The Saskatchewan Miners' Struggle of '31." History Cooperative. https://historycooperative.org/journal/bienfait-the-saskatchewan-miners-struggle-of-31/.

Bissell, Claude. *The Imperial Canadian: Vincent Massey in Office.* Toronto: University of Toronto Press, 1986.

Blair, F.C. "Dear Mrs. Freiman." October 7, 1938. Personal correspondence with Lorenz Friedlaender, October 10, 2018.

Bohi, Charles W., and Leslie Kozma. "Interwar Rail Construction in Saskatchewan and Alberta: An Evaluation." *Prairie Perspectives* 11 (2008): 45–70.

Boulet, Roger. *Vistas: Artists on the Canadian Pacific Railway.* Calgary: Glenbow Museum, 2009.

British Family Settlement in New Brunswick Canada. Ottawa: Department of Immigration and Colonization, 1929.

Brown, Alison K. *First Nations, Museums, Narrations: Stories of the 1929 Franklin Motor Expedition to the Canadian Prairies.* Vancouver: UBC Press, 2014.

Brown, Nolan. "Protecting the Individual: The Origins and Development of Saskatchewan Conservatism, 1905–1944." PhD thesis, University of Western Ontario, 2019.

Bryce, P.H. "The Immigrant Settler." *Annals of the American Academy of Political and Social Science* 107 (1923): 35–44.

Cadzow, Donald A. "The Vanishing American Indian Medicine-Man." *Scientific American* 140, no. 5 (1929): 418–20.

Calgary City Directory. 1934. Medicine Hat and District Genealogical Society: A Branch of Alberta Genealogical Society. https://mhdgs.ca/calgcity1.html.

Cameron, James D. "Canada's Struggle with Illegal Entry on Its West Coast: The Case of Fred Yoshy and Japanese Migrants before the Second World War." *BC Studies* 146 (2005): 37–62.

Canadian Folk Song and Handicrafts Festival [pamphlet]. Quebec City, May 24–28, 1928.

"Canadian Pacific Railway." In *Encyclopedia of Saskatchewan.* https://esask.uregina.ca/entry/canadian_pacific_railway.jsp.

Carter, Sarah. *Lost Harvests: Prairie Indian Reserve Farmers and Government Policy.* Montreal and Kingston: McGill-Queen's University Press, 1990.

Chan, Arlene. "Chinese Head Tax in Canada." In *The Canadian Encyclopedia.* https://www.thecanadianencyclopedia.ca/en/article/chinese-head-tax-in-canada.

"*Choshever redaktor.*" *Dos Yiddishe Vort,* October 27, 1933, 5.

Clarke, Lawrence B. *Souris Valley Plains—A History.* Souris, MB: Souris Plaindealer, 1976.

Coats, R.H. "The Growth of Population in Canada." *Annals of the American Academy of Political and Social Science* 107 (1923): 1–6.

———. *Origin, Birthplace, Nationality and Language of the Canadian People: A Census Study Based on the Census of 1921 and Supplementary Data.* Ottawa: Dominion Bureau of Statistics, 1929.

Coyne, James H. "Foreword." In *Our Canadian Mosaic,* by Kate A. Foster, 5–6. Toronto: Dominion Council YWCA, 1926.

Culliton, J.T. *Assisted Emigration and Land Settlement with Special Reference to Western Canada.* McGill University Economic Studies 9. Montreal: McGill University, 1928.

"Cunard Tourist Third Cabin Accommodations—1920s." GG Archives. https://www.gjenvick.com/OceanTravel/Brochures/Cunard-Line-1920s-TouristThirdCabinAccommodations.html.

"Deportation Just and System Legal, Declares Gordon." *Globe* [Toronto], June 23, 1933, 5.

"*Dos schwindlerishe arbet muz oifhern.*" *Der Keneder Adler,* April 8, 1926, 4.

Duncan, David M. *The Story of the Canadian People*. Toronto: Macmillan, 1922.

"Dysart." In *The Encyclopedia of Saskatchewan*. https://esask.uregina.ca/entry/dysart.jsp.

"Dysart, Sask." *Dos Yiddishe Vort*, December 5, 1932, 4.

"Dysart, Sask." *Dos Yiddishe Vort*, May 12, 1933, 2.

"Dysart, Sask." *Dos Yiddishe Vort*, October 27, 1933, 5.

Endicott, Stephen L. *Bienfait: The Saskatchewan Miners' Struggle of '31*. Toronto: University of Toronto Press, 2002.

England, Robert. *The Central European Immigrant in Canada*. Toronto: Macmillan, 1929.

———. *The Colonization of Western Canada: A Study of Contemporary Land Settlement (1896–1934)*. London: P.S. King and Son, 1936.

Faulkner, William. *Requiem for a Nun*. 1951; reprinted New York: Random House, 1968.

Figler, Bernard. *Lillian and Archie Freiman: Biographies*. Montreal: privately printed, 1961.

"File Hills Colony: A Failed Experiment." https://www2.uregina.ca/education/saskindianresidentialschools/wp-content/uploads/2017/06/ShatteringtheSilenceFileHillsColony.jpg.

"File Hills Indian Residential School." The Children Remembered. https://thechildrenremembered.ca/school-histories/file-hill/.

Fortney, Valerie. "Bennett Revisited." *Ottawa Citizen*, August 8, 2010, A7.

Foster, Kate A. *Our Canadian Mosaic*. Toronto: Dominion Council YWCA, 1926.

"Frederick Blair." Wikipedia. https://en.wikipedia.org/wiki/Frederick_Blair.

Friedgut, Theodore. "Jewish Pioneers on Canada's Prairies: The Lipton Jewish Agricultural Colony." *Jewish History* 21, nos. 3–4 (2007): 385–411.

Gardiner, James G. *The Politician: Or, The Treason of Democracy*. Saskatoon: Western Producer Prairie Books, 1975.

Gibbon, John Murray. *Canadian Mosaic: The Making of a Northern Nation*. Toronto: McClelland and Stewart, 1938.

Goodman, Joseph J. *Gezamelte Shriften/Collected Writings: Poetry, Short Stories, and Essays on the Jewish Canadian Immigrant Experience*. Edited by H. Goodman Hoffman. Translated by H. Fischthal. Bloomington, IN: Xlibris, 2011. [Originally published 1919.]

"Gordon W.A." LiPaD/Canadian Hansard Data Set. May 6, 1931; June 24, 1931; June 26, 1931; July 10, 1931; July 20, 1931; April 22, 1932;

February 8, 1933; March 27, 1933; January 1, 1934; March 12, 1934; May 3, 1934; January 28, 1935. https://lipad.ca/.

"Grand Trunk Pacific Railway." *The Encyclopedia of Saskatchewan.* https://esask.uregina.ca/entry/grand_trunk_pacific_railway.jsp.

Grayson, L.M., and Michael Bliss. *The Wretched of Canada: Letters to R.B. Bennett 1930–1935.* Toronto: University of Toronto Press, 1971.

The Great West Canadian Folk Dance, Folk Song, and Handicraft Festival [pamphlet]. Calgary, 1930.

Greenway, F., and N. Keyfitz. "Robert Coats and the Organization of Statistics." *Canadian Journal of Economics and Political Science* 27, no. 3 (1961): 313–22.

Grossman, Vladimir. *The Soil's Calling.* Montreal: Eagle Publishing, 1938.

Hall, D.J. "Clifford Sifton: Immigration and Settlement Policy 1896–1905." In *The Settlement of the West,* edited by H. Palmer, 60–85. Calgary: University of Calgary Press, 1977.

"Hangings in Montreal." Coolopolis: Montreal Alles the Uber. http://coolopolis.blogspot.com/2019/05/hangings-in-montreal-full-list-and.html.

Hanson, Stanley D. "The Estevan Strike and Riot, 1931." MA thesis, University of Saskatchewan, 1971.

Hedges, James B. *Building the Canadian West: The Land and Colonization Policies of the Canadian Pacific Railway.* New York: Russell and Russell, 1939.

Hind, Henry Youle. *Reports of Progress, Together with a Preliminary and General Report, on the Assinniboine and Saskatchewan Exploring Expedition.* London: George Edward Eyre and W. Spottiswoode, 1860.

"Hirsch." Doug Gent's History Pages. https://www.gent.name/sask:towns:hirsch:history.

"Historical Tours." Doug Gent's History Pages. https://www.gent.name/sask:towns:estevan:historicaltour:start.

"The History of Metropolitan Vancouver." https://vancouverhistory.ca/chronology/chronology-1930/.

"HMS Ausonia." HMS Ausonia: In Memory of HMS Ausonia and Her Crew. http://hmsausonia.co.uk/history/cunard-a-class-ships/ascania/.

"Hon. Wesley Gordon Takes Firm Stand on Deportations." *Globe* [Toronto], February 17, 1931, 13.

House of Commons Debates, 14th Parl, 1st Sess., vol. 3 (June 5, 1922) (Jacobs). Parliament of Canada. http://parl.canadiana.ca/view/ oop.debates_HOC1401_03/467?r=0&s=1.

"How They Framed Sam Scarlett." *Canadian Labor Defender* 3, no. 11 (1932): 2.

Huyda, Richard J. *Camera in the Interior: 1858 H.L. Hime, Photographer. The Assiniboine and Saskatchewan Exploring Expedition.* Toronto: Coach House Press, 1975.

"Immigration Act, 1906." Canadian Museum of Immigration at Pier 21. https:// pier21.ca/research/immigration-history/immigration-act-1906.

"Immigration Project Takes Egan Overseas to Confer with King." *Toronto Star*, September 11, 1928, 1–2.

"The Indian Act." Indigenous Foundations. https://indigenousfoundations. arts.ubc.ca/the_indian_act/.

"Influx of Migrants on Hard Times' Eve Scored by Minister." *Globe* [Toronto], November 20, 1930, 1.

Jamieson, E., and P. Sandiford. "The Mental Capacity of Southern Ontario Indians." *Journal of Educational Psychology* 19, no. 8 (1928): 536–50.

Jeffs, H.B. "Overseas Immigration Medical Service." *Canadian Public Health Journal* 27, no. 6 (1936): 282–84.

Jewish People's Relief Committee. "Correspondence of the Jewish People's Relief Committee with Other Organizations: 1915–1924. V. 6. Correspondence with Elias Heifitz (Cheifitz), President of the Ukrainian [Pogrom Relief] Committee, Kiev, 1919–1921." Harvard Library. https://iiif.lib.harvard.edu/manifests/view/ drs:427972949$11.

"John Murray Gibbon." In *The Canadian Encyclopedia*. https://www. thecanadianencyclopedia.ca/en/article/john-murray-gibbon-emc.

Jolliffe, A.L. "Report of the Commissioner of Immigration." In *Annual Report of the Department of Immigration and Colonization for 1930–31*.

"Juda J. Ajzensztejn." In "Passenger Lists and Border Entries, 1925–1935." LAC, RG76, vol. 25.
https://www.bac-lac.gc.ca/eng/discover/immigration/immigra- tion-records/passenger-lists-border-entry-1925-1935/Pages/ introduction.aspx.

Kazimi, Ali. *Undesirables: White Canada and the* Komagata Maru—*An Illustrated History*. Vancouver: Douglas and McIntyre, 2012.

Kelley, Ninette, and Michael Trebilcock. *The Making of the Mosaic: A History of Canadian Immigration Policy.* Toronto: University of Toronto Press, 1998.

King, William Lyon Mackenzie. *The Mackenzie King Diaries, 1932–1949.* Toronto: University of Toronto Press, 1980.

LaDow, Beth. *The Medicine Line: Life and Death on a North American Borderland.* New York: Routledge, 2001.

Land of Promise: The Jewish Experience in Southern Alberta 1889–1945. Calgary: Jewish Historical Society of Southern Alberta, 1996.

Lepore, Jill. "But Who's Counting? The Coming Census." *The New Yorker,* March 23, 2020, 10–16.

Lewando, Fania. *The Vilna Vegetarian Cookbook.* Translated by Eve Jochnowitz. New York: Schocken Books, 2015.

Mandelbaum, David G. *The Plains Cree: An Ethnographic Historical and Comparative Study.* Regina: Canadian Plains Research Center, 1979.

Marr, Norma. "House of Jacob/Bow Valley College: 325 5th Ave. S.E." *Calgary Herald,* April 22, 2003, B2.

Mawani, Renisa. *Across Oceans of Law: The* Komagata Maru *and Jurisdiction in the Time of Empire.* Durham, NC: Duke University Press, 2018.

McManus, Curtis. *Happyland: A History of the "Dirty Thirties" in Saskatchewan, 1914–1937.* Calgary: University of Calgary Press, 2011.

"Message of the Prime Minister on the Occasion of the Jewish New Year, 5695." *Dos Yiddishe Vort,* September 13, 1934. LAC, RG76, vol. 245, file 168186.

Moir, Lindsay. "Canada West: The New Homeland." *Art Libraries Journal* 24, no. 3 (1999): 12–18.

Montgomery, Lucy Maude. *Anne of Green Gables.* 1908; reprinted, London: Puffin, 2010.

"Motherwell, William Richard." In *The Encyclopedia of Saskatchewan.* https://esask.uregina.ca/entry/motherwell_william_richard_1860-_1943.jsp.

"Mrs. A.J. Freiman." BiblioArchives. https://flickr.com/photos/lac-bac/31096392455/in/photolist-PnT96v-N9zXYV-N9zXut.

"Mrs. I. Kesnick" [obituary]. *Calgary Herald,* February 6, 1935, 12. https://news.google.com/newspapers?nid=PLWDSxI5WzYC&dat=19350206&printsec=frontpage&hl=en.

Munro, Alice. "The Moon in the Orange Street Skating Rink." *The New Yorker,* March 31, 1986, 26–44.

The New Canadian Folksong and Handicraft Festival [pamphlet]. Winnipeg, 1928.

O'Leary, M. Grattan. "Cabinet Portraits." *Maclean's*, January 1, 1931, 19, 32–33.

"Opposing Move to Limit Cases of Deportation." *Ottawa Morning Citizen*, March 15, 1933. LAC, RG76, vol. 245, file 168186.

"Order-in-Council PC 1931-695." Canadian Museum of Immigration at Pier 21. https://pier21.ca/order-council-pc-1931-695.

"Order-in-Council PC 1931-695, 1931." Canadian Museum of Immigration at Pier 21. https://www.pier21.ca/research/immigration-history/order-in-council-pc-1931-695-1931.

Osborne, Brian S. "Constructing the State, Managing the Corporation, Transforming the Individual: Photography, Immigration and the Canadian National Railways, 1925–30." In *Picturing Place: Photography and the Geographical Imagination*, edited by J.M. Schwartz and J.R. Ryan, 162–91. London: I.B. Tauris, 2003.

Osborne, Brian S., and Susan E. Wurtele. "The Other Railway: Canadian National's Department of Colonization and Agriculture." In *Immigration and Settlement, 1870–1939*, edited by G.P. Marchildon, 123–28. Regina: CPRC Press, 2009.

Pagé, J.D. "Medical Aspects of Immigration." *Public Health Journal* 19, no. 8 (1928): 366–73.

Park, Norm. "Deep Lessons Learned by First World War Veteran." *Estevan Mercury*, November 11, 2014. https://www.sasktoday.ca/south/in-the-community/deep-lessons-learned-by-first-world-war-veteran-4017915.

Pitsula, James. *Keeping Canada British: The Ku Klux Klan in 1920s Saskatchewan*. Vancouver: UBC Press, 2013.

"Quality in Immigration." *Globe* [Toronto], October 25, 1928, 4.

"The Qu'Appelle Valley." http://www.cmste.uregina.ca/valley/social-history.html.

Radison, Garry. *Fine Day: Plains Cree Warrior, Shaman and Elder*. Calgary: Smoke Ridge Books, 2013.

Rampell, Catherine. "The Little People Pay Taxes." https://archive.nytimes.com/economix.blogs.nytimes.com/2011/02/23/the-little-people-pay-taxes/

"RMS *Queen Mary* Kosher Dinner Menu—8 June 1936." GG Archives. https://www.gjenvick.com/OceanTravel/VintageMenus/Specialty/KosherDinnerMenu-QueenMary-1936-06-08.html.

Rome, David. *Clouds in the Thirties: On Antisemitism in Canada 1929–1939*. Montreal: National Archives Canadian Jewish Congress, 1980.

Rosenberg, Louis. *Canada's Jews: A Social and Economic Study of the Jews in Canada*. Montreal: Canadian Jewish Congress, 1939.

———. "The Jewish Population of Canada: A Statistical Summary from 1850 to 1943." *American Jewish Year Book* 48 (1946–47): 19–50.

"Ryfka Low." In "Passenger Lists and Border Entries, 1925–1935." LAC, RG76, vol. 25. https://www.bac-lac.gc.ca/eng/discover/immigration/immigration-records/passenger-lists-border-entry-1925-1935/Pages/introduction.aspx.

"A Sheine Bar-Mitzvah in Dysart, Sask." Dos Yiddishe Vort, January 27, 1933, 5.

"The Ships List." http://www.theshipslist.com/ships/descriptions/ShipsSS.shtml.

Singer, Isaac Bashevis. *The Family Moskat*. New York: Knopf, 1950.

———. *In My Father's Court*. New York: Farrar, Straus and Giroux, 1991.

"Some Types of the New-Comers." *Canadian Courier* 7 (1910): 13.

"Souris River." Turtle Mountain—Souris Plains Heritage Association. https://vantagepoints.ca/stories/souris-river/.

Speisman, Stephen A. "Bilsky, Moses." In *Dictionary of Canadian Biography*, vol. 15. Toronto: University of Toronto; Laval: Université Laval, 2003. http://www.biographi.ca/en/bio/bilsky_moses_15E.html.

Stegner, Wallace. *Wolf Willow: A History, a Story, and a Memory of the Last Plains Frontier*. New York: Viking, 1971.

"Trafficking at Ottawa in Immigration Permits Charged by Regina Man." *Toronto Daily Star*, May 15, 1928, 1.

Trant, William. "Jew and Chinaman." *North American Review* 195, no. 675 (1912): 249–60.

Waite, P.B. *The Loner: Three Sketches of the Personal Life and Ideas of R.B. Bennett 1870–1947*. Toronto: University of Toronto Press, 1992.

Ward, Norman. "Editor's Foreword." In *The Politician: Or, The Treason of Democracy*, by James G. Gardiner, ix–xii. Saskatoon: Western Producer Prairie Books, 1975.

Weinfeld, Morton. "Introduction." In *Canada's Jews: A Social and Economic Study of the Jews in Canada in the 1930s*, edited by Morton Weinfeld, xi–xxiii. Montreal and Kingston: McGill-Queen's University Press, 1993.

Weiss, M. "Availability of Kosher Food Aboard *Titanic*." *Jewish Telegraphic Agency*, April 11, 2012. https://www.jta.org/2012/04/11/lifestyle/

availability-of-kosher-food-aboard-titanic-sheds-light-on-immigration-via-england.

"Wesley Ashton Gordon." The Linked Parliamentary Data Project. https://www.lipad.ca/search/?q=Wesley+Ashton+Gordon&pol=&par=&sd_year=1901&sd_month=1&sd_day=1&ed_year=2019&ed_month=7&ed_day=7.

White, Donny. *In Search of Geraldine Moodie*. Regina: Canadian Plains Research Center, 1998.

Winning Through: Stories of Life on Canadian Farms Told by New British Settlers. Ottawa: Department of Immigration and Colonization, 1929.

ARCHIVAL MATERIALS

All materials listed below, with the exception of the Eisenstein file at the Jewish Heritage Centre of Western Canada, Winnipeg, were accessed on physical visits to archive sites. These visits and the archival repositories themselves are a key part of this book's narrative.

1. Alex Dworkin Canadian Jewish Archives, Montreal
   JIAS, file JIAS-CA-71-17808, Rabbi J. Eisenstein
   JIAS, file JIAS-CA-72-18070–18359
   JIAS, file JIAS-CA-72-18084
   JCA, KC 87–88, Lipton Colony
   JCA, MAI DB 14, Hirsch Colony
   JCA, MAI DC 7, Hirsch Colony
   JCA, Canada Collection, L100, box 57
   JCA, Canada Collection, CJC K-46

2. Jewish Heritage Centre of Western Canada Archives, Winnipeg
   JHC 148, file 18, JIAS, "Rev. J. Eisenstein"

3. Ottawa Jewish Archives
   OJA, Archibald and Lillian Freiman Family Fonds, R6882-0-3-E, folders 18, 19 (1934, 1935)

4. Library and Archives Canada, Ottawa
MG26-I
Arthur Meighen Fonds, Series 5, vol. 159

MG26-K
"Bennett, Richard Bedford Provincial Governments—Saskatchewan 1935," microfiche M-1282
"Bennett, Richard Bedford Department of Immigration and Colonization—Saskatchewan Immigration 1930–1935," microfiche M-1315
"Bennett, Richard Bedford Senatorships—Saskatchewan—Lynd W.W. 1932–33," microfiche M-1347

MG27 III C3 S.W. Jacobs Fonds

RG2, Privy Council Office Fonds, vol. 1562
Order-in-Council 1136G, March 18, 1935, file 1310
Order-in-Council 1139G, March 19, 1935, file 1310
Order-in-Council 1145G, March 26, 1935, file 1310

RG30
Vol. 5893, Canadian National Railways—Winnipeg Office

RG76
Vol. 189, file 68829, part 1
Vol. 245, file 168186, part 1
Vol. 245, file 168186, "Canadian National Telegraphs," October 22, 1930
Vol. 349, file 376333, part 8

5. Canadian Museum of History Archive, Gatineau
Anna Feldman Fonds, 2007-F0012, box 814, folder 28, tape JS 72,73

ILLUSTRATION CREDITS

PAGE 8: Author's personal collection

PAGE 10: Author's personal collection

PAGE 11: Author's personal collection

PAGE 26: Library and Archives Canada, Passenger Lists: Quebec City (1925–35), Mikan Number 134839, Microform T-14771

PAGE 44: Glenbow Museum Archives, NA-3300-1

PAGE 48: Library and Archives Canada, Canadian National Railways Fonds, RG30, vol. 5893

PAGE 49: Author's personal collection

PAGE 51: Library and Archives Canada, C-009798

PAGE 64: Map of Saskatchewan from the early twentieth century, https://rollymartincountry.blogspot.com/2018/07/austin-to-quappelle-valley-and-regina.html?m=0

PAGE 70: Library and Archives Canada, Humphrey Lloyd Hime Fonds, C-04573

PAGE 110: Author's personal collection

PAGE 111: Alex Dworkin Canadian Jewish Archives, JIAS-CA-71-17808

PAGE 118 (BOTH IMAGES): Alex Dworkin Canadian Jewish Archives, JIAS-CA-71-17808

PAGE 133: Alex Dworkin Canadian Jewish Archives, JIAS-CA-71-17808

PAGE 136: Alex Dworkin Canadian Jewish Archives, JIAS-CA-71-17808
PAGE 149: Jewish Heritage Centre of Western Canada Archives, JHC 148, file 18
PAGE 150: Jewish Heritage Centre of Western Canada Archives, JHC 148, file 18
PAGE 154: Alex Dworkin Canadian Jewish Archives, JIAS-CA-71-17808
PAGE 158: Jewish Heritage Centre of Western Canada Archives, JHC 148, file 18
PAGE 163: Alex Dworkin Canadian Jewish Archives, JIAS-CA-71-17808
PAGE 165: Alex Dworkin Canadian Jewish Archives, JIAS-CA-71-17808
PAGE 166: Alex Dworkin Canadian Jewish Archives, JIAS-CA-71-17808
PAGE 167: Alex Dworkin Canadian Jewish Archives, JIAS-CA-71-17808
PAGE 168: Alex Dworkin Canadian Jewish Archives, JIAS-CA-71-17808
PAGE 169: Alex Dworkin Canadian Jewish Archives, JIAS-CA-71-17808
PAGE 196: Library and Archives Canada, Privy Council Office Fonds, RG2, vol. 1562, file 1310, Order-in-Council 1139, March 19, 1935
PAGE 198: Library and Archives Canada, Privy Council Office Fonds, RG2, vol. 1562, file 1310, Order-in-Council 1139, March 19, 1935
PAGE 199: Library and Archives Canada, Privy Council Office Fonds, RG2, vol. 1562, file 1310, Order-in-Council 1139, March 19, 1935
PAGE 203: Author's personal collection
PAGE 208: Library and Archives Canada, Privy Council Office Fonds, RG2, vol. 1562, file 1310, Order-in-Council 1139, March 19, 1935
PAGE 209: Alex Dworkin Canadian Jewish Archives, JIAS-CA-71-17808
PAGE 222: Alex Dworkin Canadian Jewish Archives, JIAS-CA-72-18084
PAGE 227: Jewish Heritage Centre of Western Canada Archives, JHC 148, file 18

INDEX

Abbott, Edwina, 183
Abella, Irving, 64, 93, 162, 166, 182
Adaskin, Harry, 45
Adler, Sol, 128
Alexander II, Tsar of Russia:
    assassination of, 67
Alexander III, Tsar of Russia:
    anti-Semitic May Laws of, 67
Alisero, Joseph, 193, 194
American Jewish Committee, 27
Anderson, J.T.M.: Eisenstein's case
    and, 133, 190; Ku Klux Klan and,
    135; political career of, 20,
    133–34; relief commission of, 82;
    teaching career of, 200; treatise
    on Canada's Jews, 22–24
Anglican mission, 71, 83–84
Anne of Green Gables, 175–76
Antwerp Canadian immigration
    office, 214–15
Army Officers' Mess, 174, 175, 187
Arpin, Dr., 217

Asian immigrants, 4, 76
assimilationist ethics, 33, 40
Aunt Miriam (Ciocia
    Mariam), 202, *203*, 204
Azarowa, Feige, 179

Basso, Innocente, 195
Battleford, SK, 88
Baum, Louis, 180
Beatty, William, 148, 151, 152; letter
    to Eisenstein, *149*, 149–50
Belkin, Simon, 54, 55, 57, 58, 172
Bennett, R.B.: background of, 94, 95;
    begging letters to, 183–84; cabinet
    of, 29, 99–100, 207; education of, 95;
    Eisenstein's case and, 128, 153, 165,
    166, 181, 188–89, 190; immigration
    policies of, 63, 74, 99, 100–101, 181,
    204; Jewish Canadians and, 96, 98,
    181; at Kesnick's Confectionery,
    97; Lady Lougheed and, 98; legal
    career of, 95; miners' strike and, 127;

Mława, Poland: Jewish society
in, 94, 212; photographs of,
212–13; train station, 213, 226
Molloy, Thomas, 127, 144
Montreal: Jewish quarter, 184;
life of immigrants in, 116;
neighbourhoods, 173
Montreal Peretz School, 194
Moodie, Geraldine, 88
Moodie, Susanna, 88
Moose Jaw, SK, 134
Motherwell, W.R., 113–14,
115, 200, 201, 206
MS *St. Louis,* 162
Munro, Alice: "The Moon
in the Orange Street
Skating Rink," 211–12

New Brunswick: promotion of
immigration to, 74, 75
New Canadian Folksong and
Handicraft Festivals, 40, 41, 43, 45
newcomers: assimilation of, 21,
32–33; categories of, 22–23, 31–32,
36; education of, 22; language
instruction for, 81; photographs
of, 50, 51–52; question of 'origin'
of, 30–31, 32, 33, 34; racial
desirability, 36; statistics of, 31
Niedwiedzki, Miss, 218
None Is Too Many (Abella and
Troper), 64, 166, 182
Northern Assurance
Company, 131
North-West Territories, 67,
70, 71, 83, 123–24

O'Leary, M. Grattan, 99–100
orders-in-council, 193, 195, 197
*Origin, Birthplace, Nationality
and Language of the Canadian
People,* 30–31, 36
Osborne, J., 75–76
Ottawa: businesses, 53–54; downtown
area, 174; Jewish community,
54–55; Somerset Street, 174,
185–86; train ride to, 171–72
Ottawa Jewish Archives, 187
Ottawa Ladies' Hebrew
Benevolent Society, 176
Our Canadian Mosaic
(Foster), 40–41, 45

Palliser, John, 68
Palliser Hotel events, 42, 43
Palliser's Triangle, 68, 124
Paryniuk, Maftej, 205
Pastinsky, N.M., 77
Pattee, C.B., 174
Paull, A.J.: appeal to Prime Minister
Bennett, 188–89; correspondence
of, 145; Eisenstein's case and, 114,
119–20, 121, 148, 152, 155–56, 161,
164–65; Jolliffe's letter to, *209*; letter
to Department of Immigration,
163, 167; letter to Eisenstein, *165,
166,* 190–91; letter to Gray, 221,
222; promotion of immigration
files, 155, 194–95, 220, 221
peddlers, 176
Pelletier, Georges, 196
Peretz School Orchestra, 44–45, 52
Perley, George Halsey, 199, 207
Petrokovsky, Itcha Meir, 15
Piłsudski, Józef, 19, 147

AUTHOR PHOTO: SHELLEY BUTLER

ABOUT THE AUTHOR

NORMAN RAVVIN is an award-winning fiction and non-fiction writer whose previous works include *The Girl Who Stole Everything*; *Hidden Canada: An Intimate Travelogue*; *Sex, Skyscrapers, and Standard Yiddish*; and *A House of Words: Jewish Writing, Identity, and Memory*. For fifteen years he headed the Institute for Canadian Jewish Studies at Concordia University, where he teaches in the Department of Religions and Cultures. Born in Calgary, he lived in Vancouver, Toronto, and Fredericton before settling in Montreal with his family.